A
Treatise
on
Efficacy

Jim Rustopan
December 25,
2008

A Treatise on Efficacy

Between Western and Chinese Thinking

1996

François Jullien
Translated by Janet Lloyd

2004

 University of Hawai'i Press
HONOLULU

Originally published as *Traité de l'efficacité* by Bernard Grasset, 1996

Printed in the United States of America
09 08 07 06 05 04   6 5 4 3 2 1

Library of Congress Cataloging-in-Publication Data
Jullien, François.
  [Traite de l'efficacité. English]
  A treatise on efficacy : between Western and Chinese thinking /
François Jullien ; translated by Janet Lloyd.
    p.   cm.
  ISBN 0-8248-2815-1 (hardcover : alk. paper)—ISBN 0-8248-2830-5 (pbk. : alk. paper)
  1. Act (Philosophy).   2. Philosophy, Chinese.   3. Philosophy, Comparative.   I. Title.
  B 105.A35J9413 2004
  128'.4—dc22
                                    2003025768

University of Hawai'i Press books are printed on acid-free paper and meet the
guidelines for permanence and durability of the Council on Library Resources.

Designed by Lucille C. Aono

Printed by The Maple-Vail Book Manufacturing Group

Contents

possesses a potential :
by its very nature it is destined
for some kind of development
on which we may rely
... to let ourselves be carried
along with it.

to carry a potential
to overstep their limits

Preface

What do we mean when we say that something has "potential"—not "a potential for" but an absolute potential—for example, a market with a potential, a developing business with a potential? When we say that something possesses a potential, we mean that by its very nature it is destined for some kind of development on which we may rely. Instead of having everything depend on our own initiative, we recognize that the situation itself carries a certain potential that we should identify and then let ourselves be carried along with it. This use of the expression "to carry a potential" remains somewhat vague, or at least belongs to the sphere of practice, on the edge of language, so it may not occur to us to probe deeper into the logic behind it. Yet it seems to me possible that a whole new vision of our engagement in the world can be sensed here; and even that, ill-adjusted as it is to our declared theoretical assumptions, it might offer us an opportunity to overstep their limits, to move on beyond them, to rethink them and discover different sources of "efficacy."

Those sources are different from those of the European tradition, or at least the tradition that has come down to us from the Greeks: a tradition that conceives of efficacy on the basis of abstract, ideal forms, set up as models to be projected onto the world and that our will deliberately establishes as a goal to be attained. This is the tradition of a plan devised in advance and the heroism of action. Depending on one's point of view, it is a tradition of means and ends, or of the interrelation between theory and practice. But far away in China, we discover a concept of efficacy that teaches one to learn how to allow an effect to come about: not to aim for it (directly) but to implicate it (as a consequence), in other words, not to seek it, but simply to welcome it—to allow it to result. The ancient Chinese tell us that it is enough to know how to make the most of the

to implicate it

to divert it away from
to open it up to a diff.

way a situation develops and to let yourself be "carried" along by it. You do not rack your brains, you do not struggle or strive. But that is not at all because you wish to disengage from the world; rather, it is the better to succeed in it. To describe this kind of intelligence that bypasses the theory-practice relationship and instead depends solely on the way that things evolve, let us use the term "strategic." As we study it, we shall find ourselves wondering whether we, for our part, including even those who have opted for "realism" when faced with the power of ideas or ethics—from Aristotle to Machiavelli or to Clausewitz—have ever really thought through the concept of efficacy. We may even come to wonder whether the notion of efficacy itself is not too limited or clumsy to capture the means of producing reality or allowing it to come about.

The fact is that, beneath the question of efficacy, another gradually surfaces: not the question of being and knowing, which is constantly raised by metaphysics, nor that of action, which is its ethical corollary, but the question of the conditions of effectiveness. What, strictly speaking, is an *effect?* Or how does reality realize itself?

To move on from the question of efficacy, which still bears the imprint of voluntarism, to that of efficiency, which implies an underlying fund of immanence, we need to attempt a shift. A *shift* in two senses of the term: a shift away from our normal thinking habits, a move from one framework to another—from Europe to China and back again—which will undermine our representations and get our thoughts moving; and also a shift in the sense of shifting the impediment that is preventing us from perceiving what we have always blocked out of our thinking and, for that very reason, have been unable to think about.

In order to operate this shift, we need to recast our language and its theoretical assumptions. As we proceed, we must divert it away from what it finds itself inclined to say even before we begin to speak and open it up to a different intelligibility, urging it toward other resources.

close,

The Objective of This Study and the References on Which It Draws

open

The present essay complements an earlier one devoted to ethics (*Fonder la morale,* Grasset, 1995), which was prompted by a reading of Mencius. In the China of late Antiquity, an opposition between two schools of thought became increasingly apparent. On the one hand were the "moralists," best represented by Mencius (MZ) and the *Doctrine of the Mean,* or *Zhong yong* (ZY), from the fourth century B.C.; on the other were those who can be called the "realists," who, in the frantic dash for power in which the warring states were involved, reacted against tradition and the teaching of the rites.

It was the latter group, the "realists," who developed the notion of efficacy most explicitly in China. But the moralists, in particular Mencius, while taking up opposed positions, were nevertheless in agreement with them on many points. For the notion of efficacy was shared by all, the only difference in position being the "way" in which to proceed.

On warfare, the principal text is that of Sunzi (SZ; sixth to fifth century B.C.?). The edition I use is that of Yang Bingyan, *Sunzi huijian* (Henan: Zhongzhou guji chubanshe, 1986), together with the Eleven Commentators, *Shiyi jia zhu Sunzi* (ed. Guo Huaruo, Shanghai: Zhonghua shuju, 1962). The best Western edition is that of Roger Ames, *Suntzu: The Art of Warfare* (New York: Ballantine Books, 1993).

I also cite Sun Bin (fourth century B.C.), who is likewise extremely interesting, although the text is much more corrupt. I use the edition of Deng Zezong, *Sun Bin bingfa zhuyi* (Beijing: Jiefangjun chubanshe, 1986); see also the more recent volume edited by D. C. Lau and Roger Ames, *Sun Pin: The Art of Warfare* (New York: Ballantine Books, 1996).

On politics, the text used is that of Han Feizi (HFZ, 280?–234), the most brilliant thinker on the subject of Chinese despotism, misleadingly known as "Legalism." The edition I use is that of Chen Qiyou, *Han Feizi jishi* (Shanghai: Shanghai renmin chubanshe, 1974, 2 vols.).

On diplomacy and what we would call rhetoric, although it is really more of an antirhetoric, the text used is the *Guiguzi* (GGZ, 390?–320?). In the absence of an altogether reliable edition, which is explained by the scant attention usually paid to this text, I use not only the classic commentaries (Yin Zhizhang, Tao Hongjing), but also the recent information produced by Zheng Jiewen in *Guiguzi yanjiu* (Haikou: Nanhai chubangongsi, 1993) as well as *Neng bian shan dou* (Ji'nan: Shangdong renmin chubanshe, 1995), together with that provided by Feng Zuomin in *Baihua Guiguzi* (Taiwan: Xingguang chubanshe).

Warfare, power, and speech are the three principal subjects on which I focus. The *Laozi* (LZ, sixth or fourth century B.C.?) is unclassifiable, as it covers all of them. For that reason I have sought to pluck it from the mystical context in which Western scholars have tended to place it and establish it as fundamental to thought on efficacy. The edition of the text that I have used, together with its commentary by Wang Bi, is *Wang Bi ji xiaoshi*, volume 1 (Beijing: Zhonghua shuju, 1980). The best Western edition is that produced by Robert G. Henricks, *Laotzu: Te-tao ching* (New York: Ballantine Books, 1989).

Finally, I have decided not to make use of "stratagems" such as the

Thirty-Six Stratagems (Sanshiliu ji), both so as to respect the historical unity of the corpus (since such collections are clearly of a later date and merely diffuse the contents of earlier works in the form of proverbs) and also in order to dissociate the present study from the "chinoiseries" to which some authors frequently limit themselves.

The present essay is, in truth, not a treatise on efficacy, but a treatise *about* efficacy. As such, it returns to questions already tackled in *The Propensity of Things* (New York: The New Press, 1995) but endeavors to extend their context and pursue them further.

The superscript letters refer the reader to the glossary of Chinese expressions at the end of this volume.

A

Treatise

on

Efficacy

1

Fixing One's Eyes on a Model

1

To what extent have we ever stepped outside that European schema or are we even able to—can we even question it ("we" within the European tradition who still perpetuate those early Greek categories)? It is so thoroughly assimilated that we no longer see it—no longer see ourselves. We set up an ideal form *(eidos)*, which we take to be a goal *(telos),* and we then act in such a way as to make it become fact. It all seems to go without saying—a goal, an ideal, and will: with our eyes fixed on the model that we have conceived, which we project on the world and on which we base a plan to be executed, we choose to intervene in the world and give a form to reality. And the closer we stick to that ideal form in the action that we take, the better our chances of succeeding.

We can at least spot the origin of this habitual line of reasoning.* For the assumption is that, in the first place, the creation of the world must have involved some such procedure (although, of course, the very idea of explaining the world from the point of view of its creation is itself loaded with preconceptions...). The idea of a model was itself offered as a model, one in which a particular gesture

stepped outside schema

Goal, ideal, will

---

*[Translator's note: The French here is *"ce pli ('pli' au sens où l'on dit: 'prendre un pli')."* Literally, *"pli"* means a fold. But metaphorically, *"prendre un pli"* means "to fall into a habit."]

fell into a fold

came first. In his divine goodness and operating with a view to achieving excellence, Plato's *demiurgos* was bound to "keep his gaze fixed" on "imperishable being" so as to set it up as a paradigm and in order to realize its "shape and properties" (*idea kai dunamis, Timaeus*, 28a), and all that is "executed in this way must of necessity be beautiful." The craftsman of a city operates similarly, taking the great Demiurge as his model: "keeping his eyes turned toward" the absolute of essences, he endeavors to imbue the mores of his fellows with whatever he "perceives above" (*Rep.*,VI, 500c). "Up there" are the eternal forms, the perfect virtues that only a contemplative mind can apprehend. So, when drawing up the plan for a good political constitution, the craftsman of the city is like a painter who, working from the "divine model," tries painstakingly to reproduce it. Even the orator, usually a somewhat suspect figure, as soon as he ceases to be a flatterer keeps his gaze fixed on the ideal (*Gorgias*, 304d) and is constantly inspired by it in his discourse.

Despite the process of philosophical rationalization to which the notion of this power of Forms or Ideas* has been submitted, many have tried to detect in it vestiges of a mythical concept. It has been claimed that, in that it relates the visible to the invisible and attributes to the Forms set up as archetypes beyond experience the power to inform all that which is sensible, Platonism stems from a "primitive mentality" (as is shown by the analogies between the theory of the Forms [or Ideas] and an extratemporal world with an almost etiological function—such as that of the "Demas"—which Lévy-Bruhl associated with archaic societies). In this way, Platonism would have drawn its concept of efficacy from old religious sources from which philosophy subsequently strove constantly to distance itself. As is well known, from Aristotle onward the world's status purely as a copy is dismissed. It is no longer believed that the material world is simply a receptacle fashioned according to the will of the demiurge. The norm is no longer thought to be some intangible canon

---

*[Translator's note: The French uses the word "*Idées.*"]

that comes from outside to impress itself upon the world; instead, it is now regarded as the correct mean immanent in things, which as such depends on the particular circumstances of situations. But all the same, we still keep our eyes *turned toward* something. It is still by "fixing our eyes" on the ideal, here the ideal of the mean *(mesotès),* that, in the manner of "good artists" (*Nic. Ethics,* 1106b), we conceive of action. Aristotle tells us, more precisely, that it is "toward that ideal" that, "with our eyes fixed upon it," we shall "*guide* our work." Even if the correct mean varies, since it relates both to circumstances and to individuals, it is always what we set our sights *(skopos)* on, and its perfection is established as a norm that we must then embody in facts. The function of the model set up as a goal remains intact: the model is determined on a "theoretical" basis that, once established, must be submitted to "practice."

> The model remains in sight even if it is immanent

From now on, for us theory and practice are interfolded, coupled.* And this coupling, the solid basis of which we no longer even dream of questioning, forces acceptance from us (for however we reformulate those terms, we cannot get around them). In fact, I regard this as one of the most characteristic moves made by the modern Western world (or maybe quite simply the world as a whole—if it has been standardized in accordance with the Western model): a revolutionary designs the model of the city that must be built; a soldier sets out the plan of war to be followed; an economist decides on the growth curve to target; and, all of them, whatever their respective roles, operate in a similar way. Each projects upon the world an ideal plan that will then have to be incorporated into factual reality. But what does "incorporate" mean here, given

> The implied coupling of theory and practice

*[Translator's note: The French here is *"Le 'pli' théorie-pratique: Le pli, désormais est pris."* The meaning of *"pli"* here is more complex. In addition to the idea of something that has become habitual, the author uses the notion of a *pli,* an "interfolding," to convey the idea of an implicit combination. Both Western thought and Chinese thought carry underlying implicit assumptions, and he believes it is useful to "unfold" them or bring them to the surface and make them explicit.]

that they are already operating *in reality?* First, they conceive of working "for the best"; next, they draw on their "willpower" in order to impose their models upon reality. To impose is to superimpose, as if imprinting a transfer on a new surface and using force to do so. Our inclination is to extend to everything this model-making, the principle of which was developed by science, for, as is well known, science (European science, or at least classic science) is itself simply a vast operation of model-making (mathematization in the first instance), the technique or practical application of which materially transforms the world, thereby testifying to its efficacy.

The question that therefore arises is whether what works so well from a technical point of view, by enabling us to control nature, works just as well for managing human situations and relations. Or, to express that in terms of the two separate categories established by the Greeks: is the efficacy of the model that we recognize at the level of production *(poesis)* equally operative in the domain of action *(praxis)*—in what Aristotle describes as not the domain in which we "make" things, but that in which we "accomplish" them? For even if we have distinguished between the two, we may nevertheless have copied the one from the other (as we have indeed modeled action on production). Even when "things" become human affairs, we should still like to remain in the reassuring position of "technicians"—artisans or demiurges. Now, as we are well aware and as Aristotle was the first to recognize, although science may impose its rigor on things by understanding their necessary aspects and thereby achieving technical efficacy, the situations in which our actions are performed are, for their part, indeterminate. Our actions cannot eliminate their contingency, and their particularities cannot be covered by any general law. In consequence, action cannot be classified simply as an extension of science. So just as, for Aristotle, matter, an indeterminate power of contraries, always remains more or less recalcitrant to the determination that "form" seeks to impose upon it, similarly the world is never altogether receptive to the order that we wish it to have: inevitably, there is always a discrepancy between the planned model for our action and what we,

Can one continue to operate as a technician when it comes to determining behavior?

with our eyes fixed on that model, manage to achieve. In short, practice always to some degree falls short of theory. The model remains out there on the horizon on which we fix our gaze. The ideal, up in the sky, is inaccessible.

the model remains out there on the horizon

2

But that is by no means all that there is to be said in this story (the long "theory-practice" story), since philosophy cannot accept such a failure. After hoping for so much from the human aptitude for science and after allowing us to glimpse the perfection of essences, how could it resign itself to leaving us in such a wretched state: ill-equipped to manage in the world and to maneuver so as to succeed in our projects? In this uneasy debate between form and matter or, as the tragic poets were already putting it, between "the best" and "the necessary," Aristotle thought he had discovered a faculty for dealing with practice, a faculty that, taking over from theory, could fill in the gap. This ability was at once intellectual ("dianoetic") and directly linked with action and could thus mediate as was required. "Prudence" *(phronesis)* is the name traditionally given to this practical wisdom. Whoever "is able to deliberate well about what is good and advantageous for himself" (*Nic. Ethics,* VI, 5) may be called prudent and possesses this practical ability. Given that such a person only deliberates on that which is contingent, prudence is not a science; nor is it an art, in the sense of a *techne,* since it is aimed at action *(praxis),* not production. The two defining characteristics indicate its own specific function: it operates not as an extension of science but alongside it, drawing on a different part of the rational soul. While the soul's scientific part aims to contemplate all that could not be other than it is (metaphysical and mathematical objects), its "logistic" part is designed to take charge of the need for action within a constantly changing world; it calculates and deliberates on the best thing to do. In this, it is complemented not only by "an accurate eye" but also by "an alert mind" or "good judgment" *(gnome).* It is exemplified not by scholars absorbed in their speculations, but in "the administrators of households and cities"; not by a

Might "prudence" fill the gap between theory and practice?

Thales or an Anaxagoras, whose "difficult" and "divine" knowledge is "of no practical use," but by a man of action: Pericles. Pericles is rehabilitated by philosophy thanks to his ability to manage human affairs.

So it is that, with Aristotle, and as has been pointed out ever since, philosophy returned to "things"; after aiming too high, it became realistic. But, all the same, I am not sure that this means that "prudence" really implies a "logistic" ability that can answer the perceived need and that is based on the principle of efficacy. In the first place, when it comes to defining this practical faculty according to his own criteria, Aristotle finds himself trapped in a vicious circle, as his commentators have not failed to point out. Aristotle defines "prudence" as follows: "Prudence is a practical disposition, accompanied by correct reason with regard to what is good and what is bad for man" (*Nic. Ethics,* VI, 6). But what is the source of this "correct reason" that must accompany deliberation and serve as a norm, if not—precisely—science itself? We know that, unlike Plato, Aristotle no longer believes either in the possibility of deducing the particular totally from the general or in action based on principles. So he can only define pru-

On what is prudence founded?

dence by whatever is prudent: the criterion of prudence, which cannot be established by science, can only be provided by a man of whom it is generally said that "he is prudent." Given that Aristotle no longer trusts the transcendence of the norm, by the same token he finds himself forced to the opposite extreme and condemned to empiricism. For, in the absence of any essence in relation to which it can be defined, prudence can only be discerned through the existence of remarkable individuals. Aristotle thus finds himself unable to account for prudence beyond what has always been said by common sense. It therefore turns out to be extremely difficult to establish a definition of this practical faculty that is supposed to make good the inadequacy of theory. Or is it the case that the Greek intellectual premises (from which Aristotle cannot dissociate himself, as is shown by his definition of prudence in accordance with "correct reason," *orthos logos*), by making this prudence ungraspable on the basis of a criterion, topple the theory itself?

Furthermore, and despite the tendency of the popular definition of prudence by which he is inspired, Aristotle is unable, or unwilling, to separate his own thought on prudence from ethical considerations. The position adopted by Greek philosophy orients action toward morality, and Aristotle cannot dissociate himself from this position. Although it is he who goes the furthest, in Greek philosophy, in his attempts to think through the conditions for efficacious action, the latter is always transcended by the end to which it is directed (the "advantage" for which the prudent man aims is not his own personal profit, but profit for the community; ultimately, he is concerned for the city; see *Nic. Ethics,* III). This is shown in particular by the way in which Aristotle opposes what is prudent to what is clever *(deinos)*. Whereas cleverness is an ability to combine the most efficacious means, regardless of the quality of the end, prudence, for its part, is concerned about that end. Prudence, an ethical take on cleverness, is always directed toward the good; and pure "cleverness" is set aside.

Prudence/cleverness

orients toward morality

Cleverness is dismissed

3

But how can we believe that the Greeks, with their well-known taste for stratagems, were never captivated simply by cleverness and the art of succeeding? Very early on and in a wide variety of fields of action, they celebrated *mètis,* the kind of cunning intelligence that knows how to adapt to difficulties. In their fine study devoted to this subject, Marcel Detienne and Jean-Pierre Vernant tell us that *mètis* combines "flair, sagacity, foresight, adaptability, pretense, resourcefulness, vigilance, opportunism.". . . Odysseus, clever Odysseus with a thousand tricks up his sleeve, is the hero most richly endowed with *mètis:* he is *polumètis.* And Zeus himself starts off by swallowing the goddess Mètis in order to absorb her wisdom and to be sure of avoiding all the traps that could bring about his downfall in dealings with both gods and men.

Detienne and Vernant tell us that, while the kind of intelligence designated by *mètis* is deployed at many different levels, the emphasis is always on "practical efficacy,"

The cunning intelligence of the Greeks

Odysseus

polumètis

that is to say, on "the pursuit of success in a particular field of action." *Mètis* is characterized in particular by the fact that, through some more or less fundamental maneuver and by making the most of circumstances, it is possible to win out over brute strength. By deceiving his opponent in the chariot race and seizing his hoped-for chance when it arises, Homer's Antilochus manages to turn the situation to his own advantage. As the field of application for *mètis* is the world of all that is shifting, multiple, and ambivalent, this kind of intelligence is infinitely adaptable and nimble; it is said to be "lithe" and "multicolored." Because the realities that it affects are usually tugged this way and that by contrary forces, it has to remain polymorphous and mobile; because it needs to control a constantly changing situation, it remains open to all possibilities and itself changes constantly in order to adapt to circumstances. Even more ungraspable and elusive than the world in which it operates, thanks to its malleability it is able to triumph where there are no hard and fast rules for success. Its model—or at least its favorite bestiary—combines the roles of the fox and the octopus. Like the former, it is adept at turning back on its tracks; like the latter it is able to seize hold of its victim and paralyze it. Similarly, Odysseus is so devious that he can foil the attacks of any opponent and ensnare him with his eloquence.

The "agility" of the mind when faced with the variability of things

$f \circ x \rightarrow$

$octopus \rightarrow$

Mètis, which will stoop to any means, thus seems to represent the universal model of realism. And yet, reading Detienne and Vernant, one senses that it is peculiarly Greek. For it carries a double imprint: it is at once technical and magical. It is Athena, after all, who presides over *mètis*. Its technical dimension is unmistakable in both hunting and fishing, and is illustrated by skill in the art of driving a chariot or steering a boat. A good helmsman is one whose *mètis* allows him to master even the uncontrollable heaving of the waves; and although that is certainly a matter of action, it also refers to production, for Athena not only guides the ship, but also built it. At the same time, when it comes to Athena's or Medea's machinations, one fears their *philters* and their tricks. They also make use of other powers, ones that are darker than purely human intelligence, for they have not broken with the world of spells and enchantment. The efficacy revealed by *mètis* is not yet free from the magic of myth.

Even more important, nowhere in Greece do we find any theory relating to this cunning intelligence. We can detect it at work, sometimes in obsessive fashion, in social and intellectual practices everywhere, but no text ever analyzes it for us, explaining its roots and its sources. So the only way for Detienne and Vernant to study it is to turn to the myths that show it at work, where it is detectable but always more or less below the surface, "immersed in practical operations that, even when they use it, show no concern to make its nature explicit or to justify its procedures." Insofar as it presupposes movement and elusiveness and is thus refractory to the imposition of any form set up as a model, *mètis* foils any attempt to stabilize its identity on the basis provided by Being or God, to which Greek thought is devoted. Only the Sophists made an initial attempt to open philosophical intelligence up to the disturbing features of *mètis,* and it is known that this line of inquiry was soon suppressed. Inevitably then, "*mètis* remained outside what was to become the field of Greek science" (in fact, the very word "*mètis*" soon disappeared from the Greek language). Was it simply through lack of interest in the subject that knowledge turned away from it, being primarily concerned to discover consistency in things and to impose order on the world? Or was it perhaps because the means at the disposal of Greek theory (which remain very much the means that we still use today) were inadequate when it came to pinning down the perpetual instability in which action must take place? At any rate, however important this practical efficacy was recognized to be and however delightful it was to evoke it, among the Greeks it was never theorized.

Cunning intelligence eludes thought

the word métis soon disappeared

inadeq. .. pinning down the perpetual instability in which action must take place

4

The subject of warfare provides evidence of how difficult it is to theorize how to act. Given that warfare, as action, is radical and leads to extremes, it is particularly well

Example: The failure to produce a theory of warfare

*as they
conceive
of
everything
else:
from the
point of
view of
material
production.*

suited to reveal the dead-ends into which any concept of efficacious action will lead us if it proceeds from model-making or limits itself to a technical view. As we are perhaps beginning to see, these two do tend to go hand in hand. In support of that hypothesis, let me call on the testimony of Clausewitz, at the other end of our European tradition, in the early nineteenth century, when he was assessing the attempts that had been made to produce a theory of warfare in Europe. For he considered all those attempts to have failed. According to him, the failure stemmed primarily from the fact that people were beginning to conceive of warfare as they conceived of everything else, that is to say, from the point of view of material production; and in so doing, they failed to notice the fundamentally active principle on which warfare is based. The science of warfare had begun to concentrate on the art of making weapons, constructing fortifications, and organizing armies, and the ways to get the latter to move as was required. It had thus shifted from siege strategy and military tactics toward an increasingly elaborate art of mechanics. When it attempted to systematize the material data, it either reduced superiority in warfare simply to numerical data (thereby making warfare depend on mathematical laws) or else it proceeded by way of a geometrification of one of the crucial factors (for instance, on the basis of the angle of the army's thrust in relation to its basic position—see von Bülow—or according to the theory of its internal alignments; see De Jomini). Clausewitz sternly concluded that such ways of proceeding produced "purely geometrical results that have no value at all." With a unilateral point of view that failed to take variability into account and was exclusively concerned with material factors, such theorization was incapable of "dominating real life." So, with the conduct of warfare proving to be resistant to theory, the only way to account for military successes was to invoke the natural dispositions and "genius" of those involved (which, as we all know, are beyond the bounds of theory). Clausewitz reckoned that the true conduct of warfare had thus only been revealed "in a marginal and anonymous way" in the comments penned by "eye-witnesses and the writers of memoirs."

How did Clausewitz himself, wishing to progress beyond such dead-ends, set about thinking through warfare? At first sight, his method seems somewhat surprising. He begins by conceiving warfare according to a "model" form, as an ideal and pure essence, "absolute warfare." Then he goes on to contrast this model to "real" warfare, as modified by the facts of reality. Although he considers that past thinking about warfare missed the point in setting out to make a model of something that could not be modeled, Clausewitz still cannot break free from the theory-practice notion. Unable to break out of the common rut according to which Western thought conceived of action, his only solution is to reconsider the traditional interplay between model and reality, then to set those terms in opposition and think about what divides them. According to his model, warfare implies a limitless use of force that, logically, tends to lead it, in reaction to attack, to extremes (that envisaged total destruction). Yet "everything appears in a different guise if one moves from abstraction to reality." Because warfare is never an isolated act and never depends on a single decision or leads to an absolute result, the tendency toward the extreme, which constitutes the essence of warfare, is always to some extent attenuated in reality (only Napoleon, the "god of war," succeeded in making warfare match its ideal).

The problem of this dilution is one of the most interesting that Clausewitz ever raised: what is the nature of "these nonconducive circumstances" that block the "complete realization" of the principle of warfare? Unable to shake free from the theory-practice relationship, the relation between "ideal" and real warfare, and being at the same time all too aware of the reality that that relationship failed to reflect, Clausewitz eventually manages to make use of this perception—but he does so by turning it around: he accurately perceives that this mismatch constitutes the peculiarity of warfare. The defining characteristic of warfare is precisely the inevitable distance that separates the reality of it from its model. In short, to think about warfare is to think about the extent to which it is bound to betray the ideal concept of it.

All this forces us to ask point blank what conditions

are necessary for a science of the conduct of warfare to be possible (just as, in the past, Kant asked: what are the conditions necessary for a science of metaphysics to be possible? or, going even farther back, to Newton: what are the conditions necessary for a science of physics to be possible?). And we are bound to recognize that, of all the forms of logic that rule the world of action (which are, however, copied from those that rule the world of knowledge), the most rigorous of them, that of the "law," is inapplicable to the conduct of warfare because of the changeable and variable nature of the phenomena involved.

So, in the case of warfare, it is just a matter of a "method," in the sense not of a logic but of "an average probability, judging by similar cases." This results in a way of proceeding that is "normally" adapted, which, having progressively become assimilated, becomes "customary," a "routine," and so, in the heat of action, gets to be used "more or less automatically" (hence "professionally," facilitating the progress of the military machine). It is therefore considered to be the "best" (or "least bad") way of operating even if the particular circumstances of the situation remain undetermined. However, when constantly and uniformly applied, such a "method" eventually engenders "a mechanical sort of aptitude" and becomes increasingly inappropriate as one progresses from the level of tactics to that of strategy. The trouble is that the more one is engaged in managing overall action, the more one relies on an ability to appreciate the particularities of a situation and therefore on one's own personal talent. At this level, given the inevitably singular and therefore unprecedented nature of overall military action, any formalization, which implies repetition, is extremely dangerous. And faced with the impossibility of relying on a model, theory is inevitably found wanting. In any case, Clausewitz himself, in his reflections on warfare, aspires to do no more than "educate" the mind of a future military leader or, even more modestly, "to guide him in his self-education" by providing him at least with a reference point on which to base his own judgment: in short, to "cultivate" him but not to "accompany him onto the battlefield."

Nevertheless, however wary he may be of abstract

models applied to the way that things proceed, as soon as he moves from theorizing warfare to telling us how to wage war (for he is surely not content with such a low profile), Clausewitz cannot conceive of warfare without a "plan of war" devised in advance. This, for him, remains "the framework for the whole act of war," because it determines the series of actions that can lead to the projected goal. Even in the "apparent thrust" of the moment, one should never be "deflected from" or even led to "doubt" the difficult task of "achieving" that goal. Thus, when he adopts the point of view of practical necessity, Clausewitz returns to the schema that his theoretical reflection has undermined: first one's understanding conceives the ideal form, then one commits one's will to it—an "iron will" that "overcomes all obstacles"—in order to make that project come about.... Strategy may later modify the initial plan, since "in warfare, more than in anything else, things do not happen as one thought they would and from close-up appear altogether different from how they appeared at a distance." Warfare is not a matter of willpower "applied to inert matter," as was wrongly believed by earlier theorists. Instead, it "lives and reacts," and the vivacity of reaction will necessarily foil any preconceived plan. Hence the conclusion at which Clausewitz arrives returns us to the impasse with which we are already familiar: "Clearly then, in action such as warfare, in which a plan based on general conditions is so often upset by particular and unexpected phenomena, it is necessary to leave far more, generally, to talent and to rely less than in any other domain on *theoretical recommendations*."

Clausewitz forged a concept to explain why the ideal model intended as a guide for action fails: namely, friction. He suggested that this concept was sufficiently general to make it possible to distinguish between real warfare and the kinds one reads about in books, because it is generally true that "in warfare everything takes place at a lower level because of all the countless secondary contingencies that can never be closely examined on paper and as a result of which one always falls short of the theoretical goal." The reason Clausewitz speaks of friction is that he himself clings to a mechanistic model in his thought about

algorithmic mind

The plan of war may clash with variable circumstances

def. the series

Instead, it lives and reacts

"Friction," a "machine"

action (and to the technical point of view that accompanies such a model): however well "oiled" the military "machine" may be, countless points of friction nevertheless remain, and, however minimal, these eventually produce sufficient resistance to throw the action off course. "In warfare everything is simple" (in the initial plan), "but the simplest of things proves difficult" (in practice). Clausewitz tells us that this difficulty can be compared to that which we experience as soon as we try to execute a movement as natural as walking in the water. . . . What distinguishes warfare in practice from the ease with which it may be planned is an overall difference—a difference of "climate" or "atmosphere," as it were: it would be illusory to think of reducing it by resorting to yet more theory. Only by adapting through experience, in other words, through practice, can one hope to improve the situation.

Yet in warfare even such an adaptation can never wholly eliminate the gap between theory and practice. Ever since Aristotle (or perhaps even since Plato), Western philosophy has been trying to forge some means of mediation between theory and practice, a means in which "prudence," the ethical interpretation of the *mètis* of the ancient heroes, represented the first link. However, the gap between reality and its model cannot be plugged. That is why, in the case of warfare, the best that Clausewitz could do was theorize that deficiency on the part of theory. We can see that warfare is not a science. But, Clausewitz adds, nor is it an art, and it is striking "to note the extent to which the ideological schemata of the arts and sciences are ill-suited to this activity." And he immediately spots why: it is because the activity of warfare affects an object that *lives and reacts.* But for all that, as we, along with Clausewitz, still note, however much we criticize those "schemata," it is not easy to avoid them.

2

Relying on the Propensity of Things

1

Chinese thought is a way out of our rut, for it never constructed a world of ideal forms, archetypes, or pure essences that are separate from reality but inform it. It regards the whole of reality as a regulated and continuous process that stems purely from the interaction of the factors in play (which are at once opposed and complementary: the famous *yin* and *yang*). Order is not perceived as coming from a model that one can fix one's eyes on and apply to things. Instead, it is entirely contained within the course of reality, which it directs in an immanent fashion, ensuring its *viability* (hence the omnipresence, in Chinese thought, of the theme of the "way," the *dao*). Setting out to illuminate the progress of things, by elucidating its internal coherence and in order to act in accordance with it, the Chinese sage never conceived of a contemplative activity that was pure knowledge *(theorein),* possessing an end in itself, or that itself represented the supreme end (happiness) and was altogether disinterested. For him, the "world" was not an object of speculation; it was not a matter of "knowledge" on the one hand and "action" on the other. That is why Chinese thought, logically enough, disregarded the theory-practice relationship: not through ignorance or because it was childish, but simply because it *sidestepped* the concept—just as it sidestepped the notion of Being and thought about God.

directs it on an immanent fashion (or its propensity's a function

If one no longer had to entertain the theory-practice relationship

A difference thus appears, far away in China, that we should seize upon and that might open up new possibilities and at last shift the vision in which our tradition has become bogged down—as, indeed, all traditions tend to do, including the Chinese tradition (which is certainly extremely *traditional*). For this difference could show us

A cleavage opens up

how to track back beyond our own implicit choices (that we may consider to be self-evident but that, standing back from them in this way, we could well plumb further). We could do this by associating the difference that we have discovered with the common notion of efficacy. Rather than set up a model to serve as a norm for his actions, a Chinese sage is inclined to concentrate his attention on the course of things in which he finds himself involved in order to detect their coherence and profit from the way that they evolve. From this difference that we have discovered, we could deduce an alternative way of behaving. Instead of constructing an ideal Form that we then project on to things, we could try to detect the factors whose configuration is favorable to the task at hand; instead of setting up a goal for our actions, we could allow ourselves to be carried along by the propensity of things. In short, in-

Rely on the inherent
potential

stead of imposing our plan upon the world, we could rely on the potential inherent in the situation.

From our traditional perspective, let us look back a long way and consider a proverb from the kingdom of Qi, cited by Mencius (himself a moralist), that seems, in its own way, to sum up this alternative possibility. (In the last two centuries of Chinese Antiquity, it seems to have been the culture of the country of Qi, as opposed to the more traditionalist culture of Lu, that concentrated particular interest on efficacy.) The proverb runs as follows: "However acute one's intelligence may be, it is better to rely on the potential inherent in the situation"; "even with a mattock and a hoe to hand, it is better to wait for the moment of ripening" (MZ, II, A, 1). Here wisdom and strategy come together: rather than depend on our tools, we should rely on the way that a process unfolds in order to attain the hoped-for result; rather than think of drawing up plans, we should learn to make the most of what is implied by the situation and whatever promise is held out by its evolution. For this potential is far more than—in fact something quite different from—just a collection of favorable circumstances. Caught up in the logic of a regulated evolution, it is driven to develop of its own accord and to "carry" us with it.

Two notions thus lie at the heart of ancient Chinese strategy, forming a pair: on the one hand, the notion of a *situation* or *configuration (xing)*, as it develops and takes shape before our eyes (as a relation of forces); on the other hand, and counterbalancing this, the notion of *potential* (*shi*[a]), which is implied by that situation and can be made to play in one's favor. In the ancient military treatises (*Sunzi*, chap. 5, "Shi"), this is sometimes illustrated by the image of a mountain stream that, as it rushes along, is strong enough to carry boulders with it or by that of a crossbow drawn back and ready to discharge its arrow. In the frequent absence of theoretical explanations, in China, we need to interpret such images. Thanks to its downward-sloping course and its narrow channel (which result from the configuration of the mountain landscape), the situation is itself the source of an effect (the rushing stream is said to "obtain a potential," "to make things happen"). Similarly, in the case of the crossbow, the design works of its own accord as soon as one releases the arrow; it constitutes a mechanism.

The notion of the potential of a situation

Shi :

mountain
stream

Once they had identified this potential, Chinese strategists were careful to make the most of its consequences. And those consequences call into question what can perhaps be called the humanist concept of efficacy. For what counts is no longer so much what we ourselves personally invest in the situation, which imposes itself on the world thanks to our efforts, but rather the objective conditioning that results from the situation: that is what I must exploit and count on, for it is enough, on its own, to determine success. All I have to do is *allow* it to play its part. The Chinese strategists go on to point out that if strength and weakness are a matter of the situation, courage and cowardice are a matter of that situation's inherent potential. So courage and cowardice are a product of the situation

It is the potential of the situation that renders the combatants courageous or cowardly rather than qualities of our own (and—one might add—rather than being our responsibility). As one commentator (Li Quan) glosses, if the troops obtain the strategic potential, "then cowards are brave"; if they lose it, "then the brave are cowardly." The treatise goes on to make the following point: a good general seeks success in the potential of the situation rather than demanding it from the men under his command. Depending on whether or not he knows how to exploit the potential of the situation, he renders them cowardly or brave. In other words (Wang Xi says), courage and cowardice constitute "modifications" of that potential.

A physical or strategic potential

On the European side, the only equivalent to this idea of a potential that I can think of is the example provided by mechanics: what it calls "the potential energy of the situation" (in physical terms rather than moral, as used in a scientific theorem that is applicable to the production of kinetic energy, not as a rule to guide human behavior). The parallel is borne out by the image that brings this essay on strategy to a close:

> A man who relies on the potential contained within the situation uses his men in battle in the same way one gets logs or stones to roll. It is in the nature of logs and stones to remain immobile on a level surface and to enter into movement on sloping ground; if they are square, they stop; if they are round, they roll. The potential of troops that one knows how to use in battle is comparable to that of round stones that tumble down a mountain, rolling over and over.

The slope here serves as an image of the *propensity* that results from the relations of force that the general knows how to exploit to his advantage, by maneuvering his men. The commentators insist that the effect happens *sponte sua* and is irresistible. Because the slope is part of the configuration (which includes both the relief of the terrain and the roundness of the stones), the result is "easy."

But this *potential energy within the situation* should not be limited to the terrain of military operations. For it became traditional to conceive of it more widely, that is to say, taking into account three interconnected aspects (see Li Jing). The first is that of a moral potential: "When the general despises the enemy and his troops are glad to fight, their ardor soars as high as the skies and their energy is like a hurricane." The second is that of a topographical potential: when the pass is constricted and the path is narrow, "a single man can guard the place and even a thousand men could not force their way through." The third is that of a potential through "adaptation": one can profit from the exhaustion and lassitude of the enemy when he is worn out by thirst and hunger, when "his forward positions are not yet well established and the troops that guard the army's rear are still crossing a river."... In all these cases, whoever knows how to exploit the potential of the situation can easily win the day. Or, as one commentator puts it, "with very little effort," one can produce "great effects."[b]

topograph. potential (handwritten margin note)

Little effort, great results (margin note)

The ancient treatises on strategy do not hesitate to exploit this resource to the limit, even in ways that we find shocking. For, in order to increase the energy inherent in the situation, the Chinese general does not merely exploit all the aspects of the topography and the state of the troops that may be unfavorable to the enemy. He also manipulates the situation in such a way that his own troops are driven to display the maximum degree of ardor. To achieve this, all he needs to do is to lead them into a perilous situation from which the only way out is to fight as hard as they can (SZ, chap. 11, "Jiu di"). He therefore only engages battle in "mortally dangerous terrain," that is to say, after getting his troops to advance deep into enemy territory, for then it is as if, having made them climb up high, he "removed their ladder." Being unable to retreat, they are forced to fight as hard as possible. He does not ask his troops to be naturally courageous, as if courage were an intrinsic virtue, but forces them to be courageous by placing them in a dangerous situation in which they are forced, despite themselves, to fight bravely. The reverse is equally true. When he sees that the enemy has its back to the wall and so has no alternative but to fight to the death, he himself arranges an escape route for them so

Get their backs to the wall to increase the troops' potential (margin note)

that his opponents are not led to deploy the full measure of their combativity.*

2

According to the ancient treatises, the key to Chinese strategy is to rely on the inherent potential of the situation and to be carried along by it as it evolves. Right from the start, this rules out any idea of predetermining the course of events in accordance with a more or less definitive plan worked out in advance as an ideal to be realized. (Clausewitz calls this "a strategic plan": it lays down when, where, and with what kind of armed force battle should be joined.) A Chinese general, for his part, is careful not to impose upon the course of events any notion of his own of how things ought to be, since it is from the very evolution of the situation, which follows the course that it is logically bound to take, that he intends to profit. So if any operation is to be undertaken before engaging in battle (be it in the "ancestral temple" or, as for us, "in committee"), it must be an operation not of planning but of "evaluation" (the concept of *xiao*) or, more precisely, "assessment" (in the sense of a preliminary evaluation on the basis of a calculation: the concept of *ji*ᶜ). The general must start by making a painstaking study of the forces present. This will enable him to assess which factors are favorable to each of the two camps, for these are the factors from which victory will stem.

Begin by evaluating the situation

---

*In *The Art of War,* Machiavelli makes the same observation: "Other generals impose upon their soldiers the necessity to fight by leaving them no hope of salvation save through victory. This is the most powerful and sure way to render soldiers determined in combat" (IV). The reverse is equally true: "One must never force the enemy into desperation; that is a rule that Caesar observed in a battle against the Germans. Noticing that their need for victory was giving them new strength, he opened up a way of escape for them, preferring to go to the trouble of pursuing them than to conquer them, with danger, on the field of battle" (VI). But for Machiavelli, this is no more than a remark in passing. He offers no theory to justify it. What Western strategy merely notes in passing, Chinese thinkers try to interpret and use as food for thought.

The first of the ancient treatises that we are considering thus starts off with a systematic description of the way in which this preliminary (and, as such, indispensable; SZ, chap. 1, "Ji") evaluation must be conducted. It should be based on five criteria—morale, meteorological conditions (the "heavens"), topographical conditions (the "earth"), those in command, and the system of organization—and it should pose a definite set of questions (1. Which sovereign makes the better morale prevail? 2. Which commander is the more capable? 3. Which side benefits more from the meteorological conditions and the topography of the terrain? 4. On which side are orders obeyed more punctiliously? 5. Which side is the better armed? 6. Which side has the better-trained officers and men? 7. On which side, finally, is discipline better observed?). The expert on strategy then concludes: "On the basis of the above, I know who will prevail and who will be defeated." From this antagonistic situation, as evaluated by that series of questions, by viewing it from every possible angle, he will discover a particular potential and will only need to exploit it.

The system of evaluation

This passage, moving from an assessment of the forces in confrontation to the potential that can be deduced from that assessment, is of central importance. The words of the ancient treatise deserve particularly close attention: "Once the assessment of what is profitable [made on the basis of the above seven points] has been agreed upon, one can deduce the potential of the situation, which can be helpful outside[d] ['outside' meaning beyond the rules of evaluation, on the terrain where operations are to take place]." Hence the definition that follows: that potential consists in "determining the circumstances with a view to profiting from them." Understood in this fashion, circumstances are no longer something unpredictable that will turn out in a particular way, always threatening to ruin any plan imposed upon them. Instead, thanks precisely to their variability, circumstances can progressively be turned to advantage by the propensity emanating from the situation. In this way, one escapes from a logic of model-making (where a model-plan is brought to bear) and also from the task of producing an embodiment (making a project or idea become a concrete temporal reality), and one accedes to a logic of *unfolding:* one allows the implied effect to develop by itself, by virtue of the process that has been set off. Now circumstances are no longer conceived only (indeed, at all) as "that which surrounds" *(circum-stare),* that is to say, as accessories or details (accompanying that which is essential in the situation or happening—in keeping with a metaphysics of essence). Instead, it is through those very circumstances that potential is released, the potential, precisely, *of the situation.* Conclusion: potential is circumstantial—it only exists thanks to the circumstances and vice-versa (so it is the potentiality of the circumstances that one needs to exploit).

Circumstances are no longer "that which surrounds"

Far from destroying a plan, circumstances create potential

As one commentator (Du Mu) rightly noted, even if one can be sure of victory on the basis of a preliminary assessment, the potential of the situation, for its part, cannot be "seen in advance" (i.e., before the start of operations), but only detected, since it changes all the time. Within this antagonistic process there is constant interaction: at every moment "it is on the basis of what is harmful to my opponent that I perceive what is profitable to myself" and, reciprocally, "on the basis of what is profitable to the enemy, I perceive what is harmful to me." As Wang Xi remarks, this comes down to recognizing that "the potential of the situation is whatever profits from that which is variable." With such a view of this potential, inevitably this essay on strategy moves on from the subject of initial assessments, conducted according to fixed rules, to consider how, later, to exploit the circumstances once the process has begun. The treatise now explains that, in the course of operations, one should constantly keep the enemy guessing, but also always adapt to him. If he is tempted by profit, "I lead him on"; if he is in disorder, I "seize hold of him"; if he stands fast, I "am prepared for him"; and so forth. Alternatively, if he is full of ardor, I "spread doubt among his ranks"; if he prudently adopts a low profile, I "pump up his pride"; if he is in splendid form, I "exhaust him." Given that I myself am constantly evolving in the presence of the enemy, I cannot tell in advance how I shall win the day. In other words, (Li Quan tells us), strategy cannot be determined "in advance," and

From an evaluation of the factors to the possibility of exploiting them

it is only "on the basis of the potential of the situation that it takes shape."[c]

Now let us return to the European side. When Clausewitz assessed the setbacks encountered by the theorists of warfare, he traced them back to three causes (*On Warfare*, II, 2): (1) The (Western) theorists of warfare "strove after determinate quantities," "whereas in war all calculation has to be made with varying quantities"; (2) they only took into consideration "material forces," "while all action in war is permeated by spiritual and moral forces and effects"; (3) "they only took into consideration the action of one of the combatants, while war entails a constant state of reciprocal action."

In contrast, as we can see, the concept of strategy elaborated in the ancient Chinese treatises, based on the key idea of the potential of a situation, is not affected by those three criticisms (and—from the outside—we can thus verify that the three causes are interlinked and refer back to a single logic): (1) The Chinese consider the potential of a situation to be variable; it cannot be determined in advance, since it proceeds from continuous adaptation; (2) the assessments from which the potential is deduced are adept at combining spiritual and physical features (taking into account both the morale on which the cohesion of the troops depends and also material questions of organization and weaponry); (3) the dimension of reciprocity lies at the very heart of what constitutes the potential of a situation (whatever is disadvantageous to the enemy is, by the same token, advantageous to oneself), and, in China, warfare is quite naturally thought of in terms of interaction and polarity, just as any other process is.

In consequence, Chinese military strategy is not affected by the theory-practice relationship. (The notion of the potential of the situation takes its place and, in its own way, provides the link between initial calculations and the inevitable variations that depend on the circumstances.) By the same token, it also avoids the inevitable inferiority ascribed to practice as opposed to theory, which has hitherto crippled Western theory, that of Clausewitz included. In short, it does not have to cope with "friction," since, whereas friction is a threat to any plan drawn up in

Warfare should be understood as "something that lives and reacts"

No more "friction," "chance," or "genius"

advance, adventitious circumstances are themselves precisely what make it possible for the implied potential to come about and deploy itself. The West, with its own kind of theoretical equipment, which is of a formalizing and technical nature, has proved itself to be singularly inept at thinking about the conduct of warfare, taking account only of secondary matters (preparations and material data) and failing to consider the phenomenon itself (although Clausewitz himself identified it as "something that lives and reacts"). That being so, only one option was left—one that even Clausewitz was unable to reject entirely—namely, to involve pure chance or genius. In contrast, the intelligence developed by Chinese thought is, manifestly, eminently *strategic*. By the end of Antiquity (at the time of the Warring States, in the fifth to fourth centuries B.C.), military treatises were producing a coherent account of that thinking, which was already leaving its mark on other sectors of human activity, in particular diplomacy and politics.

3

Court advisers and generals were confronted by similar problems. Whether he operated outside the court, arranging alliances, or inside it, trying to win the prince over to his own view, every diplomat had to start off by making a precise evaluation of the situation. He needed both to "appreciate" the relations of force at the political level and to "assess" the internal dispositions of his partners from a psychological point of view (*Guiguzi,* chap. 7, "Chuai"). Calculation of the relation between the forces in play thus involves a series of factors that, as before, are designed to reveal the situation clearly in all its aspects. It is necessary to gauge the respective sizes of the kingdoms involved, to evaluate their demographic dimensions, to measure their economic weight and wealth, and so forth. It is also necessary to determine which is favored topographically, which is stronger either strategically or because of the relations that obtain between the ruler and his ministers, and the like. Then it is necessary to estimate which allies one can count on, to whom the populace is best disposed, and who would profit from reversals in the

A similar systematic evaluation is required in diplomacy

current situation (see also chap. 5, "Fei qian"). By systematically completing this type of questionnaire and collating all the data, a political adviser acquires sufficient understanding of the factors in play to be certain of the result of the operation in which he then engages (and if he finds that his calculation was faulty, the treatise observes, that is because he did not yet understand the situation fully (chap. 3, "Nei qian"). Where the ruler is concerned, the adviser's calculations ought to focus on what he likes and what he dislikes so as to be sure to please him, thereby gaining his sympathy, thus winning him over and rendering him amenable to his own suggestions. As for other figures at court, the adviser needs to gauge their intelligence, their abilities, and their attitudes so as to make use of those factors in his handling of them.

In this domain, as in that of military strategy, there is no need to make a plan or to fix a norm to guide your behavior. In order to have the whip hand over another and make use of him as you please, the only way forward, after assessing him carefully, is to adapt yourself to him; whatever his personal characteristics may be, they can be used to your own advantage. If the person in question has moral priorities that cause him to despise riches, you cannot suborn him with the temptation of profit but can, instead, make the most of this by getting him to agree to an outlay of money. If he is so courageous that he scorns all danger, you have no way of frightening him but, instead, can profit by getting him to confront any dangers, and so on (chap. 10, "Mou"). This ancient treatise on diplomacy is bent on analyzing in detail how, by constantly adapting yourself to another person and by never alienating him and so never causing him to doubt or resist you, you gradually increase your power over him and so can manipulate him as you will. By remaining ever flexible, always going along with the situation, never forcing it or even countering it, you make yourself available to the situation, never predetermining anything yourself or expending any energy. When your partner has doubts, you "modify" your conduct. Whatever he knows, you "agree that it is so." Whatever he says, you underline as being the essential point. When things seem to be "going well for him," you "make them happen." Whatever he dislikes, you "adapt." Whatever he fears, you "ward off." And so on. Your partner in this way moves forward amid a continuous kind of acquiescence that progressively makes him weaker and gives you ascendancy over him. In this way, in relations with others (especially the ruler himself), you always act openly, without risk, neither planning nor forcing anything in advance, but always adapting so closely to the circumstances that, on the contrary, it is they that at every turn offer you a measure of control from which you can profit. Allowing yourself always to be carried along by the situation in this fashion, you gradually increase your control over what is happening. The treatise produces a striking image for this: a sage "spins," as a ball would, to find the "adequate" position in any situation. Because his strategy never limits itself to a single level, never commits him to any plan, it is fathomless: "fathomless" to others and "inexhaustible" to himself.

Adapt to circumstances in order to profit from them (rather than following an ideal model)

This thinking on diplomacy logically enough brings us back to the idea of the *potential of a situation* (again the notion of *shi*). For the sway that you acquire over the other person is not due to your own efforts nor to chance (neither would be successful anyway). It is due solely to the fact that you know how to make the most of the ongoing process: you rely on the determining factors that you have managed to detect in the situation and leave them to play in your favor. The formula in which this notion is expressed in this treatise on diplomacy is as decisive as those used in the treatises on the military art: "To manage things, you must establish the potential of the situation" (chap. 5, "Fei qian"). And, as we have seen, in order to establish that, you need first to evaluate the situation as precisely as possible. (In a diplomatic context, this involves determining who is on your side, detecting who agrees with you and who does not, noting what is said both "inside" the court and "outside" it, and so on.) It is the potential of the situation, which has gathered force as things have evolved, that will, in the clearest fashion, result in your acquiring maximum control rather than being defeated (chap. "Benjing yinfu"). For it is definitely that potential that "separates" "profit" from "harm," since it

The potential of the situation determines its evolution

is the factor that, through its "authority," influences how the situation will evolve.[f] We revert, quite naturally, to the image of round stones rolling down a slope and to the conclusion that the potential of the situation makes it impossible that things "should be otherwise." In diplomacy, just as in military strategy, there is a strategic *configuration*, and the objective conditioning that it produces is just as determining.

4

Now let us consider this potential in a situation within the framework of social and political organization. It takes the form of a *position of strength (shi)* that confers authority, while the gradient that produces an effect (for instance, stones rolling down a hill) corresponds to the difference in hierarchical positions. The potential in the situation creates a gradient of obedience, which is the source of whatever ascendancy is exercised. Thanks to your superior position, you are inclined to be heeded by your inferiors. However, this has nothing to do with your personal qualities or the efforts that you may make, or even the fact that you may have solicited their attention. It happens without any need to commit or expend yourself. This propensity to be obeyed stems solely from the position that you occupy. In short, the effect results from your position, not from yourself.

The place par excellence from which authority spontaneously stems is the throne. That is why one major school of thought in late Chinese Antiquity focused on the notion of authority and aimed to set up the throne as the source of absolute power. It did not do this, as happened elsewhere or was recommended by others in China (the Confucians), by invoking any kind of transcendence, in the name of any divine power, or in the name of any political contract reached between individuals in order to provide a basis for civil order. Instead, it did it solely in the name of efficacy: simply by reason of its higher position, the place occupied by the ruler emanated sufficient power to ensure that order reigned throughout the whole empire. It did so solely by virtue of the purely objective propensity

In politics, the potential is a position of authority

The slope of obedience

that emanated from it, not at all on account of the ever unpredictable qualities of any individual. These defenders of authoritarianism are known as the "legalists" (most unsuitably, given that their views were a far cry from our own idea of law): they were not concerned with legality, only with authority. What they tried to do was concentrate the potential of the situation in the position of a single figure, the prince, who was at the top of the hierarchy. Their aim was to turn political relations into a means purely for imposing authority. The hierarchical gradient from which the potential stemmed remained, but the potential of the situation, now polarized on the prince, became fixed. No longer eminently changeable, it was immobilized at a single point. The prince was carried by his people as a log perched on the summit of a mountain is carried by the mountain and dominates it (Han Feizi, chap. 14, "Gong ming").

But how was this post of command from which limitless obedience flowed conceived? From the lofty position where he was perched and purely through his authority, the prince held both "sleeves" in his grip, distributing both rewards and punishments (both codified according to strict rules—*fa*—recognized by all and sundry and regularly applied). The two levers of fear and self-interest, the one repressive, the other an incentive, on their own constituted a device that enabled the prince to manipulate human nature as he pleased (HFZ, chap. 7, "Er bing"). At the same time, these defenders of authoritarianism (who, by the same token, were also the inventors of totalitarianism) understood full well that the basic essence of the power that one exercises over others depends on the knowledge about them that one acquires by forcing transparency upon their lives: the less one can conceal, the more docile one must be. An all-seeing eye has a paralyzing effect.

A punctilious system is set up for "dissociating" opinions (which makes it possible to challenge them individually) and combined with a "solidarization" of individuals (which makes them collectively responsible and encourages them to denounce one another) (HFZ, chap. 48, "Ba jing," sections 4 and 6). This is accompanied by secret,

The position of authority constitutes a mechanism

Far more effective than Bentham's "Pantopticism" (Foucault)

subtle policing techniques that proceed, on the one hand, by means of investigations and, on the other, by the dissemination of misinformation designed to entrap people (the notion of *shu*). The prince thus turns his position into a veritable intelligence-gathering machine. Through this relentless collection of information and this meticulous gleaning of data, from deep inside his palace he is able to "see everything" and "hear everything" (given that, in these circumstances, everyone "becomes his eyes and his ears" (HFZ, chap. 14). As the first hint of rebellion is immediately denounced, he does not even need to resort to force to repress it. Basically, the art of government lies simply in making others compete in the maintenance of one's own position. The ruler himself does not make any effort at all but gets others to wish to do so for him. It is perfectly possible for him to devote himself to his task without leaving his palace or without even occupying his position there. He can perfectly well withdraw "to the seaside" yet still keep control of his mechanism of power and continue to direct everything. In other words, the position of authority needs to be occupied not in person, but only technically. It does not require any physical presence that is inevitably of a local and limited nature. It is simply a matter of issuing orders. This makes it possible to exercise power fully without expending great efforts.

> Make others compete to secure one's position

> A perfect tyrant does not need to be present

Given the totally sufficient efficacy of the position of the ruler, the only task that falls to the prince in order for him to govern is to respect that position's automatic nature and to maintain it unimpaired. Since sovereignty only exists thanks to that position and can count on no feelings of love or gratitude on the part of the people (in contrast to the paternalism of which Confucius dreamed), that sovereign position has to defend itself against any infringement and prevent the establishment of any other position that could detract from its authority. From the point of view of that position, the prince and his subjects are perceived to be in a strictly antagonistic relationship. Power thus turns out to be the object of a permanent conflict, even if this remains for the most part latent. It is a conflict that opposes the despot to everyone else: his nobles, ministers, and advisers, and also his wife, mother, concubines,

> Never allow this position to be encroached upon

bastards, and, of course, his son and heir, for all of them would like him to "lose" his position or at least to "share" it (HFZ, chap. 48, sections 3 and 8). This theory of the ruler's position thus exists in parallel to a subtle theorization of the psychology of seduction (in the sense of winning another's confidence), which stands in opposition to what we have learned of the art of diplomacy to be mastered by court advisers and which sets one on one's guard against the latter: above all the prince should beware of those who anticipate his desires and always act so as to please him, for by so doing they build up for themselves a stock of trust that makes it possible for them to shift him surreptitiously from his position of authority. They would do so not in order to overthrow the throne (that was unthinkable in China), but to usurp it, simply by taking the place of the current incumbent (to effect such a replacement would be all the easier given that individual qualities and commitment that might confer a personal dimension on power counted for nothing).

The other duty that falls to the ruler, as a way to use his position, is to allow that position to fulfill its role without interfering in the functioning of this mechanism by bringing his own generous sentiments and virtues into play. For, provided the apparatus represented by that position functions, others automatically submit to it. In contrast, because it introduces an element of unpredictability—inevitable where goodwill is concerned—and also the possibility of exceptions (to the norm), any measure of indulgence and generosity on the part of the ruler is an inevitable source of dysfunction. The human vibrations set off by such a measure would upset a system that, otherwise, works automatically. In making power depend on this, purely instrumental, position of authority, the general aim of the Chinese defenders of despotism was to depersonalize it as completely as possible (indeed it is my belief that they went farther along this path than any other cultural tradition). Whereas the ascendancy of a Confucian type of ruler stems from his wisdom and is manifested by the favorable influence that he spreads around him, the ascendancy of a legalist sovereign rests entirely on the huge inequality of his position as compared to all others and the potential that stems from this. Two criteria are possible: on the one hand, personal *merit;* on the other, the occupation of this *position* of authority. And in the legalists' view, the one excludes the other (HFZ, chap. 40, "Nan shi"). Either you rely on your personal qualities and exhaust yourself in your efforts, in which case the result is always precarious (HFZ, chap. 49, "Wu du"), or else you rely solely on that position of authority, allowing yourself to be "carried" along by it, as a dragon is by the clouds (see Shen Dao), in which case all orders are unfailingly executed (HFZ, chap. 28), in the same unfailing way that a cargo carried by a ship is bound to float....

The continuity between the concept of military strategy that has remained traditional in China down to the present day and this particular political concept is easy to see. The courage or cowardice of a fighter depends on the potential of the situation just as the submission or insubordination of a ruler's subjects do (the same notion of *shi* obtains). In both cases, the objective conditioning of the situation matters more than the intrinsic qualities and efforts of individuals. But whereas in thought about warfare this concept of a potential rested on interaction and polarity, and the situation was always considered as it evolved (in fact, its very evolution was the source of its effects), in thought about power (and how to increase it to the maximum), the defenders of despotism sought to monopolize all the potential, making it converge upon the throne in such a way as to immobilize the situation (in an exclusive—and perpetual—relationship based on submission). The system was blocked and became aberrant. Yet that did not make it totally inefficacious. It was by scrupulously following the teaching of those theorists of despotism that the Chinese empire was founded (in 221), and, as is well known, it became the world's first bureaucratic empire.

Merit versus position

3

Goal or Consequence

*[handwritten: the goal gets us to make the effort.
holds out a promise]*

1

[handwritten margin note: end ideally conceive. the means whereby the end can be made to enter the realm of]

[handwritten margin note: Can we do without the means-end relationship?]

[handwritten: fact]

In the alternative sketched out above, the first way of proceeding, the "European" way of "model-making," involves a means-end relationship. Once an end is ideally conceived, we set about finding the means whereby that end can be made to enter the realm of fact (fully accepting the presumable element of intrusion, however arbitrary and forced). Or, to put it the other way around, what we understand by a plan, in the sense of a plan of action, is an elaborated project involving a sequence of operations that constitute means designed to attain a particular goal.

Means-end: at one end, and already more or less to hand, a wide range of resources in the shape of tools and markers; at the other end, far away on the horizon, something that is at once an end and a goal *(telos)*, to which we unswervingly march, with our eyes fixed upon it. This goal draws us along, getting us to make an effort, and at the same time holds out a promise. The opposition is so well established and has become so convenient that it eludes our thought (our thinking takes it as its starting point, but we do not think *about* it). The framework that it provides is of the most general nature: our understanding is based upon it, and from it we expect efficacy. (Generally speaking, action, for us, means employing certain means with a view to achieving a given end, so efficacy is an element that figures in the means-end equation.) I would even suggest that those concerned with "management" today, although in quest of new models, cannot do without this concept, not even if they redefine one of the terms in the pairing or push it to the limit (for example, they may consider the end that is envisaged to be a fiction but nevertheless consistent enough to call for useful means). The framework that the pairing provides can be reworked and its limits can be redefined, but it is hard to step outside it. The framework remains, for it is the framework of our thought.

But then, in China, we find a way of thinking about efficacy that, since it projects no plan upon the course of things, by the same token does not need to envisage behavior from a means-end point of view. In these circumstances, one's behavior does not result from an *application* (with a theory conceived in advance being imposed upon reality in such a way as to be eventually imprinted upon it). Rather, it is determined by an *exploitation* (the best way to profit from the potential implied by the given situation). Other points of view, or at least ones that are in our interest in that they are different and shift us from our own entrenched positions, can help us to detect new possibilities. These points of view do not place a high value on setting up preconceived and systematically managed operations or on marking out their gradual progress, according to a program devised to achieve a predetermined goal. In short, there is no foreseen outcome, perfect in itself, to dictate the way of proceeding and guide us on our way. The "way" itself (the *dao*), as conceived traditionally in China, is a far cry indeed from our Western method (*methodos*, which is a "way" to be "pursued" that leads "toward" something).

Let us return, from this standpoint, to the matter of our own theoretical preconceptions. The "prudent" man introduced by Aristotle to mediate between theory and practice is defined as someone capable of "deliberating" on means with a view to achieving a given end. How does Aristotle conceive of that deliberation? He takes as his model the construction of mathematical figures. You start from the constructed figure and work back, through a regressive analysis of the sequence of necessary operations

The framework remains, for it is the framework of our

More on the divergence

Thought

(Oc)

At the origin of the means-end relationship: "prudence," an ability to deliberate on means (so that the last term discovered by the analysis turns out to be the first from the point of view of the genesis of that sequence). In exactly the same way, you start off from the supposedly achieved goal and then work back to determine the sequence of means that lead to that achievement (and the last means discovered is thus the means with which it will be necessary to begin). At the same time though, Aristotle is well aware that the model borrowed from mathematics is not totally suitable for human action (see the interpretation produced by Pierre Aubenque in his study of prudence): (1) Unlike mathematical reversibility, which makes it equally possible to move either forward or backward along the sequence, human action takes place in irreversible time, and, so long as it is not verified by experience, the instrumental causality of the means remains hypothetical. (2) There is always a danger that, between the means and the projected end, unpredictable events may intervene, blocking the supposed efficacy of the means and rendering the end unattainable. (3) Conversely, taking into account the relative autonomy of the means vis-à-vis the end, there is also a danger that, in the development of its causality, the means may overshoot the intended end (as an example of this adjacent or parasitic kind of causality, Aristotle suggests the case of a remedy intended to heal that accidentally kills the patient).

It would thus appear that, in Europe, we always return to the following typical pattern of behavior: we start off with an ideal model (preferably one provided by mathematics) and then envisage to what extent practice differs from it. The reason the mathematical model cannot be completely applicable to our behavior "in questions of medicine or in money matters," Aristotle tells us (*Nic. Ethics*, III, 1112b), is that we are faced with several means that are possible but, by that very token, remain conjectural. It is only by comparing those conjectures that we can find which, of all the means envisaged, "is the one that is the most rapid and the best." For a mathematician, there is only one solution to a problem. In contrast, people generally find themselves faced with a number of concurrent possibilities but cannot be certain of the outcome of any of them. Deliberation (concerning means) can nei-

Work backward from the end achieved through the sequence of means employed (Aristotle, on geometry)

Conduct and conjecture

ther be based on knowledge nor, on the contrary, depend on divination; it can neither be founded on what is necessarily so, nor can it rely on chance. It must therefore confine itself to an approximate knowledge of "opinion" as it compares the respective efficacy of the possible means and can never rule out the possibility of failure.

The gap between the end and the means is further widened by the fact that they depend on two different faculties. On the one hand, will, understood to be an aptitude to desire what is good *(boulesis)*, determines the hoped-for end (which, however, may remain simply a pious hope); on the other hand, our capacity to choose *(proairesis)* causes us to opt, following deliberation, for the most suitable means (but, given the circumstances and the obstacles, this capacity can only be directed toward what may *possibly* be effective). The two questions consequently need to be considered separately: on the one hand, the matter of the quality of the end, which, in the last analysis, is of a moral order; on the other, that of the efficacy of the means, which is morally neutral and of a technical order, as is illustrated by the arts of medicine and warfare, or even by gymnastics. So deliberation on whether it is opportune to go to war has nothing to do with knowing whether the envisaged war is just or not (*Eudemian Ethics*, 1227a). From this Aristotle concludes that there are two domains, not just one, "in which the best action can be produced." One consists in determining the correct end *(telos)*, considered as the object to be aimed for *(skopos)*, the other in "discovering the means that will lead to that end" *(ta pros to telos)*. But it is perfectly possible for "the end and the means to be at odds instead of in agreement (or "in symphony," *sumphonein*, as Aristotle puts it). "For it sometimes happens that the end is good, but, in action, the means to attain it are lacking; at other times, one possesses the appropriate means, but the end that is projected is bad." Platonism was concerned solely with the excellence of the end (culminating in the supreme end, the idea of the good) and so regarded the administration of the means merely as immediately subordinate to the attainment of the end. But Aristotle no longer believed that means stem so easily from the idea/end and regarded

Means that are intractable to their ends

their adaptation as problematic. For an action to be good, it is not enough for it to be well intentioned: it must also be successful; and in view of the indeterminacy of things, that *realization* cannot eliminate all perils and risks.

2

In his thought on warfare, Clausewitz was similarly unable to get around this problem and settled on formulating it in the most general of terms: "Theory must endeavor to consider the nature of means and ends" (*On War*, II, 2). In military tactics, the means are the armed forces used in combat, and the end is victory in the engagement; but it is well known that, from the point of view of the strategy, this tactical success is itself only a means, since the ultimate aim is to dictate one's own conditions for peace to the enemy. In the last analysis, warfare itself is a means, and politics is the end. Thanks to this interaction, the two ends of the chain are neatly kept in hand; and until such time as the ultimate end is attained, every particular end, because it is subordinate to a more general one (cf. the difference between *Ziel* and *Zweck*) itself serves as a means to the latter. So the "war plan" itself is arrived at quite simply by working backward along the chain. However subtle and profound Clausewitz's analysis may be, and however conscious he may be of the irreducible difficulties encountered when thinking about warfare, he never breaks away from what seems, at every turn, to impose itself as an indisputable fact: efficacy in warfare, as in everything else, must surely be a matter of "knowing how to organize the warfare in precise conformity with one's means and one's ends, without doing either too much or too little." In support of this, he offers the example of Frederick II, who is to be admired for knowing how to do "*just what was necessary* in order to achieve his end." In comparison to Charles XII, or even Napoleon, he proves himself to be the best general of all, the one who was most successful precisely because he was economical. Already as a young man, Clausewitz had made such economy a guiding rule, a practical maxim in a Kantian mode but designed for practice that would aim

Means-ends also provides a framework for military strategy

The strategic imperative expressed in terms of means-ends (by Clausewitz)

solely for efficacy and in the end broke all links with morality: "You will aim for the most important and most decisive goal that you feel you have the strength to attain; and to that end, you will choose the shortest path that you feel you have the strength to follow."

What Clausewitz here tentatively recommends as a recipe for efficacy might be verifiable from an opposite and retrospective point of view when, instead of conducting warfare, it is a matter of learning from the wars of the past. In the military domain, a "critique" consists simply in "testing out the means employed" in order to evaluate them. Clausewitz tells us that to have any hope of arriving at a general theory, we need to know "what effects are produced by the means adopted" and whether those effects "were intended by the person who adopted those means." However, as soon as we embark on this critical examination, everything becomes confused. The means-end relation, which we flattered ourselves we could control so well and which seemed to us to be self-evident, once again confounds the theory (see II, 5, the particularly convoluted chapter devoted to the "critique"). In the first place, it becomes manifestly clear that a means can never be altogether isolated from the context within which it is used and is therefore never completely analyzable, never perfectly identifiable. Just as any cause, however minimal, will "extend its effects right to the end of the act of warfare," "modifying the final result to some, however slight, degree," similarly, "every means will produce effects that will extend right up to the attainment of the final goal." As it spreads and intermingles with the complexity of other phenomena, the particularity of the means is dissolved and changed and is no longer measurable. Furthermore, a critical examination should not limit itself to analyzing the means actually employed but should also address—by way of a comparison—"all the possible means," which it is first necessary to specify, that is to say, basically, to "invent." Clausewitz is not afraid to use that word. When an analysis of what really happened is no longer sufficient, the evaluation of other possibilities calls for considerable "initiative," even "creativity," on the part of a critic (even a military one!). In these circumstances, it

But, given that a means melts into the course of things, is it ever completely identifiable?

is not easy to see things exactly from the point of view of the person whose actions one has set out to praise or to blame.

On closer examination, the means-ends relation thus turns out to raise as many difficulties as the relationship of causality from which it is inseparable; and what we begin to glimpse from a retrospective and "theoretical" "critical" analysis rebounds upon the practical situation of a man deliberating on the means to attain a predetermined end. We cannot help wondering *whether in effect it ever happens* that, engaged as we are in all the complexity of situations still in the process of evolving, we are ever in a position to "choose" means that are sufficiently clear and distinct, like (Descartes') ideas, and whose future effects it is possible for us to foresee in order to compare them and "deliberate" upon them. It is no longer good enough to recognize, with Aristotle, that the means of action that we envisage are always more or less conjectural, since deliberation, the source of the "prudence" that should illuminate our choice, itself becomes something of an illusion. In other words—and it is no longer possible to duck this question—is there not something *magical* (if I can venture, tentatively, to use the word) about this distant testing out of possible means to project upon the future in anticipation of a particular end?

At this point, it seems particularly opportune to consider how Chinese thought on efficacy might manage to sidestep these difficulties (albeit, no doubt, only to run into others; I do not expect it to resolve the complications encountered by Western theory but hope, rather, that, thanks to the displacement that it occasions, it will allow us to perceive the reasons for those difficulties more clearly). As we have seen, a Chinese general does not elaborate a plan that he projects upon the future and that leads to a predetermined goal and then define how to link together the means best suited to realize that plan. Instead, he begins by making a minute evaluation of the relation of the forces in play so that he can make the most of the favorable factors implied in the situation, exploiting them constantly, whatever the circumstances that he encounters. We know that circumstances may often be unforeseen,

Is not deliberation about "means" bound to be illusory?

even unforeseeable, and unprecedented, which is why it is not possible to draw up a plan in advance. Rather, they contain a certain potential from which, if we are agile and adaptable, we can profit. That is why the Chinese general projects and constructs nothing. Nor does he "deliberate" or need to choose (between equally possible means). This suggests that, for him, there is not even an "end" set up in the distance as an ideal, but he continues to make the most of the situation as it unfolds (guided simply by whatever profit there is to be gained). More precisely, his entire strategy consists in allowing the situation to evolve in such a way that the effects result progressively of their own accord and cannot be avoided. As we are beginning to see, this may involve gradually exhausting and paralyzing the enemy so that, when he finally does engage in battle, his opponent has already given up the fight; alternatively, he may, on the contrary, lead his own troops into a situation from which there is no escape, a deadly terrain, so that they are forced to fight to the death, with no hope of retreating (SZ, chap. 11, "Jiu di"). "Having penetrated deeply into danger, they are no longer afraid"; "no longer knowing where to turn, they resist"; "with no alternative, they fight." Having reached such a point, the situation *contains its own effect*: ". . . without one needing to maintain order, they are attentive"; "without one needing to bind them together, they show solidarity"; "without one needing to give orders, they obey."

We, in the West, have stressed the conative and probationary nature of the means that we construct in order to ascend toward a goal ("toward" as in *pros to telos*), with that whole construction at every moment liable to collapse. Chinese thinkers, in contrast, have stressed the legitimacy of the inevitable result. For us the means are always relatively artificial, a deliberate construction designed to exert pressure on things so as to bring about the desired end. For them, once the situation's potential has developed, it becomes a *situation of strength* (in the same sense as in the expression "a position of strength" that has been used above). This is expressed in a variety of formulations: "the situation is such that it cannot be otherwise";[g] "without one seeking it,"[h] the result is obtained. If the worst of

A Chinese general does not deliberate on means

But he makes the most of the way the situation evolves

The situation itself leads to the result

enemies embark on a ship together, and the wind comes up and they are confronted by a storm, you will see them cooperating as closely as your own two hands usually do. In exactly the same way, in armies, cohesion grows out of the perilous situations into which they are thrown (SZ, ibid.). The Chinese writers tell us that, in order to make his troops resist and prevent their taking flight, a general does not "rely on" material means (such as "hobbled horses" and "embedded wheels" as in our Maginot Line). Instead, he is content to allow the situation into which he has led them to operate in its own way. For once the situation has begun to develop, it allows no other way out; one "is bound" to go along with it.

Two different modes of efficacy result from these two different logics: on the one hand, the relation of means to ends with which we in the West are the more familiar; on the other, a relation between conditions and consequences, which is favored by the Chinese. When strategy consists in getting a situation to evolve in such a way that, if one allows oneself to be carried along by it, the effect results naturally from the accumulated potential of the situation, there is no longer any need to choose (between means) or to struggle in order to attain an "end." Abandoning the logic of model-making (founded on the construction of an ideal end), you can switch to the logic of a process (note the importance of *ze*,[1] "as a result," in the construction of Chinese discourse). On one side, the causal system is open and complex, and an infinite number of combinations are possible; on the other, the process is closed, and its result is implicit in its evolution.

Conditions-consequences: a different perspective

Ze

(logic of a process)

3

The distance separating the two logics can be gauged by the way in which success is perceived: as hypothetical on one side, as inevitable on the other. On the Greek side, thought, born from epic and fashioned by tragedy, is sensitive to the threats by which human action is menaced. The general engages in battle as the pilot embarks on the high seas; both operate within constantly shifting fields, full of unpredictabilities, to the very end never certain of

For a pilot or a general, the undertaking remains chancy (on the Greek side)

triumphing over the enemy or making it to port: reversals are always possible between the two enemy camps, as are changes in the direction of the wind; and accounts of battles and journeys make the most of this dramatic suspense and such reversals of fortune. To succeed, the hero usually needs help from elsewhere. However fertile in cunning ploys, *mechanai*, their minds may be, the Achaeans at the gates of Troy are unable to secure victory without the assistance of the gods. And Odysseus, wandering over the "untamable waves," buffeted by hurricanes and doomed to shipwreck, would have been overcome by all those vicissitudes were it not for Athena's complicity. Even in the classical period, Greek treatises on strategy continued to recommend appealing to the gods as a last resort. "Remember that, in choosing their acts, all men are guided only by conjectures, never knowing what will turn to their advantage," the old king tells his son (Xenophon, *Cyropaedia,* I, 6). That is why, whether it is a matter of conquering the enemy by force or by cunning, "I counsel you to work with God" (Xenophon, *Cavalry Commander,* V). Rounding off the Greek rationalization of human action, Aristotle too classified the art of military strategy alongside that of navigation and declared that chance as well as skill played a part in both (*Eudemian Ethics,* VIII, 2, 1247a): *technae* can complement *tuche* but never exclude it.

Clausewitz explained why chance can never be excluded from warfare. It is because real warfare is never absolute warfare (i.e., never in total conformity with the model and the concept of it); "mathematical rigor is excluded from it," and it is not possible to achieve "logically necessary" results. The diversity of relations that are interwoven in warfare and the uncertain nature of their delimitation means that many factors that cannot be evaluated exactly come into play. In particular, as is well known, the art of warfare applies to "living and moral forces" that elude the quantifiable definition to which physical effects lend themselves. As a result, "along every strand, be it thick or thin," from which the web of warfare is composed, a complex game of possibilities is played out, and this makes "warfare the human activity that most resembles a game

If the course of warfare cannot be "modeled," does that mean that it is illogical?

of cards." That is why, despite the horror that it arouses, it tempts and excites us, and its radical unpredictability, which defies all calculations, never ceases to fascinate us. Objectively, we cannot eliminate its chancy character, and, subjectively, the person in command finds himself constantly "faced with difficulties other than those that he expected." Consequently, he cannot help but "doubt" the plan that has been drawn up and in order to abide by it needs to call upon his willpower. At best, a general must work with probabilities, and "wherever certainty is lacking, he must trust to destiny or chance, whatever he chooses to call it."

Compared with this gaping hole that the argument of indeterminacy and chance leaves at the heart of Western theory, the hard-and-fast position adopted by the ancient Chinese treatises may come as something of a surprise.

In warfare, as in other things, once the situation begins to unfold, its evolution is unswerving

For whoever knows how to rely on the potential of the situation, "victory in battle is unswerving" (SZ, chap. 4, "Xing"). The fact that it is "unswerving"[i] means that what he then does "will lead him inevitably to success." According to the glosses, there is no possibility of things going "awry" (Zhang Yu), no "two" possible evolutions of the situation (Li Quan; cf. the "constant capacity" that is unswerving in *Laozi*, section 28). Given the evolution of the relation of forces, the outcome is predetermined even before battle is joined. As a commentator explains, "if one tried to win by force," that is to say, relying solely on one's physical strength, "however great," there would always be "moments when one could be beaten." But a good general intervenes upstream in the process. He has already identified the factors favorable to him "before they have actually developed" and in this way has got the situation to evolve in the direction that suits him. When the accumulated potential reveals itself to be completely in his favor, he engages resolutely in battle, and his success is assured.

intervenes upstream

before they have actually developed

Success is predetermined by the situation

The reason for this is simple: as this ancient treatise goes on to point out, he conquers an enemy "already defeated." Victory is predetermined and cannot swing off course, because it is implied in the relation of the forces present even before the battle is joined. That is neatly conveyed, in a back-to-front way, by the following remark:

"The victorious troops thus begin by winning and only then engage in battle, whereas the defeated troops begin by engaging in battle and only then try to win." The maxim may seem paradoxical, but it is not; it simply projects onto the opposed behavior of the two sides the breaking point that is bound to come in the evolution of the antagonistic relationship from which success is bound to stem. Troops who seek victory only when they begin to fight are defeated in advance. For, as will by now be clear, the battle itself is merely a result. Its outcome is simply a clear manifestation of the propensity already implicit in the situation even before the battle began. It is because he relies on that propensity that the victor is already decided even before battle commences.

"If I know my opponent and I know myself, in a hundred battles I have nothing to fear" (SZ, chap. 3, "Mou gong"). This idea may not seem very meaningful, indeed may seem so trite as not really to qualify as an idea at all. But Chinese strategy thought it through rigorously, pursuing all its consequences to their logical conclusion and delving deep beneath what seems self-evident. Like any other process, the course of warfare depends purely on the factors in play: if I know enough about the relationship of forces between my opponent and myself, I can insist on not joining battle until such time as I am certain that the potential of the situation operates completely in my favor. All strategy thus depends on a systematic intelligence operation and evaluation of the information that it obtains (hence the importance attached to spying and its different categories of agents, all of which are meticulously classified: "native agents," "internal agents," "double agents," and so on; see SZ, chap. 13, "Yong jian"). One needs to "calculate," "measure," "count," and "assess" until such time as the difference in weight between the forces present tips the scales suddenly to one side (SZ, chap. 4). The victorious troops, we are told, in the manner of adage (see also GGZ, chap. "Ben jing," section 4), are like a ton weight compared to a feather. By accumulating potential, the general increases the imbalance, and, when he joins battle, all he needs to do is allow free play to it. In view of all this, there is no longer anything strange

[handwritten margin note:] propensity implicit (forced in)

The originality of Chinese thought is to have found depth in this truism, to have dug deeper into what may seem self-evident or uncertain about warfare. It is reduced to a process that, set in train purely by the interaction of the (opposed and complementary) pair of adversaries, becomes perfectly coherent. That being so, no room is left for indetermination and chance, nor can the course of the warfare be determined by any external powers (such as the gods or destiny). For the writers of the Chinese treatises on strategy, the heavens are nothing but a meteorological and climatic sky, conceived as a purely natural phenomenon that operates normally as a factor to be considered in any evaluation of the relation of forces in play (see SZ, chap. 1, "Ji"); and if defeat results, it can under no circumstances be a case of a "celestial calamity," but is always the fault of the general (see SZ, chap. 10, "Di xing"). As for the "foreknowledge" that he needs before engaging in combat, a Chinese general never dreams of getting it from "spirits" but obtains it from his information services.... That is why, we are told in lapidary fashion, he needs to

Ban omens, dismiss all doubts

"ban omens and dismiss all doubts" (SZ, chap. 11, "Jiu di"). Not only does he reject *omina* before a battle, the kind of omens in which the whole of Western Antiquity trusted, but he does not even countenance the kind of doubt that, Clausewitz tells us, invariably assails a general when, having drawn up his plan, he launches into action. The whole of this Chinese thought is prompted by a single concept: whatever happens "in any case" "cannot not happen" (once all the conditions are ascertained); in other words, it is "ineluctable" (bi^{k}).

Propensity is crucial in morality as well as in strategy

This idea of the ineluctability of processes and so also of success for whoever is capable of profiting from it recurs constantly throughout all Chinese thinking. Even a thinker such as Mencius subscribes to this logic of consequentiality, despite the fact that he adopts a position altogether opposed to the theses of the strategists, since he considers that sovereignty depends not on the relation of forces and therefore the art of warfare, but on the sway exercised by morality. Or rather, morality is itself a force, and a particularly strong one, because it possesses great influence and uses this to effect, in a diffuse and discreet fashion. Be concerned for your people, Mencius tells the ruler, share your pleasures with them, and you will inevitably progressively come to rule over all other princes. That is because all peoples will desire to pass under your authority; they will open their doors to you and will be unable to resist you. Through violence, you will inevitably eventually come to grief, for the power at your disposal is limited and arouses rivalry. In contrast, if you depend on the propensity that stems from your own ascendancy, you will be swept to triumph by others (MZ, I, A, 7). The conclusion is the same as that drawn by the strategists, even if the starting point is quite the opposite (moral well-being as opposed to personal profit): there is no need even to "seek" this result, as the effect of encouraging favorable conditions will naturally follow and will become "irresistible." The whole of Chinese thought about efficacy reverts to a single act: that of "returning" to the fundamental "basis,"[1] that is to say, the starting point of something that, as a condition, subsequently carried forward by the evolution of things, will gradually impose its sway of its own accord. In such circumstances, an effect is not merely probable, as it is in a *constructed* relation of means to an end, but will unfailingly result, *sponte sua*.

As we can begin to see, the gap between the two kinds of efficacy is so wide that it must be explained by a more general difference. The deliberation that leads to the means-end relation is primarily a social and political procedure that the Greek world promoted, a procedure that even became its principal institution (from the time of Homer's *boule,* the Council of the Elders, right down to the democratic deliberations of the assembly). Along the way, the process of deliberation became internalized. It was by "deliberating within oneself" that an individual, establishing himself as "the origin of the future" *(arche ton esomenon),* planned his action. China, in contrast, did not set major store by deliberation in the organization of its political functioning. Instead, it founded its view of the world on regulation. As a result, it never conceived of efficacy on the basis of action, as an identifiable entity, but regarded it as a transformation.

In the background to this difference lies the fact that Greek deliberation is part of a political tradition

4

Action or Transformation

1

What assumptions
underlie thought
about action?

Is there truly anything in our behavior that can be said to be so complete—consistent in itself and independent of any context, in particular of a before and an after—as to be singled out, as such, from the web of our existence? Is there anything in reality that can be attributed to a particular person and identified as his or her action? The Chinese thinkers may well have thought not, for they considered human behavior, like everything else, in terms of a regulated and continuous process. For them, everything was interwoven: the course of nature and the course of human behavior (both *tianxing* and *renxing*), the human *dao* as much as the *dao* of the world. Thought on action implies two assumptions: (1) human behavior is envisaged as a specific deed (*ergon, praxis,* and here again the technical model of production provides the reference); (2) action is conceived as an entity on its own, which it is possible to *isolate* and which serves as a basic element of human behavior.

The "act" of war

Take Western thought about warfare. Clausewitz regards it as an act, "the act of war." We have already seen how military strategy is defined as a "plan," which itself relates to a "goal," but the basis of that strategy is action, for it provides "the means." In warfare, action that stems from a plan and leads to a goal is called an "engagement,"

The engagement is a
unit of the action

and it is on the basis of this "element" that warfare is analyzable. "Tactics" are regarded as the theory relating to the use of armed forces in the engagement, and "strategy" is the theory relating to the use of such engagements in the service of the war. Or, to put it another way, tactics are to do with the "form" of the engagement, while strategy relates to its "significance." "So there is only one single way of looking at things," Clausewitz concludes. One must determine, "at every moment in the war or campaign what will be the probable result of whatever major and minor engagements the two opposed parties may be proposing." In fact, it is at this point that Clausewitz' thought is at its most subtle—but, at the same time, it is possible that it overspills its framework and becomes endangered. For if the mere possibility of an engagement is taken into account, even a hypothetical engagement may have a crucial effect on the sequence of operations. In the last analysis, even if the engagement never takes place, its *consequences,* which are what is taken into consideration, are certainly real.

At any rate, only action, that is to say, an engagement, makes it possible to obtain "true efficacy," that is to say, the "direct efficacy" that makes the intended effect attainable. And Clausewitz leaves no doubt as to the nature of that effect: in warfare, the sole object of an engagement is the destruction of the enemy forces. Clausewitz belongs to the military tradition that originated with the pitched battle of Western Antiquity (a clash of phalanxes marching against each other in serried ranks), the type of battle that Napoleon is said to have likened to the absolute form of warfare (cf. Austerlitz). Clausewitz constructs his theory with just such a battle in mind: its sole objective is the annihilation of the enemy (*On War,* I, 2: "The destruction of the enemy's armed forces is thus always seen as the supreme and most efficacious means before which all others must give way").

> Destroy the enemy
> (Clausewitz)

The ancient Chinese treatise on warfare recommends the exact opposite. One of its early chapters begins by laying down the following principle: "In general, the best way of proceeding in war is to keep the [enemy] country intact." To destroy it is not the best option (SZ, chap. 3, "Mou gong"). And that remains true whatever the scale of

> Or prefer to keep it
> intact (the Chinese
> option)

the action: "To keep the [enemy] army intact is better than
to destroy it"; and, to make this quite clear, the author
repeatedly declares that the same applies at the level of
every batallion and the smallest platoon. The contrast with
Western tactics is flagrant. "Thus, those who are expert in
the art of warfare overcome the enemy army without engaging in combat. They capture towns without attacking
them and ruin a country with no prolonged operations.
The way to conquer the world is always to keep it intact.
In that way, weapons are not blunted and the profit is
total." As one commentator (Li Quan) sums it up, there is
no "value" in killing. Rather than destroy the forces of the
enemy, it is better to have them come over to your side. By
advancing deep into their territory, separating them from
their bases, and cutting off their communications, you
force the enemy to surrender of his own accord. Moreover, not only do you capture the enemy country intact,
"you also keep your own troops intact." Nothing could be
more economical.

It is important to see that this is no paradox. It is not
out of the goodness of your heart that you avoid mas-
sacring the enemy, but purely for the sake of efficacy. From
the point of view of action, the objective of warfare is the
destruction of the enemy, but from the point of view of a

Destruction or
deconstruction

transformation, the objective is a *deconstruction*. Now we
can begin to glimpse an opposition to which we shall have
occasion to return again and again: the efficacy of action is
direct (the means lead to an end), but it is both costly and
risky. In contrast, the efficacy of transformation is indirect
(the conditions lead to the consequences) but progressively
becomes irresistible. The Chinese classic declares specifically that the ideal in warfare is "to attack the enemy in
his strategy," then "in his alliances" (or "when his armies
meet up"), next "in his troops," and lastly "in his places."
The very worst procedure is to embark (directly) on siege
warfare, both because it pins down your troops and also
because they are then at their most exposed. Such an im-
mobile standoff represents the most abysmal strategy. Proper strategy consists in attacking the enemy in his "mind,"
as the ancient commentators put it, rather than in his
physical forces. For, becoming little by little increasingly

demoralized, the enemy eventually surrenders of his own accord. He is vanquished without a blow being struck, simply as a result of his resistance becoming paralyzed, not through the physical force of any "engagement."

The notion of an engagement seems to have suited Clausewitz for another reason too: it allowed him to analyze warfare purely as such, *stricto sensu,* in isolation from all that surrounded it or was intermingled with it yet remained separate from it. In other words, it enabled him to distinguish, in his own terms, between warfare in the strictest sense, that is to say, "the use of armed forces" and the "servicing of those forces," which could be regarded as merely "a preparation for combat" and could accordingly be excluded from strategy. Clausewitz could not deny the importance of those "preliminaries" (or what he felt bound to classify as such since, as he recognized, "such preparations affect the action closely in that they bring in their train the action of warfare, and, in practice, they alternate with it"). However, he needed to introduce that separation in order to think about "the concept" of warfare in isolation, as pure action.

Can an "act of war" be isolated?

In contrast, the ancient Chinese military treatises integrate into their strategic thinking not only matters to do with organization and supplies, but also the economic cost of the war and the moral and practical state of the country involved in it (see, in SZ, the important chapter 2, "Zuo zhan"). All the above are factors that impinge on the course of the war and affect it. They cannot be excluded as "concomitant circumstances," as they are by Clausewitz, since those circumstances are part and parcel of the potential of the situation and turn out to be decisive factors in the evolution of the forces present. In consequence, they modify the very nature of the engagement. For Clausewitz, only the engagement itself, in the heat of battle, is truly decisive. For him, that is the moment when everything comes into play, and, on that account, it in itself constitutes the "essence" of warfare. As we are now beginning to see, in the eyes of the Chinese strategists an engagement is simply a result in that it is the consequence of a transformation that began some way upstream from the action itself.

Thinking about warfare as he does, purely from the point of view of an engagement, an isolated action, Clausewitz can only conceive of the duration of a war as "a number of successive actions" or, at best, by connecting these together more closely, as "interlinked engagements." This means that he only envisages the time taken up by warfare, whether it be merely a campaign or a full-scale war, in terms of *the sum of the moments of action.* Any lapse of time between those engagements can only divert the war and dilute its essence. For anything that is not action can only be negative, "a suspension of action"—in other words, "inaction." Anything that does not constitute warfaring action becomes merely "a temporal dilution of the war."

The Chinese, in contrast, who were very much aware of the effects of even the briefest operations that might have a decisive impact, emphasized the progressive duration of a transformation in the course of which the potential of the situation accumulates. The time in between engagements is by no means sterile, so to speak, "dead time," however inactive it may seem, for this unfolding of time allows for an evolution thanks to which the relation of forces may eventually incline to one's own advantage. Time brings about not a "dilution," but a "maturation." The effect is not diluted but, on the contrary, deployed. For indirect efficacy requires a long time—a *slow* time—in order to operate. The Chinese, who conceived of warfare not as action but as a process can thus teach us to make good use of time.

.2

So perhaps we should think again about the Western myth of action, particularly given that action is the main subject of *muthos,* which is conceived to be, precisely, an account of action thanks to which European civilization began. Let us take another look at those images, which are among the first to figure in the history of Western reasoning. God— whether the god of the Judeo-Christian tradition or that of the *Timaeus*—brought the world into existence by a creative act; and the distinctive feature of a hero is likewise that he faces up to the world and affects it by his action. Literature began, in the epic, with an account of memorable acts, magnified as exploits; tragedy then set these on stage (and, although, as Aristotle reminds us, there was no term at the time for those whom we call the "characters," the specific function of theater was to represent men "in action," *prattontes*). To us, this may seem an altogether obvious observation, but from the Chinese point of view, it is less so. China never did construct a great story about genesis, nor was it concerned to explain the coming-to-be of the world by some demiurgic action (the story of Nü Wa fashioning figures out of mud never fueled any significant line of Chinese thought). Nor is there any trace of the epic in Chinese Antiquity, nor, consequently, the kind of theater that, in the West, followed from it. Those absences are worth considering when it comes to discovering the source of our own (Western) representations. For we find that not only did Chinese thought never develop a cult of action—either heroic or tragic—but also, more radically, it never chose to interpret reality in terms of action. On the contrary, its most ancient work (the *Yijing*, or *Book of Changes*), which is constructed on the basis of the opposition between two types of strokes, the one continuous, the other broken, representing the two poles of every process, interprets reality as a continuous transformation. Within a series of diagrams, figures can be converted into one another simply by a permutation of those strokes, and by consulting them a sage can learn to appreciate the field of forces that are present in any situation and that constitute its potential. The purpose of this was not to turn them into an object of contemplation (whereas in Greece thought about action went hand in hand with the abstraction of being). Instead, it was to *harmonize* the development of a situation with the evolution of things in general. As we shall see repeatedly, in China efficacy is effective through adaptation.

As we know, Aristotle, moving on from his thought about tragedy, came to conceive action on the basis of two opposed modalities. Either it is accomplished "freely and willingly" *(hekon)* or "unwillingly"; either its principle lies within us or we act "under constraint" or "out of

The Chinese view

[handwritten marginal note: Book of Changes: by 2 strokes, one continuous and broken; reality, as a continuous transformation]

ignorance." In this way, he drew attention to the nonattributability of the subject and indicated a level at which deliberation enabled that subject to "choose" how to act. (From this, Western thought was later able to develop its notion of the will as an autonomous condition of liberty.) It is interesting to note that the Chinese language, for its part, never categorically opposes the active and the passive (there are not two separate voices). In most cases it leaves that difference undecided and describes operations from the angle not so much of the agent as of the "functioning" (that of the *yong* in relation to the *ti*).ᵐ Take, for example, efficacy through influence, which results from conditioning (as when the potential of the situation renders us courageous in battle): how can that be attributed to ourselves? We do not "choose" to be so, nor does it come about as a result of some kind of "violence" against us (encouraging us to deploy our energy); it is both integral to us and at the same time inclines us to such behavior. The active-passive divide, as defined in our Western grammar books, is too narrow to apprehend this. For whatever "inclines" me in this way is neither within me nor imposed upon me; rather, it "passes through me." Whereas action is personal and refers back to a subject, this transformation is *trans*individual, and its indirect efficacy dissolves the subject. Naturally, this benefits the category of the process.

We in the West too sometimes have to address a case in which the result comes about without it being possible for us to consider that it is due to ourselves personally. We have a traditional solution to this (but of course Chinese thinkers have no need of this): we were "inspired." This success for which I am not personally responsible results from an action that is external to me—but it is still action, for all that, whether it be that of the gods or of demons. Reason has to strain to accept such a solution. Aware that it is irrational, it nevertheless tolerates it for the sake of convenience, for it is a solution that compensates for the rationalization necessary to set up an acting subject as an autonomous element, yet it does not force us to abandon the idea of an agent (even if it does set it at one remove). Following in Plato's steps, even Aristotle resorts to this solution (just as we ourselves, surely, continue to do). He

That which is neither chosen nor undergone

Neither active nor passive

Neither me nor not me

The dissolution of the category of the subject benefits that of the process

Behind the myth of action lies that of "inspiration"

declares that those who, "whichever way they launch themselves, are successful without even thinking, are inhabited by a god (*Eudemian Ethics,* VII, 1247a). Good fortune *(eutuchia)* is a "gift" from Heaven, in the same way that noble birth is. However, little by little, from Aristotle onward, Western thought developed a different concept of chance (see *Nic. Eth.,* VI), now seeing it as an effect not of providence but of contingency, due not to inspiration from some god but to the indeterminacy of matter. Now chance was no longer the name that we, in our ignorance, gave to the mysterious force beyond the causes that we can perceive, a force that seemed to direct everything. Instead, it became something that, in the lacunae left by divine action, made it possible for human initiative to find a place. Lacking guidance by a god, one can—indeed should—resort to deliberation. There is room for human action to intervene in the order of the world, since that order is incomplete. Prudence *(prudentia,* which Cicero considered to be a contraction of *"providential"*), taking over from an inadequate Providence, is the only means left to us to direct action toward success.

> A change in the European definition of chance

European thought thereafter continued to widen the breach thus made in the indeterminacy of things. From the Renaissance onward, in particular, by dissociating the world of human affairs from the notion of final causes (with contingency now playing far more than the residual role assigned to it by Aristotle), it came to associate action and efficacy ever more closely. With the human world seen as a world of instability, doomed to discontinuity, ephemerality, and mobility, and without any intrinsic or transcendent principle of order, the only way thinkers could conceive of efficacy was in terms of a risky intervention that, thanks to its audacity, might cope with the unpredictability of things—or even profit from it. As is well known, for Machiavelli, politics was essentially action, just as warfare was, and from start to finish *The Prince* sings the praises of an ability to take action. The matter of politics, being contingent, is—by the same token—malleable and, in consequence, also technically transformable. A man can gain a hold on it and, despite the dangers involved, can hope to give it form by imposing his own designs upon it.

> Bold action is the only means of coping with unpredictability

Since political chaos is open to all initiatives, a man can react to danger with all the virtuosity of innovative action. In this way, by the time the ancient notion of creation had undergone a considerable secularization, the criterion by which to measure a hero (whether Cyrus, Theseus, or Romulus—or even Moses) was considered to be determined and resolute, foundational action, on a strictly human level. Through his action, a man could become the creator of "new order."

3

However, the Chinese tradition was undeniably skeptical of efficacy ascribed to action. This applies right across the board of Chinese thinkers, irrespective of how emphatic they are. It is as though they all shared a common intuition upon which their thought was based (that is to say, which it constantly exploited), an intuition so manifestly well founded that it could hardly be questioned and was, in consequence, never fully justified. I shall therefore venture to elaborate upon it. For the very reason that action intervenes in the course of things, it is always external to it and constitutes an initiative that is intrusive. Because it impinges from outside, introducing a plan/project (ideal), it is always to some degree external to the world and is therefore relatively incompatible and arbitrary: both arbitrary and importunate, for, by forcing itself into the course of things, it inevitably to some degree tears at the tissue of things and upsets their coherence. In fact, by imposing itself, it inevitably provokes elements of resistance, or at least of reticence, that it cannot immediately control and that, tacitly forming common cause, block and quietly undermine it. The shock that it thereby produces is deadened, makes little impact, and its effects are absorbed.

Moreover, action from the outside always intervenes at one particular moment and not at another, applying force in one particular spot and not in any other. It is always local and momentary (even if it lasts for ten years, as the Trojan War did). It is always a "one-off." Because it is arbitrary and isolated, such an action stands out in the course of things; it attracts notice. By forcing the course of things, it also forces attention. Furthermore, because action is personal and relates directly to a particular (even if collective) subject, it is easy to spot. It constitutes an event, suggests a meaning, becomes the basis of a story. It focuses attention, crystallizes interest. The interconnections that it picks out from the unfolding of things serve as the framework for a narrative, and the difficulties that it encounters create a fascinating suspense. Its *asperity*, in a word, provides a hook on which to hang a story. But this spectacular aspect is simply the counterpart to its lack of impact upon reality, its *arti*- and *super*ficiality. In short, it is just an epiphenomenon that momentarily appears, like a shower of spray, against the silent background of things, and then is gone. The tension that it produces may well satisfy our need for drama ("drama," in Greek, means action), but it is not efficacious. As our very language, too, suggests, by its ability to evoke an opposite, every agent (or actor), by breaking into the order of things, behaves as an "energumen," a fanatic (*energein*: to act), instead of the demiurge that he thinks he is. All action is *naive*.

So, to confirm his control over the world or to acquire some sway over it, a sage never takes action (in this respect, his role is like that of a general). Instead, he "transforms" (*hua*[n]). For, in contrast to action that, even if it is prolonged, is necessarily momentary, the duration of transformation is extended; and it is this continuity that produces effects. Chinese thought constantly returns to this theme. However imperceptible the starting point, by slowly accentuating its propensity, one can end up with the most decisive results. Chinese thought is particularly sensitive to the way in which any process that is not interrupted is inclined, on that very account, to "deploy" itself, to "thicken" and to become "more dense" and, through this regular development, to take on more and more consistency (see ZY, section 26). Eventually, this becomes "evident" to us, without ever ceasing to be totally natural. As one Chinese saying neatly puts it, "it becomes manifest without ever having to show itself."[o] The result is increasingly perceptible, even becomes patently clear, but that is precisely what it is: simply a result that has never attracted our attention and does not need to be pointed out.

All the above is borne out by the way that we become aware of a person's "ascendancy"—in particular of the ascendancy of a sage. This is a phenomenon that has been analyzed in far greater depth in China than in the West. Perhaps we Westerners are ill at ease when it comes to analyzing it. We simply envisage it as something not quite definable, a classic *"je ne sais quoi,"* as Gracian puts it ("They win over the hearts and words of others through some *je ne sais quoi* that elicits our respect"; *The Courtier,* XLII). The transformation of oneself and the transformation of others are both progressive processes, and the one follows from the other: it is because that "inner authenticity" is ever unfailing that it eventually comes to "inform" a person's entire behavior; next it becomes externally "transparent" and then so completely "manifest" that, as its objectivization becomes more intense, it acts so forcefully on those who surround him that the sage, without ever intending to, ends up by "shaking" and "transforming" them all (ZY, section 23). The process leading to the manifestation of the inner principle through its eventual outer effects is regular and continuous. Because he does not betray the confidence that others place in him and continues never to betray it, that confidence in him grows increasingly solid and increasingly deeply anchored. Because it is never shattered, it develops, becomes a part of reality, causing no surprise, never in question. Eventually the sage has no need to "make any move in order to be respected," no need "to speak in order to be believed," no need "to recompense people in order to encourage them" or to "become angry in order to be feared" (ZY, section 33). In short, he need make no "move" (to one side or to another, either of which is always relatively arbitrary) in order to modify reality. In other words—and this is a most striking way of putting it—he need not "act" in order to make things "happen"[p] (ZY, section 26).

Change thus occurs of its own accord, in consequence of the continuation of the process, with no need for anyone to exert pressure on the situation or to expend any effort. Reality is inclined, not forced, in a particular direction and thus prompts no resistance. The same applies when we move on from the domain of moral preoccupations to consider, in a more practical fashion, how an adviser at court acquires ascendancy over his prince (by becoming progressively more familiar to the latter) and how he gets a situation to evolve as he wishes it to (by constantly modifying it). The ancient formula for wisdom is just as valid for military strategy: "through duration, transform and make things happen"[q] (GGZ, chap. 8, "Mo"). To make things happen (or rather allow them to happen, since "make" is too injunctive a term) is not to seek to impose an effect, as when one acts, but to allow the effect, as it takes on shape and mass, to impose itself through a progressive process of sedimentation. So it is no longer I who imperiously wish for that effect; rather, the situation progressively implies it. An injunction has deftly infiltrated the course of things, where it is no longer detectable.

Furthermore, unlike with action, which is always "one-off," transformation affects the concerned collection of elements at every point. In fact, this is one of the aspects of reality to which the Chinese were always most sensitive and that the ancient classic *The Book of Changes* constantly stresses: transformation is "without locale."[r] Not only is it not local, as action is, but it is impossible to localize; its deployment is always global. In consequence, its effects are diffuse, all-pervading, never limited.

Because it is continuous and progressive and operates everywhere at once, transformation normally passes unnoticed. Since it is not attributable (to any individual's will) and not localizable (to a particular place or a particular moment), it is not possible to isolate, not demarcated, and so escapes notice. In contrast to action, which is always spectacular, even dramatically so, its effects dissolve within the situation. Time and again it is said of the sage that, under his influence, "the people day by day evolve toward the good without realizing who is making this happen" (MZ, VII, A, 13). But this applies equally to the court adviser, managing things to his own advantage: "It is necessary to direct things in such a way that it happens gradually, from one day to another, unnoticed by others"[s] (GGZ, chap. 8, "Mo"). The fact that any injunction is so

Do not impose effects but allow them to impose themselves

Transformation is global, so it cannot be seen

fully infiltrated into the course of things as to be hidden there makes it all the more efficacious. For, being unnoticeable, it does not weigh upon people's consciousness, so they do not react against it. A similar formula applies to the general: "One must direct military affairs in such a way that one triumphs little by little, progressively, without causing the others any alarm" (ibid.). It does not even occur to "the others," that is to say, our enemies, to fear us, because they do not notice the situation changing and becoming dangerous (and by the time they do, it is too late; we have them at our mercy). The transformation has been so imperceptible, through a progressive "accumulation" (of "positive power" or "capacity"), that even in one's own camp, one "relies upon it" without even knowing where the advantage is coming from. One simply follows naturally along the "way," "without realizing how this comes about."

In short, efficacy is all the greater the more *discreet* it is. A sage transforms the world through whatever he allows to emanate from his personality, day by day, which then passes from one person to another with no need for any justification or to be held up as an example (ZY, section 33). In similar fashion, a good general needs no praise—either for his "foresight" or for his "courage" (SZ, chap. 4, "Xing"). We Westerners may find that surprising, but the affirmation is categorical: no one would ever dream of erecting a statue to the best of generals. For he will have gotten the situation to evolve in the desired direction so successfully, gradually intervening well in advance, that he will have made the victory seem so "easy" that it does not occur to anyone to praise him for it. Once the engagement has taken place, people will say, "Victory was a foregone conclusion," thereby reducing the merit of the commander. Yet, without realizing it, they will have paid him the greatest of all compliments. It is because his merit is so complete that the victory seems natural and therefore attracts no notice. Here again, what seems to be paradoxical in truth proves the point: "In the old days those who were skilled at warfare only won easy victories." That was because they did not engage in combat until, by getting the situation to evolve to their advantage, they had ensured that victory would be "easy" and so were certain of winning the day. Instead of success being snatched in the heat of action and by dint of feats of prowess that made it quite exceptional (and that were commemorated), here it was implied in the transformation of the relation between the two adversaries, a transformation that was set in motion much earlier so that it was indistinguishable from the natural evolution of things. In the absence of suspense and eventfulness, there was nothing to make it stand out as remarkable or dramatic, no reason to turn it into a great story. It is not hard to see why China produced no epic.

In the ways that the Greeks and the Chinese respectively thought about efficacy, the former in terms of action, the latter in terms of transformation, the referents are reversed. The Greeks thought of natural transformation on the model of human action. Although Aristotle distanced himself from Plato's fable of the creation of the world, in his biological works nature is constantly personified. Aristotelian nature is "ingenious," "demiurgic," "fabricating"; and it "paints," "models," and "organizes"; it too has a plan. However much it is distinct from the products of art, given that its principle lies within itself and proceeds in an immanent mode, nevertheless, like all action, it operates through means that lead to ends. Even if it does not deliberate (but we should remember that it is only because of ignorance that an artist needs to deliberate), it nevertheless has a kind of "will" in that it "looks" toward the goal that it has fixed for itself. In contrast, the Chinese thought of human efficacy as a natural transformation. A general made the situation evolve to his advantage in the same way as nature makes a plant grow or a river continuously hollows out its bed. As in such natural modifications, the transformation that he brings about is both diffuse and discreet, imperceptible as it operates but manifest in its effects. The Chinese believe not so much in the transcendence of action, but rather in the immanence of transformation. We do not notice ourselves aging or the river hollowing out its bed. Yet the reality of the landscape and of life stems from that imperceptible evolution.

There is one particular image that manages to convey

implied in the transformation

Nothing to recount

China and Greece, the one the reverse of the other

Greek nature "fabricates"

Greek: its principle lies in itself (not in site)

A Chinese sage "transforms"

diffuse and discrete: believe in the immanence of transformation

Transformation is like an invisible wind (the effects of which are perceptible everywhere)

this diffuse efficiency of transformation (but I shall have to return to this term "efficiency"). It is the image of *wind* (see ZY, section 33: "He knows whence comes the wind"). One does not see the wind passing as it constantly insinuates itself everywhere, but as it passes, "the grasses are flattened" (Confucius, *Analects*, XII, 19). This is not the breath of inspiration—the divine *pneuma*—that arises momentarily, like a tidal wave surging out of the torpor of existence, giving rise to the great blast of a heroic act or poetic creativity. Rather, it is a continuous flow that, ever renewed, passes constantly through the world and, carrying things along with it, spreads its influence there on every side. Greek literature began with the *Iliad*, a story inspired by unequaled high deeds of action, a goddess singing of the anger of Achilles, and a series of dramatic clashes. The first section of the first literary work of China (the *Shijing*), which dates from approximately the same period and is entitled "The Winds of the Kingdoms" ("Guo feng"), presents a striking contrast. It consists of a series of short passages that are interpreted as evoking the transforming influence, stemming from the personality of the sovereign, that spreads throughout his kingdom and affects the country's mores. The sovereign's influence is manifested in every last aspect of his people's feelings and behavior, as these take on the same orientation yet are never apprehendable in a concrete fashion and are always impossible to pin down—just as the wind is.

5

The Structure of Opportunity

1

On the one hand, there is chance; on the other, skill; and positioned in between *tuche* and *techne,* a third term is relevant to thought about action: opportunity *(kairos).* Whether it be a matter of navigation, medicine, or military strategy, the three domains that Plato lists together (*Laws,* IV, 709b), opportunity seems to provide the link between, on the one hand, the field of fortune (or the deities) and, on the other, the field of that which is "ours" (technique or skill); and it is from that link that efficacy stems. Opportunity means the favorable moment that is offered by chance and that skill enables us to exploit. Thanks to opportunity, our action is able to insert itself into the course of things, causing no friction but managing to graft itself there, profiting from its causality and aided by it. Thanks to opportunity, the concerted plan takes shape, the opportune moment offers us a hold, confirms our control. Plato recognizes that, in politics too, "I always waited for the right moment for action" (Letter VII). Opportunity is always a requisite, even in a risky venture such as the Sicilian expedition, if one is to have any hope of putting "theory" into practice. Goal–action–opportunity: the schema is now complete, with the third term, opportunity, adjusting the second in order to achieve the first. For the "end of the action" also "relates to opportunity," as Aristotle reminds us (*Nic. Eth.,* III, 1110a14).

Between skill and chance: opportunity

Goal–action–opportunity: the schema comes full circle

So, to plot efficacious action, the remaining coordinate to be taken into consideration is that of timing. For an opportunity arises when action and the right time coincide so that suddenly that moment becomes a chance, the time is propitious and seems to come to meet us, *occurit*, occurs. The time is favorable, leading into a safe harbor: it is "opportune," but it is also fleeting. It is a minimal as well as an optimal time, hardly perceptible between a *not yet* and a *no longer*, a time that must be "grabbed" in order to achieve success. The sciences are concerned with what is eternal (that which is always identical and can be demonstrated: always the ideal in mathematics). In contrast, what is useful is eminently variable, as Aristotle recognizes: for something may be "useful today but not tomorrow" (*Magna Moralia*, I, 1197a38). "With a view to what is necessary," one should therefore determine both the means

The good according to the category of time

to adopt and *when to do so*. For since "the good" varies according to the relevant category, once belief in a general Good is discarded, in the category of time an opportunity becomes "the good," that is to say, "the time that is the right time." Even within the category of time, "different sciences study different opportunities," and an opportunity in medicine will be conceived differently than in military strategy. In the last analysis, there may be as many specific opportunities as there are situations. But at the same stroke—and again it is a counterstroke (or a "downside") in Aristotle's critique of Plato—an opportunity may

Can there be a general concept of opportunity?

be impossible to seize. For, scattered as they are across the wide range of their occurrences, can opportunities ever be an object of "science" or even of a "technique," given that technique also needs to be of a general nature?

However that may be, throughout Western Antiquity the importance of opportunity—*kairos*—is affirmed. "To

Kairos is all-powerful

recognize it is more useful than anything" (Pindar); it is "the best of guides in all human endeavors" (Sophocles); and its "all-powerful" nature is constantly emphasized. Monique Trédé tells us that, right from the time of the earliest poets, Homer and Hesiod, *kairos* appears to be linked with the definition of an action, and "this, it would seem, is the key to the very notion," a notion that was to be fully developed in the fifth century as technical skills became more highly valued. From Gorgias to Isocrates, orators, in their efforts to win over their audiences, besides making use of reasoning to draw attention to whatever was probable *(eikos)*, were also keen to make the most of the circumstances by seizing opportunities to voice whatever best suited the moment. Similarly, Hippocratic doctors were wary of over-general precepts and, in the absence of "stable" *(kathestekos)* elements, strove to adapt their therapies to the particular features and "disparities" of the cases that they encountered. They did so not only with a view to prescribing the right doses, but also so as to intervene at the right moment in the course of treating an illness, in response to the "crisis."

Beneath the fabric of evidence that they eventually wove, thanks to which our thought (or perhaps our nonthought) about opportunity came to seem to go without saying, we begin to perceive the theoretical assumptions made about this "opportune time"—in other words, we begin to discern the Greek components of opportunity. For in the background lies ontology, setting being in opposition to becoming and that which is "stable" in opposition to that which is "shifting." It is in order to adapt a rule to the instability of things—or rather, so that the latter eventually seems to conform to a rule—that one "waits for" an opportunity. Similarly, the concept of "opportunity" rests so firmly on the relationship that most marked the rise of philosophy, that is to say, the relation of the particular to the general, that it even radicalizes that opposition (and, taking refuge in particularity, as in Aristotle, it eludes theory altogether). In a world denied the fixity of essences and abandoned to time, in which we are obliged to act, it thus becomes our last resource. And, given that an opportunity is, after all, pervaded by harmony, it certainly does constitute a resource: midway between too much and too little, an opportunity is *summetros;* it tallies with the Greek ideal of number and proportion. In the last analysis, opportunity is conceived on the basis of the *technai* and also in relation to action. A question that cannot be avoided is therefore the following: what remains of this concept of opportune time (indeed, is it even still a matter of "time"?) when it is extricated from those implicit choices, that is to

The Greek components of opportunity

say, once it is no longer envisaged from the point of view of action but, instead, in accordance with that other logic that we have begun to investigate: the logic of transformation? "Opportunity" is certainly a factor that is still present, but, as we can already see, its structure is conceived quite differently.

2

However, in China too, we find the notion of an opportune moment that is perfectly adapted and not to be missed (for if it is, all its strategic efficacy is lost). Here, as in the West, "the good" covers a wide spectrum of aspects: for the mind "the good" is "depth," for "business" it is "capacity," for "setting things in train" it is "the right moment" (LZ, section 8). And the moment of "activation" must not be "delayed" (GGZ, chap. 8, "Mo"). Now let us look more closely at the way in which the ancient literature on military strategy understands that moment (see SZ, chap. 5, "Shi"). The potential of a situation is first illustrated by the image of a mountain stream that, in its rushing flow, even has the force to carry rocks along with it; next, that moment of activation is evoked by the image of a bird that, homing in on its prey, shatters the latter's bones in one fell swoop. It strikes at the moment that exactly correlates with the distance that separates it from its target (cf. the notion of *jie'* that initially designated the knot in a bamboo stem and later came to be applied to the right circumstances and the correct mean). If the bird's attack is so intense that it cleanly snaps the victim's body, that is because the maximum potential has accumulated. For, as one commentator (Wang Xi) explains, "the lightening force of the bird of prey results from the potential of the situation," just as does the power of the stream that can carry rocks along: "the right moment to attack is determined by the potential of the situation." As the canonical text puts it, the potential creates the vertiginous tension from which the force springs, and after that the right moment is extremely "short." The gradual preliminary buildup stands in sharp contrast to the very brief instant in which to strike. But the two are inextricably linked, as another image

Opportunity conceived as an activation of the potential

conveys: "the potential of the situation can be likened to the bending of the cross-bow and the opportune moment to release the mechanism."

This conveys a different concept of "opportunity." Here it is seen not as a fleeting chance resulting from a favorable conjunction of circumstances that prompts action and favors its success, but as the most suitable moment to intervene in the course of a process that has already begun (so that, such is the pressure leading up to it, in the last analysis it is not really a matter of an intervention), the moment that sees the culmination of all the potentiality gradually acquired and that makes it possible to derive the greatest efficacy from it. As a commentator (Wang Xi again) explains, this potential of the situation "comes from afar," even if the moment for attacking is so brief. Seen from the point of view of a transformation, an opportunity is simply the end result of an evolution and has been prepared by the duration of that evolution. So, far from coming about unexpectedly, it is the fruit of an evolution that must be taken in hand as soon as it begins or as soon as it is discernible.

> As such, opportunity is the end of a process

This kind of opportunity is different from the Western variety, or rather it is double, as it is detectable at both ends of an ongoing process. Behind the opportunity that seems to arise unexpectedly and that one needs to know how to exploit instantly can be glimpsed another, way upstream, that is the starting point of the process from which the later opportunity eventually emerges. What we have here, in fact, are two crucial moments, not just one (one at the beginning, the other at the end of the transformation): the moment at the end, when one at last falls upon the enemy with such intensity that the latter is immediately defeated; and the moment at the beginning, which was the point of the appearance of a cleavage that caused the potential gradually to shift to one side rather than the other. By the last stage, the opportunity has become glaringly obvious, but at the beginning it is barely perceptible. Yet it is the initial demarcation that is the more decisive, since that is the origin of the potential effect, while the final opportunity is, after all, simply a consequence of it. Logically enough, then, in China thought on military strategy

> *2 : beg. end of transf.*
>
> There are two crucial moments, not just one
>
> *the cleavage*
>
> *barely perceptible*

deflected its attention away from the moment of the launching of an attack in order to focus on the initial moment when the tendency that culminated in that attack could first be glimpsed. According to one precious formula (GGZ, chap. 7, "Chuai"), military thought is concerned with spotting the "potential of a situation" at its "embryonic, initial" stage." For, as we have seen, a general will then be able to count on the development of the potential and allow himself to be carried along by it. The sooner he spots the initial appearance of the potential, the better he will be able to profit from it. Everything is at stake at the stage of the most infinitesimal occurrence, and from Lorenz to Prigogine the slightest event, be it "the flight of an insect," "the wriggling progress of a worm," or even the flutter of a butterfly's wing, involves a series of repercussions.*

On this point too, the sage's wisdom and military strategy are in exact agreement. For whether it be a matter of the sage inwardly conforming with morality or of the general deploying efficacy in the outside world, both are led to scrutinize the starting point of a tendency—in fact, that is the very first of their concerns. As soon as a tendency, however slight, begins to develop, it is bound to modify the situation. So the sage watches for the slightest signs of an inner deviation, for, unless he corrects it immediately, it will lead him farther and farther from the correct way (see ZY, section 1). Likewise, the general watches for signs of the slightest favorable propensity becoming established in the external world, for, as soon as he has detected it, he can depend upon it until its full development is reached. At the moment of inception, nothing is as yet detectable, but already an orientation is engaged. Or, as a commentator explains, in connection with morality (Zhu Xi, commenting on ZY, section 1), no perceptible mark is yet visible, but movement has already begun and this infinitesimal tremor will, unless noticed, have infinite consequences. For

The stage of the infinitesimal beginning is decisive

Scrutinize the starting point of a tendency

---

*[Translator's note: Edward Lorenz and Ilya Prigogine worked, in the 1960s and 1970s, on chaos theory and the laws of chaos, noting that "a small variation in the initial conditions will produce wildly different results." *The Cambridge Encyclopedia*, ed. David Crystal (Cambridge: Cambridge University Press, 1990).]

no sooner does it start than already it affects the course of things (or of one's conscience) and, for as long as it continues, its effects will gradually be felt farther and farther afield. The lesson provided by this precious notion of an inception is not hard to learn. The potential of a situation that suddenly surfaces as an opportunity should have been detected at the moment of its earlier prefiguration. If it is, instead of being presented with a fleeting opportunity, one is in a position to follow every step of its development and certain—and ready—to strike at the right moment.

The notion of an inception

All the general's strategic attention should therefore be focused on the initial stage, well "upstream" from the point where an opportunity surfaces, for although it is by no means easy to discern, that is the discriminating moment that will imperceptibly incline the situation in a particular direction. It is the stage from which success will gradually stem. That secret startup of a process is hard to detect, but it dictates what happens later; in the most subtle fashion, it "decides" what will later swing the entire situation one way or another[v] (GGZ, chap. "Ben jing"; cf. the telling discrepancies between the text and the commentary over the interpretations of "*ji*" and "*wei*"[w]). If an opportunity is conceived as twofold, the notion of a "crisis" (*krisis*, in the sense of "decision") also needs to be rethought. For the crucial moment no longer occurs at the stage when the opportunity becomes manifest (cf. Hippocratic medicine, in which the crisis is the moment when the illness can be "judged"). Instead, it is shifted farther back, upstream, to the earliest, almost imperceptible stage (that of the "inception") when a particular tendency that will be decisive begins to become distinguishable. Now the moment that is crucial is associated not with the spectacular, as in the action of Greek drama, but with the greatest degree of discretion. And if that moment can but be detected, it will be possible to foresee and manage subsequent developments. The crisis can therefore be diffused.

The discriminating moment, upstream from the visible opportunity

Dissolution of the crisis

3

An ability to foresee "opportunity" is certainly the most common requisite of strategy both in the West and in

China. Learning from the example of Rome, Machiavelli
too recognizes that by "perceiving disaster from afar," it is
easy to remedy it (*Prince*, 3), whereas by the time it has
become glaringly obvious, "it is too late," for "the sick-
ness has become incurable." But it is at this point that the
attitudes of the West and China first diverge. Machiavelli
values such foresight purely for negative reasons as a
defense against whatever may threaten (not because it
allows one to make use of any positive aspects of the situation). For instance, when "a secret venom lies hidden"
beneath advantageous appearances, one must be able to
spot it in advance, for otherwise one may fall victim to it
(ibid., 13). Furthermore, there are two ways of conceiving
of this necessary foresight. Either one constructs a line of
reasoning (relating the opportunity to action), or else one
relies on the logic of an evolution (relating the opportunity
to a "transformation"). A good example of the first case
is provided by a historian such as Thucydides who, in classical Greece, pursued the rationalization of opportunity
the furthest. His heroes, Phormio and Brasidas, deduce

Foresight on the basis
of reasoning or on
that of an unfolding

future opportunities from calculations (*logismos*) based
on a number of conjectures. On the one hand, they assem-
ble as much data as possible; on the other (and next), they
elaborate a number of hypotheses and select the one that
seems the most probable. An argument based on likelihood (*eikos*) thus enables them to reconstruct the enemy's
state of mind, foresee his intentions, and evaluate the
chances of success. Their reasoning is based on various
factors: their understanding of the psychological, strategic, and political principles involved, and also a most precise assessment of the situation. The merit, but also the
danger, of this method lies in its determination to correlate
two different levels. In Greece, the task of thought yet
again is to connect the particular to the general. Through
this art of rational foresight (*pronoia*), the Greek general
is able to proceed beyond appearances and arrive at "what
seems most true," which—as he well knows—is also "what
is least visible" (*alethestaton/aphanestaton*). (As ever, the
Western quest is for the "truth" that is concealed beneath
a veil: a quest for hidden Being.)

In contrast, a Chinese general makes no conjectures,

elaborates no arguments, constructs nothing. He sets up no hypotheses, makes no attempt to calculate what is probable. On the contrary, all his skill lies in the earliest possible detection of the slightest tendencies that may develop. By spotting these almost before they have begun, secretly, to orient the uninterrupted course of things and so before they have had time to emerge and manifest their effects, he will be in a position to foresee where they may lead. Already aware of the inception of a tendency, he knows in advance what it will produce. The commentator on the treatise on diplomacy explains (GGZ, chap. "Ben jing"): "The setting in motion that has hardly begun" but that in itself is already "crucial," "evolves from being very subtle to being manifest."[x] So a general with foresight is one who apprehends that tendency at the initial stage, "when it is not yet patently visible and has not yet become actualized."[y] At this stage, the storm has not yet broken; the "eruption" of the crisis is still "hidden." But, as everyone knows, just as "clods of earth accumulate," an effect inevitably leads to a result.

This idea is sometimes illustrated by a process of cracking (see GGZ, chap. 4, "Di xi," which is devoted to this image). First, the slightest fissure produces premonitory indications and symptoms that enable an attentive eye to detect it. Then, unless it is immediately plugged, the tiny fissure naturally develops: it opens up and it deepens. It becomes a "crack," a "gap," then a "crevasse." The development from a crack to a wide breach is predictable, because it is implied from the start; the change is bound to happen; it is all just a matter of time. So it is at the initial stage of the fissure that the "danger" begins. As is well known, the whole world consists of union and separation (from the very first, the Sky and the Earth were at once separate and conjoined). The development of a fissure is thus encompassed in the great logic of reality; it is always at work beneath the surface fabric of things, which is constantly liable to tear and cries out to be permanently put back together again (either by being "plugged" or "recut" or "blocked" or "concealed"...). That is why a general is always "on the lookout" for a crack—especially, of course, one on the side of his opponent. The whole of military

Rely not on what is likely (a construction) but on the tendency that has begun to develop

Crack, gap, crevasse (see Butor, *La modification*)

Seek out the slightest
crack

Know how to wait

strategy, when confronting an enemy, could even be summed up by the following double maneuver (see GGZ, chap. "Ben jing"): never present the slightest crack to the enemy so that he can never get a hold on you and will be bound to slide about with no means of penetrating your façade; at the same time, be on the watch for the development on his side of the slightest crack, which, progressively widening into a breach, will eventually make it possible to attack him without risk. The diplomatic treatise explains that it is by thus "tracking the faults in the adversary's position" that one must "move."[2] Otherwise, one would have to make an arbitrary intervention that would be perilous because it would be forced. The fact is that all you need to do is simply push into the crack[aa] and allow it to develop. The enemy will then inevitably be defeated.

However, there is a drawback to such a strategy. What if the enemy himself likewise presents not the slightest crack? Then what is to be done? But, far from calling into question the original thesis, that quandary simply validates the logic by radicalizing it. The point is, precisely, to do nothing—nothing but "wait." The treatise (GGZ, chap. "Ben jing") insists that you have to "wait for a crack on the other side before you make any move at all" rather than even think of attacking until such time as the enemy position is already destabilized, for to do so would be both costly and risky. *Waiting* is the corollary to foreseeing. As is well known, in the logic of things, something is bound to give, so you can be sure that, sooner or later, the enemy will be at risk. So long as the world is smooth, presenting no handhold to grab, no crack to penetrate, the general "holds himself in reserve and waits for an opportunity" (GGZ, chap. 4, "Di xi"). He waits for that first beginning of a crack that will later open up into a breach and will eventually, when the time comes, allow a sudden thrust into the enemy's position. Yet again, the art of warfare corroborates the art of diplomacy. At first, you must be like a "maiden," discreet and reserved, until such time as the enemy "opens his door; then, once this is open, you spring through as swiftly as a hare, and the enemy is no longer able to resist" (SZ, chap. 11, "Jiu di").

This is usually what happens when no factor in the sit-

uation carries a favorable potential. If the situation is completely unfavorable to him, showing no sign of any potential in his favor, the sage *waits*. He takes up his position on
the touchline, for it is important for him to preserve his
strength. (Today, in China, he retires to the country, lets it
be known that he is ill, and so on.) The formula used to
convey this is worth close attention: "The sage, through
nonaction, waits until there is capacity"[bb] (GGZ, chap.
"Ben jing"). In other words, he waits for the situation to
develop a positive charge. For he knows that a renewal is
at work and that, in time, a new coherent pattern will
stem from it, a pattern that, given that the process continues of its own accord, can only come about through a
switch. New factors will therefore emerge and are bound
to be less negative than those that obtain at present, since
they will be compensating for them. The bad times will
pass; a new deal is secretly already in the offing; so the
sage waits serenely for it once more to carry him forward.

4

The difference between the Chinese and the European
views with regard to the structure of opportunity thus
seems to lie in their respective concepts of "time." On the
Greek side time, from the start, was seen in relation to
the key opposition between theory and practice, so time inevitably came to be split into two: two opponents emerged,
Chronos and Kairos, implacable enemies but both sons of
Aion, eternal Time. On the one hand, there is the time that
is constructed by knowledge: regular, divisible, analyzable,
and, consequently, controllable; on the other, there is the
time that is open to action, which is constituted by an
opportunity: chancy, chaotic, and, consequently, "uncontrollable." Aristotle, already, defined this opportunity type
of time, which stands in opposition to the other variety, in
terms of its undirected, hesitant, and vacillating character.
And, as is well known, modern thought has further accen-
tuated its contingent nature or, rather, has radicalized
it. Machiavelli tells us that the "perfection" of the power
of Rome was only made possible "by the occurrence of
accidents." However, the time of processes, as conceived

Time that is neither of the "*chronos*" nor the "*kairos*" variety in China, is, strictly speaking, neither an object of knowledge nor an objective of action (cf. Aristotle: the *telos* of action relates to *kairos*). It is neither time whose extension you are content to contemplate in a disinterested fashion, nor is it time in which you seek to intervene forcefully, through an eruption of will, in the hope of profiting from its disorder. Rather, it is an unfolding process with which you continuously try to keep in step and to each of whose stages you adapt. By dint of careful scrutiny, you identify the inception of the process and then you act as befits each stage as it evolves. This is not regular time like that of Greek science, docile time; nor is it accidental time that is wide open to action, rebellious time. Instead, it is *regulated* time: it maintains a balance in the course of transformation and remains coherent even as it continues to innovate. This is time that is oblivious to the distinction between theory and practice; it is neither the time of *chronos* nor that of *kairos* (neither regularly periodic nor chancy). It never repeats itself, yet you can count on it. I think the best name for it is "strategic time."

Neither regular nor chaotic, but regulated

It is because its unfolding is regulated that the general can foresee and wait (foresee the time ahead and wait for it to improve). He is at once a sage and a strategist: that is a common theme to which Chinese thought constantly returns and that it continues endlessly to elucidate (see ZY, section 24; GGZ, *passim,* and, of course, the "Great Commentary" of the *Zhouyi*). The logic behind it might be summed up as follows: the sage/general has made his conscious mind accessible to everything, because he has dissolved all the focal points to which ideal forms and plans inevitably lead, and he has freed it from the particular obsessions that, through a lack of flexibility, it is liable to foster. In this way, he has liberated it from both the partiality and the rigidity in which any individual point of view, once it has become exclusive, becomes trapped. In other words, finally to put the matter plainly, he has allowed his conscious mind to take in the entire globality of processes, and he keeps it in a state that is as mobile and fluid—ever evolving—as the course of reality itself. The sage/general is thus in a position to identify with the overall coherence of becoming and can confidently antici-

A readily adaptable mind senses the global character of the process, and this leads to an ability to anticipate

pate future changes, as if—we are told—he experienced within himself the absence of any objective. Because he knows that, seen from this overarching point of view, the renewal constantly affecting reality is never aberrant, he confidently expects the necessary balance to be restored between all reality's adverse tensions, even before that renewal begins. Perhaps *detection* is the most appropriate term.[cc] By "scrutinizing" the present as closely as possible, he detects the presence of what it holds even before this becomes apparent.

The ancient treatise on diplomacy opens with the following observation: a sage/general "considers" the alternation of "opening" and "closing" between the two poles of reality (that is to say, the opposed and complementary factors, *yin* and *yang*); he can "calculate" the "end" that is at the same time a "beginning," at the heart of the "myriad species"; and he is, at the same time, receptive to the "inner logic of consciousness." That is how it is that he is able to "perceive the precursory symptoms of change" and can "guard the door" between "life and death" and between "success and failure." On the one hand, "change is endless"; but on the other, every phenomenon in existence "eventually reaches its proper point of achievement."[dd] So, thanks to the alternation that regulates it (*yin* and *yang*, "hard-soft," "open-closed," "tension-relaxation," and so forth), reality is eminently controllable. So the "foreknowledge" in question does not proceed from a hypothetical argument, nor from any magical procedure; it is content simply to illuminate that which "is going to happen" in the light of that which "has just happened," for the former is constantly implied by the latter. According to one well-known saying in China, which the treatise repeats in this passage, the "end" is at the same time a "beginning"; the present is a continual transition (and the world a perpetual variation). So if I work back from the unfolding that is taking place, I can "sense" in advance the unfolding that will result from it, and, in this way, I can control it (see GGZ, chap. 4, "Di xi," beginning).

A cleavage thus appears in the concept of opportunity, one well worth looking into not in order to pin down the difference (since I hope, on the contrary, to pass be-

[margin handwritten notes:] opening closing between 2 poles of reality

[margin printed note:] By going along with the logic of the unfolding that has already begun, one is able to anticipate

yond that), but, by playing momentarily upon the contrast, to seize on and, above all, find words to explain what it is that Chinese thought always—even while adopting a wide variety of positions—conveys as if it goes without saying (for one of the most difficult things about Chinese thought is what it constantly conveys and implies without ever spelling out). This is a particular logic of efficacy that is not, fundamentally, strange to us (a number of aspects of it are really quite familiar) but that Chinese thought has never needed to explain and has always taken for granted. Although, in a way, we consider it an integral part of our experience and have even turned it into a kind of wisdom, we ourselves have never taken the trouble to formulate a theory about it—or perhaps, given our assumptions, we have been unable to do so. To make the most of the parallel suggested above and to draw the lines a little closer, let us continue the comparison. In Machiavelli's eyes, time is accidental, and, as it is therefore unstable and discontinuous, he expects no benefit from it (except, perhaps, with hindsight, that of stabilizing political bodies, thanks to the legitimating effect of tradition). He doubts that one can "enjoy benefits from time" even if, as he recognizes, that is "what we are constantly told these days by the sages" (*Prince*, 3). "For time drives everything before it and is able to bring with it good as well as evil and evil as well as good." So, in such troubled times of change, chance, and danger, the sole resource lies in initiative and an ability to improvise. When a chance opportunity arises, the response must be bold action, striking while the iron is hot (as Caesar Borgia did at Sinigaglia and Jules II did against Baglione); any delay is suicidal. In contrast, if you believe that efficacy stems not from action, but from transformation, and that opportunities are dissolved by regulation, you can rely on time to produce results. However, to refuse to take the risks that are run by resorting to prompt action does not necessarily mean that you "temporize" (putting off the moment for action, for it is not a matter of prevarication); you simply wait until such time as the evolution of the process already in train brings you as close as possible to the hoped-for result (which, however, it is important to distinguish from a predetermined goal).

A further cleavage

Machiavelli: the response to a chance opportunity must be bold action

But perhaps one can count on regulation to produce success

In this way, by intervening as little as possible and thanks purely to the propensity of things, you are swept along to success.

It is true that, in Europe too, etiquette for rulers recognizes the value of long periods of maturation. It advocates "submitting" to time, "going along with it," accepting that it proceeds step by step, *gradatim*. Gracian's statesman is well aware that "time's crutch is more effective than Hercules' club." He knows that he must traverse the vast quarry of time in order to reach the hub of opportunity (*Universal Man*, 3). He too knows how to "wait." Yet even this kind of waiting is still somewhat different from the pure expectation of the unfolding of a situation. For the latter is not based on the principle that "patience" is preferable to "haste," that an intelligent delay (a stalling for time) is to be recommended, and that "slowness" is better than precipitation (since in the end those opposites— Spanish slowness and French vivacity, stolidness and ardor, and so forth—should balance out). When Gracian sings the praises of delaying, he conceives of it as a personal quality, a moral character trait. His allegory is of a psychological nature. An ability to delay constitutes proof of the control one has acquired over one's passions (or the constraint one must impose upon oneself in order—as he puts it—"to explode only when it is appropriate to do so"). This kind of waiting is part of the humanist ideal of self-control; it does not depend entirely on the unfolding of a situation. Gracian's waiting belongs to the logic that is based on a goal and on human action, even if it does come quite close to that based on transformation. Strategic waiting involves far more than—or rather something quite different from—waiting for "plans to mature" as opposed to "haste that makes everything go wrong." Indeed, it is neither slow nor hasty; it too is regulated, but precisely because it steers clear of concocted plans and so is unaffected by impatience and is, throughout, at one with the timing of the process.

All the same, even in the heroic view of our Western humanists, Machiavelli included, although bold and risky action is advisable, it would be wrong to rule out the idea of some kind of regulation, if only in the somewhat banal

[margin note:] Gracian

[margin note:] humanist ideal of

Strategic waiting

[margin note:] self-control

shape of the "wheel of fortune" (after all, the Capitol stands close to the Tarpeian Rock, so one minute you may be up, but the next you are down). That is a notion that is still with us today. Good fortune may depart, but we must remember that "it will return"; the wheel "will turn again," "raising some up and casting others down." Therefore, no disaster should make us despair (we must not lose hope), nor should any success make us confident of the future (we must resist arrogance). In Machiavelli's work, beyond this explicit theme, there even lies the idea that the nature "of the things of the world" is such that, although every existence is variable and ephemeral, the world itself is stable. We should not forget that, in the last analysis, time is "the father of all truth."... Yet once again, the comparison falls short, for we are bound to recognize that this representation of a wheel of fortune remains largely mythical (a compound of belief and skepticism, impossible to liberate completely from popular imagery). Above all, in Machiavelli, it remains on the horizon, at the rim of the human world, on a different level from that of bold human action. The fundamental invariability of the image surrounds the variability of the present but never penetrates it. So it does not modify the accidental quality of an opportunity. It cannot turn human time into time that is regulated.

5

Opportunity conceived either as a coincidence or as a result

There are thus two ways of understanding an opportunity, or, at any rate, sometimes one aspect is favored, and sometimes the other. It is seen either as a conjunction of circumstances or as a result. On the European side, the relation between necessity and chance has predominated, and it is this that lies in the background to the thought of a writer such as Machiavelli: the human world is a tissue of necessary but discontinuous—so disjointed—successions in the interstices of which an opportune conjunction of circumstances may arise. Or, in more dramatic terms (and how we have loved drama . . .): it is thanks to opportunity, which arises from time to time, that a rent is repaired—a rent that, arising from an ancient religious idea, seems, in the last analysis, to be simply the fact of our existence. So whether it is a matter of knowing or of acting, or better still of creating (in which case the coincidence results in inspiration), one thinker has suggested that "the happy simultaneity of an opportunity" is constituted by a momentary coincidence that brings together two distinct chronologies (see Vladimir Jankélévitch, *Le Je-ne-sais-quoi et le Presquerien*, 1, *La manière et l'occasion*). Quite exceptionally (in the nick of time, as they say), an "intersection" occurs between the moment of an "occurrence" and that of an "intervention." In other words, an opportunity can be considered as an "intersection" that replaces chronic, ever inefficacious disjunction by a timely conjunction *(kairos)* that should be exploited. However, it is so "fragile" that even to speak of a coincidence or a conjunction of circumstances is to overdo it, and Vladimir Jankélévitch is tempted to revise those terms, since this hardly amounts to an intervention; rather, it is no more than a fugitive and fleeting "infinitesimal" point of contact. It flashes by like a streak of lightning, in "next to no time.". . . If we abandoned the Greek idea of cyclical time and eternal periodicity, we would probably be more intensely conscious of the exceptional nature of an opportunity. An opportunity is fundamentally tragic, and rhetoric skillfully deploys its pathos. In time that is irreversible, an opportunity is "unique," "without precedent and unrepeatable." It is neither predictable nor does it ever recur. We can neither prepare for it in advance nor recoup it afterward. It is always a first (and last time), always "impromptu." We cannot be taught how to cope with it; all we can do is improvise when it occurs.

The pathos of coincidence

Yet at one point in his argument, Jankélévitch considers the possibility that "in order to loosen the urgent constraint of such an impromptu situation, we might closely espouse this new curve of development: in default of time to adjust, such unison might enable us to regain control over the occurrence. . . ." But he does not pursue this line of thought and his suggestion trails off in a line of suspension points. He spots a hypothesis, a possible deviation from the main line of his thought, and allows us to sense the possibility of an alternative logic, which, however, we are unable to develop. The glimpsed alternative fizzles out, because, although dimly perceived, the form in which it presents itself does not fit into any coherent system capable of sustaining it and imparting consistency to it. So Jankélévitch stops short, leaving the idea up in the air. However, as the reader will no doubt have realized, that glimpsed possibility is precisely what the Chinese tradition, for its part, did develop: you accompany the process that is unfolding through each of its stages, right to the end, so as to be constantly in step with it (cf. above, "we might closely espouse this new curve of development," in "unison" with it). The accidental intersection of a coincidence thus becomes a coincidence that is continuous with the course of the whole process. Instead of being a fleeting, hazardous moment, inviting action, the opportunity is coincidental with every stage of the ongoing transformation. There was an intersection right at the beginning when the process (the initial *ji*) began, but given that this was spotted very early on, one can thereafter rely on it; it initiates a development from which one can progressively profit. The initial coincidence is "decisive" because it gives rise to possibilities that can be realized and, at the other end of the process, the final realization of the opportunity is richly laden with an accumulated potential: in between the initial coincidence and the final opportunity that stems—indeed results—from it, the entire duration of the process is intercalated, and you have a grip on that process and so can inflect it in the desired direction. By the end of the process, and thanks to the way that it has evolved, what was initially accidental has progressively become an "ineluctable consequence." So, instead of initiating some kind of risky action, intervention has remained minimal.

By the end of the whole process, one finds that what might have constituted an "event" has simply dissolved. The battle—usually an unforgettable event to be celebrated—is now no more than a necessary conclusion. By this stage, victory brings no credit to a great general. On the European side, in contrast, an opportunity is most certainly an event par excellence, both as a happening and as an embodiment. It both constitutes an eruption, for it *arises*, breaking through the continuity of becoming; and at the same time, by there and then identifying a latent, preexis-

Unless we can "espouse" the unfolding process

From the inception of the process to its final realization

The event has been dissolved

tent cause, it enables this to accede to temporal reality and be realized there (or, as Jankélévitch puts it, "it occasions the causation"). The Chinese, for their part, never envisaged the moment (of opportunity) either as a purely gratuitous occurrence or from the point of view of causation (the unfathomable *causa sui* that has never ceased to haunt Western metaphysics and from which Jankélévitch was never able to detach himself). Instead, they conceived of it as a transition: as the momentarily visible emergence of a continuous transformation. For many centuries, the Chinese have thus been familiar with the concept of a long, slow duration *(la longue durée)*, a concept in which Western theories of history have only recently taken an interest. The Chinese have another name for it, but it is one that conveys the meaning very well, in fact that even illuminates it. They speak of "silent transformations."ᵉᵉ

6

By linking opportunity with action, conceiving of it as a timely coincidence and setting it up as an event, Europe turned it into the nub of its thought. It is true that Greek intellectuals at first tried hard to rationalize opportunity. On the basis of the twofold authority of *metron* and *logismos,* in other words, relying on their estimates of what was probable, doctors, orators, and generals, seduced by the infinite control that, thanks to the *technai,* was beginning to seem to be within their grasp, saw themselves as "engineers of opportunity" (as Monique Trédé has put it). Cicero continued to echo that optimism, believing that there was such a thing as an exact science of the best place and the best time (a "science of the opportunity of the right moments for action"; and Panetius, before him, had spoken of "a science of the right opportunity for action"). In Greece, however, by the late fifth century B.C., such confidence in human beings' ability to control opportunities was already under threat. Chance, which Thucydides had been unable to eliminate, now took center stage and was considered responsible for opportunity. *Kairos* met up with *tuche,* and the two tended to become confused. Aristotle went along with this linking of opportunity to contingency and regarded the latter as the particular setting for human action. As noted above, opportunity eludes theoretical understanding, for it seems to be something that it is impossible to pin down and that cannot be generalized. As the rhetor Dionysius remarks, when all is said and done, no philosopher or rhetor has ever said anything of use about *kairos*. Confronted by opportunity, reasoning is at a loss, willed control is out of the question, even intelligence can play no more than a limited role. The irrational nature of opportunity has led people to conclude that success is equally irrational. The paths leading to efficacy become obscured. As Aristotle recognizes, some people succeed not only "without reasoning" but even "contrary to all the teaching of science and reason." And Machiavelli for once echoes Aristotle: a poor understanding of both men and circumstances, which gives rise to an irrational attitude, may succeed where reason despairs and a carefully calculating man fails.

> The irrationality of a coincidental event

In response to such irrationality and the better to exorcise it, the West had to invent a mythology of Opportunity and to personify it. Lysippus sculpted it (in Aristotle's day), and Poseidippus wrote in praise of it: Kairos, "who overcomes all," advances "on tiptoes" or "wanders this way and that in his flight," clasping a razor. A lock of hair flops over his brow (and should be seized when he draws near), but the back of his head is bald (and nobody can hope to catch hold of it). For Machiavelli too, Opportunity was a goddess constantly in motion "who keeps one foot on the wheel." All the indications thus suggest that we must seize this Opportunity on the wing, "by the hair," without pausing to deliberate or even to think at all. We must simply grab it. However, I think that there is more to this matter, as is in fact suggested by the pleasure we derive from its allegorization. Even if opportunity defies reason, we still need to seize upon the meaning that it opens up and the tension that it creates. For the image of opportunity represents more than simply irrationality, as becomes clearer still when viewed from the Chinese standpoint. This view reveals aspects and a source of motivation hitherto unnoticed.

> Opportunity was accordingly personified (in Greece)

> There is more to Opportunity than pure efficacy

In the first place, an opportunity calls for boldness as

well as perspicacity. It requires one to respond to its challenge with audacity and implies that one must now surpass oneself. In the ancient Chinese treatises, this surpassing of oneself is not exalted, at least not as a personal virtue, since it is regarded as an effect not of willpower but of conditioning (as in the case of troops that are obliged to fight to the death because they have been left with no other alternative). But whereas the notion of audacity is not to be found in Chinese military treatises (as we have seen, a sage/general guards against a taste for deeds of prowess), in Greece, audacity *(tolma)* is constantly invoked in the context of warfare (cf. Hipparchus, 7; and even in the case of a general as "experienced" as Brasidas) and also in that of rhetoric (across the board from Gorgias to Isocrates). It is precisely this boldness in the face of fortune that Machiavelli turns into virtue par excellence. He calls it, quite simply, *virtu: O per fortuna o per virtu,* either through luck or through talent. If opportunity played its part in the success of city founders, it was partly—or even chiefly— that it served to reveal their merit by giving them a chance to be *daring.* For Fortune is female and more likely to yield to "fierce men" than to "cold men," preferring those that are young because they are bolder. The surprise of an opportunity provokes a rush of energy. The very risk involved makes the exploit possible: every opportunity seized is a chance for glory; it inspires heroic action. In contrast, as we have seen, Chinese strategy is not concerned with glory and is wary of heroism. Or rather, strategy is, in principle, nonheroic; it must not be heroic.

When seen as a happy coincidence, an opportunity raises one above oneself, even makes one sublime; it likewise allows time to surpass itself, makes it extraordinary: a previously unthinkable hope opens up, something outside the ordinary is sensed, something that is a dizzying possibility. By creating the chance of a breakthrough, such an opportunity also becomes a chance for freedom; it liberates new possibilities. In contrast, Chinese thought never really embraced such an externality (since whatever is the opposite is always complementary, as implied in the logic of interaction). So it knows nothing of the ecstasy produced by coincidence. Equally, it does not seem sensitive to the

A coincidence-event prompts boldness

The alternative: heroism or strategy

A coincidence-event opens up the possibility of the extraordinary

*everything
to play
for,
ardently,

in the

incandescent
moment*

A coincidence-event
is a gamble, a risk, an
adventure

*C. thought
has always
avoided*

*seems
to*

Pleasure/efficacy

*operate
more in
connection
with desire*

*than
efficacy   as for a woman*

poignant, even captivating aspect of an unpredictable present in which there is everything to play for, ardently, in the urgency of the moment—what Jankélévitch calls "the incandescent now." Chinese thought has conceived of the benefit to be derived from evolution in the long term but has not reflected on the way that such an exceptional instant can fill a person with passion and energy. For the accidental character of opportunity is itself attractive (and we are fascinated by all its aspects that are beyond our understanding). After perforce recognizing that in warfare uncertainty is inevitable and deducing from this that any strict theory about it is impossible, Clausewitz unexpectedly discovers a reason for finding that uncertainty admirable. By prompting an enthusiastic surge of energy, it opens up a new space and allows new aspirations to be fulfilled. He recognizes that, although warfare is a "gamble" and cannot be treated as an object of science, it is "the element that in general best suits the human mind." For, "instead of complying with mediocre necessity, it deploys itself in the realm of possibilities." "Courage rapturously takes wing," and audacity and danger become an element into which the human spirit launches itself "as an intrepid swimmer launches himself into the current." That is precisely the kind of gamble accompanied by risk and danger that Chinese strategy has always avoided.

As conceived in Europe, an opportunity generates the kind of pleasure afforded by risks, surprise, and the unknown, in a word, the pleasure afforded by *adventure,* which is also the source of the pleasure afforded by stories (that generally set in opposition images of warfare and images of love, in all of which opportunity turns out to play an important role). When regarded as a risky coincidence, an opportunity operates as a stimulus and triggers aspirations and so, in the last analysis, seems to operate in connection with desire more than with efficacy. Or rather, the logic of its irrationality seems to stem from a different level, that of the imaginary and of passion, as is conveyed by allegorical images of *kairos* and indicated by common expressions such as "the whims of Fortune" and also by Machiavelli's advice to approach it—or rather take it by storm—as though it were a woman.

On the one hand, then, a logic of pleasure; on the other, a logic of efficacy: there is definitely a parting of the ways here. Pursuing what initially seemed to be the European path of efficacy (based on the interaction of a goal-action and an opportunity), we now find ourselves moving in a direction that eventually turns out to lead to heroism rather than to strategy. Could it be that Machiavelli himself and Clausewitz are less concerned with efficacy than is usually claimed? For both of them, there seems to be a persistent surplus or extra element over and above the pure function of efficacy, an element that seems to have more to do with the exaltation of an individual's personality and human glory. Perhaps we never did emerge from the world of the epic.

We must now temporarily abandon the study of these parallel, alternative paths and concentrate on the Chinese side in the hope of reaching a fuller understanding of how an effect develops discreetly of its own accord, in conformity with its status as a consequence and purely through immanence. It is also possible for the imaginary and passion to operate as a source of efficacy, but only by dint of *effort*. Let us now see how efficacy might result with no expenditure of effort at all.

The ultimate
alternative

more to
do with
exaltation

Perhaps we
never did

The next question to
consider must be
immanence

emerge
from the
world
of the
epic

6

Do Nothing
(with Nothing Left Undone)

A detour by way of
the *Laozi* (and away
from metaphysics)

1

I believe the West has often misunderstood the "nonaction" recommended by Daoists, or at least nonaction as conveyed by what is considered to be the founding text of the Daoist school, namely, the *Laozi*. It is the briefest of the great Chinese classics—barely five thousand words in all— and is also the Chinese text most translated into European languages, no doubt because it seems to be at once the most revealing and the least translatable (the one perhaps implies the other), the most crucial yet also the most disconcerting. It carries a message that is the more precious because it has never quite got through to us Europeans and because we suspect that it has been more or less lost (so we are now forced to interpret it as best we can). It is a message of wisdom forever distant from us, buried beneath the endeavors of rationality, or at any rate obscured by that rationality: we feel that only the aphorisms of this text retain the original freshness of that lost wisdom. Their meaning seems at once so simple and so mysterious, and therein lies the secret of their inexhaustible fascination. Their very simplicity—or radical nature—renders them the more mysterious.

Such is the "East," or rather its mirage, the eternal, exotic East that the "West" has chosen to represent as its polar opposite, an opposite that so conveniently fuels its own fantasies and that it constantly exploits to compen-

The East that the
West exploits

sate for its own failings. The irrationality of this East seems to serve as a convenient escape valve from the machinery that science has by now definitively established. Its imagistic (and "poetic") tone seems momentarily refreshing in the stuffy atmosphere confined by the walls of Western concepts and logic. Yet the West itself does not venture beyond those walls, never conceives of any "other," outside way of thinking. Because the *Laozi* is regarded as an apophasis similar to those that we use (and the "other" of our own theoretical discourse), we have thoughtlessly labeled it "mysticism." Likewise, because the West has linked efficacy with action, it has been inclined to interpret Chinese nonaction simply as the reverse of its own heroic action, casting it as renunciation and passivity (the "active" West dreams of Eastern respite . . .). However, far from advocating disengagement from human affairs and from the world, the nonaction of the *Laozi* teaches one how to behave in this world in order to be successful. For one thing at least is clear by default: this Daoist thinker could never invite us to flee this world, since, as he sees it, there is no other in the name of which to reject this one, in the hope of which to trust, and the expectation of which might make this life endurable. Along with the other great texts of Chinese Antiquity, the *Laozi* addresses its aphorisms to the ruler, for they constitute political—or even strategic—recipes. Nonaction is promoted solely in the expectation of tangible profits—the promise of "obtaining" the world and getting order to reign there—and so purely on the grounds of its effectiveness.

> The precept of nonaction does not lead to disengagement

> On the contrary, it teaches one how to succeed

To be convinced of this, we need only to read the formula in its entirety: "do nothing and let nothing be left undone"[tt] (LZ, sections 37, 48). Although I have here translated that formula using the most neutral of conjunctions (a simple "and"), in truth it links together two propositions that might appear contradictory—at once contrary and consecutive. The formula could also be read as "do nothing *but* let nothing be left undone" or "do nothing *so that* [to such a degree that] nothing is left undone." The "empty word" *(er)* that links the two parts of the sentence together serves to express both the nonexclusion of contraries and the connection between them.

And in that second meaning, which, however, is not, strictly speaking, a meaning, it not only represents what follows on as a result of what precedes it, but furthermore introduces between the two a dimension of unfolding and (by means of its "emptiness") conveys the time that the process takes. Taken as a whole, the formula means not just that nonaction does not exclude effectiveness, but even that it is by refraining from action (knowing not to act) that we can best bring about what we desire. At this stage (where "there is nothing that is left undone"), the double negative in advance eliminates the possibility that the future result might be limited or incomplete, and guarantees it total success.

That is why, for a prince as for a sage, nonaction is an essential condition. Nonaction, in itself, embodies their ambition. The reason why a ruler has to "make sure that" clever men "no longer dare to act" (section 3) is, of course, because the initiative of such "intelligent" action upsets the spontaneous course of things. (In fact, both speech and action do so. In this respect, speech is like action: limited, obvious, and forced. Sages no more speak than they act; see section 56. Or, to reverse that comparison: acting is like speech; it is as *superfluous* as speech.) As soon as one acts, one introduces "another beginning" into the way the situation is evolving, one creates "the beginning of something" (see the commentary of Wang Bi, the most philosophical of the *Laozi*'s commentators, third century B.C., sections 45, 56). Through what it introduces from outside (such as a projected model or intention) and through what it thereby inaugurates that was not originally implied and so necessarily constitutes an interference, such action is inevitably a source of embarrassment: it *inter*venes as a hindrance. The reason why "one dares not act"ʳᵍ (end of section 64) is primarily so as not to prevent that which, otherwise, would come about of its own accord. Whereas the European tradition has always, with varying degrees of emphasis, ascribed merit to audacity, the Daoist thinker, for his part, praises "nonaudacity." And he does so purely on account of the danger that may result from initiating such action (given that it causes an infraction). If

[margin notes: Knowing not to act]

[margin notes: Acting or speaking]

[handwritten margin: superfluous / c? / speech]

[margin notes: Praise for nonaudacity]

one is "so courageous as to dare," one will not die a natural death; whereas if one has the strength "not to dare,"
one has a chance of ensuring what is essential—first and
foremost that one remains "alive" (section 73).

Two logics stand in opposition here: on the one hand,
a logic of activism, which involves an endless expenditure
and accumulation of "more and more," constantly learning more and more (section 48) and seeking to go farther
and farther (47); on the other, quite the reverse, a logic
according to which one constantly cuts back on one's
involvement and reduces one's activity. It is in the light of
this opposition that we should understand the initial formula: "reduce more and more, right down to the stage of
nonaction: do nothing, and *(er)* there is no longer anything that is left undone" (section 48). At the zero degree
of action that one thus reaches, efficacy holds total sway:
one can only ever "win the world" by "not busying oneself." Doing reveals what is not done. The more one does
everything, the more a gap opens up between what one
does and what one does not do. As soon as one does some
things, inevitably there are others that one fails to do, and
one will never be able to catch up with them. Moreover,
all that has not been done not only reduces what one sets
out to do but, above all, it works against what one does
do, prepares its undoing, *undoes* it[hh] (section 64). In other
words, there is a downside to all doing, just as anything
to which one "clings" one is bound to "lose," for every
attachment implies that one will eventually have to let go.
Making this connection, the commentator concludes, "The
more one does, the more one loses" (Wang Bi, section 5).
So only if one is careful to do nothing can there be nothing that is not done or that is undone, in other words, only
so can one avoid both want and failure.

The commentator (Wang Bi, section 29) explains that
whoever "spreads" his action by "executing" plans is
obliged to "become attached" at one point and so to
detach himself at another. Such opportunism is arbitrary
and furthermore forces one to "exclude" from reality anything that is extraneous to his particular plan." Moreover,
all action necessarily momentarily blocks reality even

[margin notes:]
Constantly
Cutting back on one's
involvement

Doing reveals what is
not done

What is not done
undoes what is done

the more
one does.
the more
one loses

Action is artificial

though all the indications are that it is constantly evolving. The contrary of taking action (which is negative) is therefore to espouse the course of reality and conform to it (*yin* as opposed to *wei*).[ll] It is best always to go along with reality so that it can evolve as suits it—and, *at the same time,* as suits us. The old master thus declares, peremptorily, "I can see very well that those who wish to win the world by taking action are bound to fail" (section 29). They have not understood that the human world is not a "pot" that they can hold in their hands: it is made up of things both visible and invisible; everything in it now appears, now disappears; nothing is fixed once and for all.[kk] In short, the world "cannot be an object for action." It certainly can be used (as can a "pot"), but its instrumentality cannot be codified, which is why, in order to use it, one must always conform to it.

That is why the world is not an object for action

We thus come back to the difference mentioned earlier. If one restrains oneself from taking action, it is so as to allow things to happen (section 47) and to allow the world to "change" of its own accord (section 37): an *implicit transformation* takes the place of *direct action.* This rejection of planned action is a valuable ploy, particularly in politics. The more rules and prescriptions proliferate, the worse the state of the world becomes, precisely because they constitute an exacerbated expression of political "doing." The more prohibitions, the more impoverished a country becomes, the more laws, the more bandits proliferate (section 57). As the writer puts it, in an ironic mode, getting order to reign in a great realm is like cooking a tiny fish (section 60); one should refrain from touching anything: "Remove neither the innards nor the scales" (He Shanggong), or else everything will be reduced to a soup. . . .

Reject planned action

For "there to be nothing that is not in order" (just as there is "nothing that is not done"), and so that this order, which results not from a predetermined harmony but rather from regulation through continuous transformation, should extend to everything and remain "constant," it is necessary to "practice nonaction," or—to be more precise and as the writer repeats—to "do nondoing" ("act with nonaction"),[ll] as the formula used in the *Laozi* puts it (sections 3, 75). This apparent paradox confirms that such nonaction by no means implies any lack of interest with regard to the world and in no way distances us from reality (in other words, it is not "mystical"). For the negation applies not to the verb itself but to its complementary object. Action is maintained (in its aim for effectiveness); only its object is removed (for the danger is that it contains partial and fixed elements). Liberated from the rigid and limited aspects that it usually implies, activity thus accedes to its fullest potential, merging with the course of things instead of obstructing it: if you drain action of its activism, at the same stroke you suppress any chance of disorder. *You act by not acting.* You do not take action (to implement a predetermined plan, in exceptional circumstances, in order to force an issue), yet nor are you inactive, since you unfailingly go along with reality as it unfolds (keeping in step with it, partnering it). Once the world is no longer an *object* to act upon, you become an integral part in its becoming: you act, but now you do not clash with it[mm] ("clash" is the *Laozi*'s very last word, section 81). This pure action ("pure" in the sense that love is sometimes said to be "pure") is action that no longer involves any expenditure of effort or any friction; it is action without activity. Having shed all aspects of discontinuity and rigidity, it turns into evolution that is endless, just as tasting can be endless. As such parallel formulations indicate, one can "act without acting" just as one can "taste a nontaste" or be "busy without busying oneself" (section 63). For just as a nontaste ("blandness") constitutes the latent basis of the most diverse of savors (and contains them all in a virtual state), a sage acts upon the very root of becoming, positioning himself upstream from its full deployment. Acting, like tasting, can then extend of its own accord, excluding nothing; it is "inexhaustible."

2

One point has been underlying this thinking from the very start. We have been circling around it all the time, just as Chinese thought itself constantly returns to it, as if it could never have enough of exploring it. It is this: once a process

it own im-
petus
corries it.

but needs
to be
afforded

Assist whatever is
natural

the
right
conditions

The efficacy is indirect

plants:
the
meta
phor

has begun, its own impetus carries it onward; something that has begun seeks only to "become." *Of its own accord* means that the impetus in question is contained within the existing state of things; it *goes without saying* that it should be "thus"; it is natural ("natural" in the sense of *ziran*[nn] in the *Laozi*). However, the fact that it is *implied* does not, of itself, mean that the process will be realized, for it still needs to be afforded the right conditions for its unfolding. To express this, the *Laozi* provides a new formulation of acting-without-action (section 64, end): instead of "daring to act," the thing to do is to "help the spontaneous development of all the existing elements," in other words, to *assist* whatever happens *naturally*. This formula, which borders on or even slips into a contradiction, suggests a possible meaning that, as it is further developed, produces a steady stream of corroborative evidence: "evidence" in such quantity, in fact, that it is hard to take it in without first contracting it. It is this corroborative evidence that Chinese thought, from one angle or another, strives continually to elucidate. The aphorisms of the *Laozi* certainly return us constantly to it, as if to the source from which they well.

Let us try to get a firm grip on this formula. As the process in question comes about naturally, we must avoid intervening by daring to act (for that might impede the spontaneity that is at work). But at the same time, it is important to assist that natural propensity by encouraging its impetus. In contrast to action (that is direct, willed, with the aim of achieving a goal), acting-without-action has an indirect efficacy. It stems from conditioning and is realized by transformation. The model (or at least the favorite example) for this is provided by the growth of plants (we should remember that the Chinese are agriculturalists, not herdsmen). As the *Mencius* (II, A, 2) points out, one must neither pull on plants to hasten their growth (an image of direct action), nor must one fail to hoe the earth around them so as to encourage their growth (by creating favorable conditions for it). You cannot force a plant to grow, but neither should you neglect it. What you should do is liberate it from whatever might impede its development. You must *allow it to grow*. Such tactics are equally effective at the level of politics. A good prince (for the *Laozi*'s main concern is such a one) is a ruler who, by eliminating constraints and exclusions, makes it possible for all that exists to develop as suits it. His acting-without-action amounts to a kind of laisser-faire but not to a policy of doing nothing at all. For what he needs to do is *act in such a way* that things can happen of their own accord. Even if the doing becomes minimal, so discreet as to be hardly discernible, *allowing* things to happen constitutes active involvement.

Meanwhile, this discretion makes the "doing" very hard to apprehend. However much one conceives of it as a contrast that sets up an opposition between that which is "organized" (by others) and that which "constantly comes about of its own accord" (section 51), what happens constantly of its own accord is, in itself, hardly detectable. Once action, by liberating itself from all activism, comes to merge with the spontaneous course of things, it is no longer detectable. Given that it is diffused as the course of things evolves, there is nothing about it on which to focus or that catches the eye. It adapted itself at such an early stage to the principle of the spontaneous course of things that it is no longer distinguishable from it. This acting-without-action presents no sharp edges. The frontier between doing and what is done is effaced. It is impossible to trace the effect back to anyone or anything. Anyone involved could in good faith claim to be its source. When, thanks to the prince's acting-without-action, "the effect comes about and gives rise to a particular situation," all concerned declare, "It just happened" (section 17). Thus, all that is known of a really good ruler is that he exists ("there really is someone up there..."). As we by now understand, his merit is all the greater the less it is perceived (not because he makes any attempt to hide it, out of humility, but because others simply have no way of perceiving it). That is how it is that, when efficacy becomes natural, one can "hardly" tell it is so, or rather it is its "hardly" perceptible nature that testifies most strongly to it[oo] (beginning of section 23). By refraining from speaking of it, one allows it to pass unnoticed; its presence is simply implicit. Or, to put that another way,

By merging with the spontaneous course of things, this acting-without-action becomes undetectable

given that acting-without-action has much in common with tasting-without-taste (tasting blandness), that very "blandness" is perhaps the way of evoking this kind of action (see Wang Bi's commentary, section 23). The less distinctive the taste, the closer one is to finding in the neutral state the undifferentiated basis of all things—which is also the basis of all their virtualities.

This acting-without-action is "bland"

Working our way back through the various levels on which reality comes to be, we can successively distinguish all the following (section 25; cf. Wang Bi and the *Zhouyi*'s "Great Commentary"): the level of concrete accomplishment, which is that of actualization (the "earth") that humankind "imitates"; upstream from this, the level of the still faint lineaments of things that prefigure their actualization and inform them (the "heavens," which the earth imitates); farther upstream still, the endless course of things, in which they pass from latency to actualization and back again (the "way," which the heavens imitate). Finally, upstream even from the way, is "that which is natural" (that can come about *sponte sua*). This is not another level but the perfect mode of the "way"—which is also that in which efficacy has full play. This is the ultimate "term," the "extreme" limit (Wang Bi), for that which is natural imitates nothing; there is nothing beyond it, nothing farther upstream. It is distinguished from everything else by the fact that it relates to nothing but itself. One might think (and it has been thought) that such a schema of reality can be interpreted in a Platonic mode. But, in the first place, the fact that a stage "imitates" the preceding one does not mean that it reproduces it (as a painting of a bed reproduces a bed made by a craftsman, who himself reproduces the Idea or Form of a bed); rather, it is inspired by the preceding stage and takes over from it (so there is no problem of any weakening in the transition between the two). Above all, it is a matter not of levels of being, but rather of stages or levels of coming-to-be (as we have seen, the Chinese view of the world is not ontological; rather, it envisages reality as a process). So this ordering of reality culminates not in the form of transcendence (a transcendent form, that of the Good), but in the capacity that is the "basis" of reality and constitutes a *fund* from

Track back to the source of efficacy

In the absence of metaphysical construction, the levels of the coming-to-be of reality culminate in the "natural"

*full play
the
extreme
limit*

The levels should be conceived not in terms of being, but as a process

The fund from which the process stems

which the process stems (from which the process of all that exists continually proceeds, for therein lies its capital and its source). That capacity is the absolute mode of the "Way," its "virtue" of immanence, one might say (in accordance with the actual title given to this text, the *Dao de jing,* or *Classic of the Way and of Virtue*).

We need a more precise understanding of these terms. Here, virtue should not be understood in the moral sense, as a disposition to act in accordance with the good; and the Daoist master forthrightly says as much: a sage does not claim "to be humane" and to act well any more than the world ("heaven and earth") does (section 5). For neither action nor the good is relevant here. If one is humane toward others, one is led to focus one's behavior on good actions that are individual and momentary, so one soon falls into action that is spectacular but with scant effect. What is called "the good" is simply a norm (moral "rectitude") projected onto the world, a norm that leads us to split the world in two, setting up an opposition within it (good-evil) and, in the last analysis, mutilating it. For to denigrate one side and set a high value on the other is to fail to do justice to their interdependence and to lose sight of their coherence (sections 2, 49). Virtue should therefore be understood in a different sense, one that relates not to how things ought to be, but rather to effectiveness: it is a quality that can engender a particular effect or that is capable of producing it (as one speaks of the curative virtue of a plant or the healing virtue of time or as in the expression "by virtue of..."). According to one of the most classical of Chinese glosses and one that can be applied to the *Laozi* (see Wang Bi, section 38), *de,* virtue, is interpreted by the verb that means "to obtain," a homonym that has become a synonym: "virtue" is something that is efficient. As for the notion of immanence, this is suggested rather than defined (to define it, of course, would be to lose its meaning). Three expressions, linked to form a spiraling crescendo, are twice used to convey it (sections 10 and 51): "It brings things about but without taking them over, acts but without applying pressure, makes things grow but without directing them." In other words, the virtue of immanence does not take over what

The virtue of immanence

Scan effect

It has nothing to do with the oppositions drawn by morality

mutilation it

Virtue in the sense of effectiveness

virtue: to obtain (efficient)

How can immanence be described?

it helps to exist (it remains uninvolved); it acts through action that is neither dependent nor expectant of any return (without applying pressure); it makes things develop (but without exerting authority). It functions but without being transcendent. Similarly, "all things that exist depend on it in order to come about, but it does not direct them (a better translation than "it does not reject them"). The effect comes about without making a name for itself; "it clothes and nourishes all existent things but does not operate as their master"[pp] (section 10). This is a capacity that springs from the depths of ("the abyss of"[qq]) reality, a capacity upon which, to be efficacious, a sage must draw. He must "assimilate" to that capacity if he is never to "lose" (section 23).

In Chinese thought, this efficacy through immanence is a recurrent theme. Where efficacy is concerned, the difference between the two great opposed traditions, those of the Confucians and the Daoists (all too frequently set apart from each other by overdistinctive labels), lies in the fact that the Confucians tend to merge the two meanings of the notion of virtue. (According to Mencius, it is the virtue of humanity that, by attracting all peoples to it, allows a ruler to triumph over all others.) The Daoists, in contrast, seem to separate them. But whether they favor inner rectitude or purely being at one with the spontaneous course of things, the two groups agree on the need to achieve nonaction (which is not specifically Daoist, even if the theme is expressed far more emphatically in Daoism). The moral progress advocated by the Confucians likewise eventually leads to spontaneity, at which point assiduous effort is finally converted into—and resolved by—perfect ease (cf. ZY, section 20). Similarly, Confucius says of Shun, the paragon of good rulers, that he "got order to reign without taking action" (*Analects*, XV, 4). And "getting things to happen without taking action" and "manifesting oneself without showing oneself" constitute another fundamental combination for both schools of thought (LZ, section 47, and ZY, section 26).

Basically, the Daoists and the Confucians differ not so much over their conceptions of how reality comes about, but rather over what they envisage as the starting point for

The notion of immanence is common to the various currents of Chinese thought

reality. The Confucians envisage reality coming from a fund of initiative and reactivity that is continuously at work in the great process of the world, never deviating, never becoming exhausted (this is the notion of *cheng*, the counterpart to the notion of *ren*[r]), the fund of "humanity" and solidarity within us that directs the course of the world in a constantly regulated fashion. Meanwhile, the Daoists envisage reality as starting from an undifferentiated basis (this is the notion of *wu*) from which every individual thing that exists (*you* in relation to *wu*[ss]) comes to be and to the plenitude of which the natural way—the *dao*—leads them to return. However, they agree about the immanence of effects: whether through a moral influence or through natural propensity (since that moral efficiency, too, is natural), the tendency realizes itself of its own accord, it "happens of itself, without prompting" (LZ, section 73); the result is unfailing (MZ, IV, A, 9). Whether by the "way" of the *dao* or by that of morality, that is the process to which the world ineluctably returns or (to convey the ambiguity of *gui*[t]) to which it also returns. That *return* seems, here, at the same time to mean that the world returns, so to speak, to its original source (whether that be undifferentiated or the source of humanity: see LZ, sections 22, 34; *Analects*, XII, 1; MZ, IV, A, 4 and 13) and also that it does so because that is profitable and justifiable, for it is the result of the way's efficacy. On this point, prescriptions of wisdom all concur: the return to immanence cannot fail to be profitable. In China, a sage is one who, by returning to the naturalness of processes, ensures that the world is rightfully his.

3

Given that the nonaction advocated by Daoism offered possible strategic advantages, it is not surprising that court advisers, with their own interests in mind, tended to resort to it. This was no distant teaching of the sages, of value solely to a ruler, but was useful to anyone seeking success in ordinary life, even at the most modest level. Or rather, it was through nonaction that—once attention-seeking action was rejected—the importance of events was

The formula of non-
action in personal
and self-interested
relations

dissolved and all times seemed "ordinary." Situations
change, but they do so "silently." In the management of
diplomatic or political affairs, the simplest degree of nonaction may, as we have noted, be simply waiting: "The
sage, in/through nonaction, waits until there is a capacity
(GGZ, chap. "Ben jing"). That is a formula worth further
thought, for in the light of Daoism, it takes on added significance. When the evolution of a situation favors no particular development, there is nothing to be done but wait,
and it is by "daring" not to take action that one can preserve oneself (which is essential whatever follows; indeed,
for there to be any follow-on at all). (Note the Daoist
attention paid to the all-important, primordial matter of
staying alive.) But above all, when there is nothing favorable that can be done, it is by not doing anything at all, by
taking care not to intervene, that, by not upsetting the
regulation that is at work by your activism, you can best
help it to achieve its fulfillment. Again we come back to
the lesson best taught by Daoism: namely, that it is not
efficacious to intervene forcibly in any situation. To do so
may constitute heroic—or at any rate spectacular—action,
but it is pointless. It will come to naught. A court adviser
should, on the contrary, "first distinguish what is easy
from what is difficult" and only then "determine his strategy" (GGZ, chap. "Ben jing"): his activity diminishes as
he follows the line of least resistance and is not impeded
in doing so. The treatise on diplomacy then goes on to
explain that it is by "conforming with the spontaneity of
the processes taking place," that is to say, the natural *dao*,
that he will render his strategy "effective." The better he
espouses the course of reality, the better that action of his
is able to merge with reality and, by so doing, be effective,
along with that reality.

In diplomacy, the principle of nonaction is thus generally applicable. If, in one's dealings with others, one
knows how to adapt to the difference between one case
and another, one can, in one way or another, always profit from the situation that develops and thus, "without taking action," succeed in "directing" it (GGZ, chap. 1, "Bai
he"). Where personal relations and interests are con-

cerned, what nonaction means here is that one exercises one's authority simply by adapting to the situation, drawing on the serenity that gives one inner strength (in the Daoist mode), that is to say, by taking care not to project any ideas or intentions onto the situation or, as this treatise elegantly puts it, by keeping these "under wraps" rather than concentrating on them (GGZ, chap. "Ben jing"). There is one image in particular, that of a snake or, better still, a dragon, that successfully conveys the mobility of mind that makes it possible to allow things to evolve freely without the slightest difficulty or effort (*evolution stands in opposition to action*). The dragon's flexible body has no fixed form; it weaves and bends in every direction, contracting in order to deploy itself, coiling up in order to progress. It merges so closely with the clouds that, borne constantly along by them, it advances without the slightest effort. Its movement is hardly distinguishable from that of the clouds. In the same way, strategic intentionality should have no fixed goal, is fixed on no particular plan, and so can adapt to every twist in the situation and profit from it. The general does not act, does not dissipate or expend his energies in any predetermined action but, instead, in the manner of the infinitely supple body of the dragon, makes the most of the ever-changing situation so as to advance continually along with it, *in a state of constant evolution.*

As is not hard to see, the relations between diplomatic thought and the nonaction of Daoism are somewhat fraught (even perverse). Whereas Daoism set its sights on the common order of things, the court adviser who here infiltrates the image of the "sage" (the same term is used) thinks only of his own personal interest (mediated by the ruler), and he does so with no hint of the slightest scruple or shame. Above all, whereas Daoism deliberately rejects intelligence (on the grounds that it upsets a primitive simplicity; LZ, section 19), the court adviser absorbs nonaction into strategic wiles that are generally recognized to operate under cover and to favor cunning machinations (GGZ, end of chap. "Mou"). Notwithstanding, both subscribe to the idea of adapting to the situation in order to

Acting-without-action is transformed into a capacity for evolution

the dragon's flex. body like clouds, in a constant state of evol.

Reaction instead of
action

Carried
along on
the
back.

get the most out of it. Merge with the spontaneous course
of things and respond to it "in a feminine manner," as the
Laozi recommends (using the terms *shun* and *yin*""). This
enables one to see strategic behavior in terms not of
action, but of reaction (*ying*"). And that shift is enough to
change one's overall perspective. Action is risky, for it
means venturing into a new situation, and furthermore it
is costly, for it demands an initial investment of initiative
and energy. However, the acting-without-action involved
in reacting is altogether different. Such reaction is not
risky, since the situation has already been tested out and is
already manifest; nor is it costly, since one is carried along
on the back of whatever one's opponent has already
invested in the way of activity (rather than starting off by
drawing on one's own fund of initiative). Finally, whereas
action is always marked by the arbitrary nature of its
inaugural move and has to use some degree of force in
order to infiltrate reality, reaction is, from the start,
always justified by whatever gives rise to it. Action is necessarily mediated (it must be prepared for by intention and
motivated by will), whereas reaction can be immediate (it
simply adheres to the action of one's oppponent, with no
further input of ideas or will). In other words, whereas
action is transcendent to the world, being marked by a
certain externality (which obliges it to *impose* itself), reaction immediately reabsorbs us in a logic of immanence,
which we need only to espouse. This is reflected in the
respective modes of operation that are employed. Whereas
action, fixed on its plan, must concentrate on one particular point and cling to it, the reactivity of a reaction keeps
it alert and mobile. Like the body of the snake-dragon, it
reacts from every point (cf. the Mount Chang snake suggested as a model for strategy: "when attacked at the
head, its tail rears up; when attacked at the tail, its head
rears up; when attacked in the middle, both ends rear up
at once"; SZ, chap. "Jiu di"). Summing up, this treatise on
diplomacy observes, "Reaction is not limited to any particular spot"""" (GGZ, chap. "Ben Jing"); it can take place
at any point, at any moment. In a word, it cannot be
"pinned down"; it is at one with the operational ubiquity
of transformation.

Reaction absorbs us in
a logic of immanence

reacts
from
every
point

4

The paradox—which, however, is no more than apparent—
can be taken further. Even dictatorial thinking can be
inspired by nonaction. Whether one turns for evidence to
tradition or to texts, it cannot be denied that the political
authoritarianism of the Chinese "legalists" stems directly
from Daoist thought. But really this is in no way surprising (so, as Leon Vandermesh has shown, there is no need
to sift through all the texts in search of evidence). Given
that authoritarian power, once it has become totalitarian,
extends to everything at every moment and imposes the
strictest constraints upon all and sundry, it never needs
to take any particular action. The conditioning that it
imposes once and for all is enough to ensure that submission will unfailingly result, with no further need to apply
willpower or force. When his tyranny is successful, there
is no more for a tyrant to do. He can just let things take
their course. Subjection to him is spontaneous; a regime of
perfect reactivity has been successfully imposed, and, once
carried to the limit, his transcendence is converted into
pure immanence.

A perfect despot has no need for action

There can be no doubt that, when the Chinese "legalists" established a power of the most authoritarian nature,
they expected efficacy to stem from its immanence (efficacy that, for them, meant obedience). As the most subtle
of its analysts notes (HFZ, chap. 8, "Yang quan"), the
nature of that power, which results from an imposed conditioning, was such that there was no need for it to "show
itself," and whoever held it could himself remain "empty,
taking no action," content to allow the power to operate.
For, in contrast to "activity, which deploys itself in every
direction," "what is essential remains at the center" which,
as we have seen, constitutes the position of authority. This
authority is the source of the whole apparatus of power.
On the one hand, it makes it possible for the ruler to institute a system of rewards and punishments that affects all
and sundry and causes every individual instinctively to
react out of fear and self-interest. On the other hand, it
enables the ruler to maintain control over the entire pop-
ulation, thanks to meticulous procedures that establish

collective responsibility, mutual hostility, and interdependence. Given that this apparatus of power acts, or rather reacts, purely mechanically, the ruler no longer needs to bother to pass judgments. Punishments and rewards are automatic. Nor need he bother to maintain surveillance, since denunciations also become automatic. Eventually, once this regime has been perfectly assimilated, even punishments are no longer necessary, since every individual, intensely motivated by desire and repulsion, spontaneously observes the imposed law. Every individual now fulfills his function as naturally as "a cock serves as a night watchman" and a cat "serves to catch mice." The "sage" (here the despot) therefore no longer needs to "busy himself" at all. It is enough that he "keeps a tight hold" on the mechanism for "everyone, from all four corners of the world, to come and offer him support." He can simply "wait" for this to be forthcoming and for all and sundry to devote themselves to his well-being.

It is easy enough for the theorist of despotism to show how productive the system is. Thanks to its automatic nature, the functioning of power is constantly satisfactory

The automatic nature of the system

(cf. "since everything is set up in this way around him [the prince], as soon as he opens his door, everything adapts to him"). The ruler's power functions in a constantly regular fashion. Fully implied by the mechanical system, it no longer has to rely on the goodwill of others or of the ruler himself. The system is constantly renewable: the machine continues to operate in this way without ever coming to a halt; it functions in a "coherent" and regular way. An overall efficiency is thus achieved. The ruler is all the more powerful because he never needs to intervene; in fact, "at the top as at the bottom," at the level of the people as at that of the ruler, "no more action is needed." With each individual occupying his or her assigned place, everything runs smoothly of its own accord. Once set in motion, the wheels turn automatically.

It is in this sense that the power that is exercised is decribed as "void" (cf. "void and without action" and "void, he waits for others to deploy their activity on his

The despotic power is "void"

behalf"). "Void" means that the ruler *allows* the mechanism of power that he holds in his grasp to function, never interfering, never making any personal contribution. It remains *purely* mechanical. He is careful never to manifest or even feel the slightest preference, for the arbitrary nature of such subjectivity would impede the impeccable functioning of the system. He is also careful never to bring his intelligence to bear on it, for introducing an element of interplay would inevitably confuse the system's rigorous self-sufficiency, which stems from its coherence. It would, moreover, lead others to compete with him in intelligence, thereby pulling him down to their level and setting up a competition for power (which would ruin its efficient functioning). Such a perfect despot is wary of all "interventionism," for to recommend a particular line of behavior is to impose a momentary and partial order ("partial" in both senses of the term) on the overall order definitively established by the system. Any interference on the ruler's part would introduce intentionality into a system that is supposed to work automatically, that is to say, purely as is necessary. Above all, so as never to upset this immanent order, which, because it is immanent, is self-sufficient, a good despotic ruler must guard against the temptations of virtue. If he were to manifest clemency or generosity, he would call into question the regularity of rewards and punishments. That is why his role is described as "void" and also why the very best of sovereigns is "never noticed." Speaking of the despot, the theorist of authoritarianism repeats what the Daoist sage said: all that is necessary is that it is known that "up there, he exists" (HFZ, chap. 38, "Nan san").

> A perfect despot is not interventionist

> In fact, he becomes unnoticed

despot: travesty

Yet this despotic version of nonaction turns out, once again, to be a travesty. For Daoism recommended nonaction on the part of the ruler with a view to allowing individuals to flourish, liberating them from the bonds imposed by rules and prohibitions (that were considered to go hand in hand with the development of civilization). "Legalist" despotism, on the contrary, plays exactly the opposite role: it enslaves the entire mass of individuals to the power of a single figure who embodies the State. Whereas Daoism was inclined to bring the social order ever closer to a natural simplicity, the "legalists" organize power in a completely artificial fashion (it is completely

The artifice of power, pushed to the limit, reinstalls a regime of pure reactivity and thus of spontaneity

independent of the sentiments of the ruler and rests solely on the norms that are imposed and the control that is exercised). However, they then expect this *artificial* and technically installed system to operate *on its own;* and by so doing they totally recuperate the nonaction of Daoism and once again plug into the natural element that processes possess. Once again, the ruler needs to do nothing but allow things to take their course. Obedience results of its own accord, and the social order is spontaneous. The "legalists" find themselves again at one with the "Daoists" in their critique of intelligence and their rejection of virtues, since they too attribute efficiency to such spontaneity. Nevertheless, excessively sensitive as they are to the speeded-up development of civilization at this time in late Antiquity, they no longer believe it possible to return to the patriarchal society that was advocated in the *Laozi* (section 80) and are by now anxious above all to allow their ruler to acquire more power than any of the rival kingdoms in order to reunite China under his sole rule. To this end, they are led to invent new—despotic—conditions in order to recover the virtue of immanence along with all its efficacy. It is by radicalizing power to such a degree that they end up restoring its discretion (it is discreet in that it is indistinguishable from the functioning of the apparatus). By conferring upon it the implacability of a natural law, they succeed in imposing it as though it were inevitable. Daoism had pointed to the way of immanence that led to liberation from social constraint. Legalist despotism, for its part, forced a return to the virtue of immanence by making constraint absolute.

Once absolute, constraint resumes the virtue of immanence and becomes natural

The reversal is total, but (or rather, so) the logic is the same. In the extreme mode of legalist tyranny we find the very same relation between conditioning and consequence that structures the entire Chinese concept of efficacy. As the legalist thinker, too, remarks (HFZ, chap. 28, "Gong ming"), if the right conditions are lacking, the result will be disappointing: however heroic one may be, "it is impossible to make an ear of grain grow in the winter." But as soon as the conditions are correctly adjusted, the result comes about purely through immanence—without any

need to "strive," "exhort," "apply pressure," or "push."
Just as "water flows and boats float," a despotic ruler
"preserves the natural way" and so is endlessly obeyed.
That is why he can be called an "enlightened" sovereign.
All he needs to do is to allow effects to come about.

7

Allow Effects to Come About

[handwritten margin note, top right] under what conditions is an effect possible

1

[handwritten margin note, left] perhaps the most crucial question of all

Now we must address a crucial question. It is perhaps the most crucial one of all, in fact, since success depends upon it, but as we come to realize, it is one that is not often asked. The question is how—that is to say, under what conditions—is an effect possible (so far as we are concerned and vis-à-vis a situation that confronts us)? Or rather, it is a question that is often raised in the context of the sciences and technology, that is to say, in circumstances where we can construct an object that is both stable and clearly defined; and it is also raised in the domains of art and discourse—aesthetics and rhetoric—where it is a matter of producing a particular effect (beauty or persuasion). But we seldom pose it in a more general fashion, in relation to the indefinite and shifting world of human behavior, and with a strategic perspective: nobody has produced a work on the art of succeeding (even *The Prince* does not qualify as such); we have not theorized *mètis*. That is because we have remained focused on action, virtuous or wondrous action, the subject of morality and epic.

However, when we turn to the teaching of ancient Chinese wisdom, we begin to suspect that an effect should not be measured by what we can see, by what we are aware of, and therefore talk about, for the visible aspect of an effect is of minimal importance. Instead of merging with reality, it remains superficial, and, by attracting atten-

[margin note] The notion of effectiveness should not be confined to purely technical domains

[margin note] Think about how effectiveness works (the *dao*, the "way")

tion to itself, it generates antagonistic reactions. Endless confrontation results, in which we get bogged down. The masters of wisdom of ancient China on the contrary teach us to make use of reality with cunning—not so much to deal with others with cunning, which we Westerners have always regarded as the acme of cleverness (Odysseus, Renard the Fox, and so forth), but rather to *deal with the situation with cunning,* relying on the logic of its unfolding. The point is at once to allow the situation's effects to come about, without having to make any effort or expend any energy, and also to prevent any rejection on its part, in other words to get it (the situation) to tolerate us. The latter is a condition of the former, and in the *Laozi* the two go together and are apprehended jointly as complying with three main criteria: an effect must not be forced, one must not try to take it over, and one must avoid saturating it.

On the subject of behavior that is efficacious, there is perhaps no more to say than what has always been said and is endlessly repeated on all sides, expressing an age-old prudence that underlies all wisdoms, a "popular" or "universal" prescription that antedates all theorizing and simply states the obvious: namely, that excess should be avoided. The image that the *Laozi* takes as its starting point is that of a receptacle that stands upright when empty but tips over as soon as it is full (section 9): one can "keep it upright" (by force) in order to "fill it to the brim," but as soon as the hold is released, it spills; thus it is "best to stop" before it is full, so that it retains its balance and there is no cause for it to overturn. Another image is that of a point that, because it is too sharp, will not last and eventually snaps. Never (pour in, sharpen, and so on) too much: that is a common precept both in Greek *(meden agan)* and in Chinese *(qu tai)* (cf. LZ, section 29). But already, underlying what might seem to be a commonplace and a subject of universal agreement, a divergence becomes detectable. In contrast to Western gnomic lore and the theme of which Greek choruses so often sing, on the Chinese side such excess is not condemned because its immoderation transgresses the human condition and trespasses on a different domain (that of the gods), implying *hubris.* It is not condemned on the grounds that it will

not be
forced

not try
to

What are the
conditions for
effectiveness?

to

take it over

avoid

A commonplace:
avoid excess

Saturating
it

China is not concerned with *hubris*
(it has no tragedy)

provoke forces that are superior to us and because it inso-
lently tempts fate. Although it goes beyond the limit, it is
not regarded as a transgression. All that matters is the internal logic of the situation: simply the fact that a vessel that
is too full will overflow (and too sharp a point will snap);
excessive effect is counterproductive. Too much effect kills
effectiveness. The Chinese point of view introduces no
background moral or religious factors (which are always
more or less a matter of magic). It is concerned purely with

A description of what
makes an effect
possible

efficacy. When an effect is pushed to the limit, strained, or
forced, it passes beyond reality's threshold of tolerance; it
can no longer be integrated and so undoes itself.

It is therefore essential that the effect carry no super-
charge imparted by whoever produces it. That person
must be careful not to add any personal or affective element to its pure effectiveness (section 30): he "must not
dare" to use it to increase his own standing but must be
content purely with the effect, without showing that he is
"proud" of it, without using it to "improve his own repu-

Effect and
countereffect

tation" or "boasting" about it. The "fruit," or end result,
is sufficient. The effect must appear to result purely from
the situation and to merge with its coherence. It must be
accepted by all as being ineluctable—as if it was bound to
happen and was in no way imposed." No show of force
must be added to emphasize the effect. For any hint of
force renders the effect dependent on the reversals that any
recourse to force invariably invites. Furthermore, the effect
then becomes subject to the ineluctable wear and tear that
the application of force inevitably implies. In short, any
such reinforcement of an effect tempers it. It weakens it by
contamination, since force is merely the other side to weak-

To link an effect with
force weakens it

ness and always provokes it on the rebound. By inclining
to the side of force, an effect becomes caught in a force-
weakness tension in which it may well swing to the opposite side. The imposition of force thus renders the effect
precarious. Since any manifestation of force is bound to be
temporary, any effect that depends on force will soon be
exhausted; it is condemned to ephemerality.

The fact is that anything that emphasizes an effect is

Defining how an
effect works

parasitic upon it, puts a strain on it, and inhibits it. The
Laozi mentions "elements of relief" and "protuberances"

in this connection (section 24). "Whoever stands on tiptoe is not steady, and whoever takes huge strides cannot walk properly." As the saying goes, if you overdo it, not only are your efforts in vain, but you undermine even the possibility of an effect. Too much turns into too little, for excess not only acts as a dead weight, not only threatens to reverse or exhaust the effect, but furthermore impedes what might have happened—one might even say what was just waiting to happen. The effect is quite simply prevented from *resulting*. A double price is then paid: internally, that surplus effectiveness undermines the effect, creating an obstruction; meanwhile, externally it causes the effect to be "detested." For, instead of passing unnoticed, the excessiveness of the effect draws attention to it, provokes resentment, and attracts resistance, causing it to be rejected.

Excessive effectiveness blocks the possibility of an effect

The *Laozi*'s prescriptions go even further: "When the effect comes about, do not dwell on it" (section 2). A sage/general is not proprietary, claims no credit for an effect. As soon as one claims credit for an effect, one engages in a logic of appropriation that is bound to be counterproductive, given that anything that is "occupied" is destined eventually to be "abandoned," so that appropriation rebounds against the effect, causing it to be challenged. "To occupy an effect" (section 77; cf. GGZ, chap. "Mo") implies that by taking up such a proprietary position one trespasses on the position of others, and, as a result of that rivalry, the effect is compromised; its duration is jeopardized. If you but refrain from "occupying the effect," it will, on the contrary, "not abandon you." Instead of rendering it precarious by binding it to your own person, you allow it to belong to the world that brought it into existence; you restore it to its immanence. Elsewhere, another formula captures that strategic discretion admirably: "Let the effect result while you yourself withdraw" (section 9). It precisely conveys two points at once: first, that an effect "follows on" as a result—it is a consequence, not a planned project—second, that instead of presenting oneself as the author of the effect and deriving prestige from this, one should step aside to allow free play to the factors that sweep the effect forward.

To link an effect to oneself renders it precarious

Once again, all this is a far cry from heroism. An effect must not be constrained or forced; one must not seek to

Antiheroism

draw attention to it; one must refrain from laying claim to
it and from expecting glory from it. Above all the effect
should be allowed to merge with the evolution of things
and be absorbed by it. Once discreetly absorbed by reality,
it too becomes real. The purpose of this rejection of any
deliberate, activist attempt to intensify and draw attention
to an effect is explained by the very nature of an effect; it
is only effective if it proves naturally inclined to deploy
itself, to work away and *become* effective. For this to happen, it is essential that it should not be saturated: one should
not only not force the limit of an effect but should beware
of even pushing it to that limit. The *Laozi* declares: "The
five colors, all at once, blind the eye" (section 12), "the
five notes, all at once, deafen the ear, and the five flavors,
all at once, spoil the palate." These declarations have been
interpreted, in moral terms, as an appeal to reduce desires
(He Shang gong). But their rejection of things that are perceived by the senses (cf. the opposition of the "stomach"
to the "eye" as the source of human capacities) can also
be given another interpretation: the less insistent a sensation is, the more effective; when an effect is *brimful* and so
overflows, it no longer works. To put that another way, an
effect comes about not when it overflows, but when it
begins to happen. When sensations are at their peak and
the senses can absorb no more, an effect is no longer felt
and so ceases to be effective. Nor is it felt if it comes about
immediately. But when there is still room for a transformation and it is still possible to move from one stage to
another, overcoming any deficiences so that an effect
comes about rather than a noneffect—then an effect does
make itself felt. It does so as a gradual decantation, a gradual change (section 15), in the same way that "troubled"
water, by "becoming still," "gradually becomes clear"; or,
in reverse, something that seems "dormant," through a
long shaking-up process, "little by little returns to life."
Such is the *dao* that "whoever keeps to this path does not
seek plenitude." There is no future for whatever is full; it
can only overflow. Whereas that which is not full aspires
to plenitude and in this way can "renew itself."

That is why, in the last analysis, true efficacy *seems
deficient.* As the *Laozi* remarks (section 41), "A great work

theory
nature of
an

Do not saturate an
effect

effect:
only effective
if it proves
naturally
inclined
to deploy

An effect is only effec-
tive when in the
process of coming
about, when it is not
yet realized

itself

overflows:
no longer
works

puts off completion" (a better reading than "happens in the evening"). As we have learned from modern painting, setting a high value on a preliminary sketch makes it possible for *what appears to be lacking in it* to allow the work to continue to evolve and to produce an effect; the unfinished element is what keeps the effect active. Elsewhere, the *Laozi* notes that "a sound may be minimal but its sonority great." In contrast to the "five notes," which when all together and raising sensation to its highest pitch deafen the ear and prevent it from feeling any effect, this small sound allows its harmonic effect to reverberate all the better, because the sound itself is restrained, holds itself in reserve, in abeyance. In other words, if it is to make an impact, true efficacy seems the reverse of a completed effect; it never quite achieves its result, which is precisely why it continues to result. "Full achievement is never quite attained, so is never used up," "total plenitude is as it were empty, so it is never exhausted by being used" (and equally "total straightness seems bent," "great ability seems clumsy," "great eloquence seems restrained," and so on). Note the terms "as it were" and "seems." The point is not that efficacy is really lacking, but it is legitimate that it should seem to be, so that, by having to continue to operate, it continues to follow an urge to come about and yet never allows itself to become completely actualized. For if it were to be definitive and fill the entire horizon, it would block off all expectation and all elicitation, and could no longer fulfill its function. To put that another way, resorting to another favorite theme of the *Laozi*—the valley—true efficacy always seems hollow (cf. "full capacity is, as it were, insufficient," which may be compared with "the most perfect capacity resembles a valley," section 41). Through the hollowness of the valley, the "spirit" passes, thanks to the emptiness that always remains to be filled. It is the same with efficacy: instead of imposing itself fully, thanks to the emptiness that it contains, it can exercise its full effect.

Why does an effect have to seem incomplete in order to be effective?

An effect is hollow

It is the emptiness that makes the full effect possible

2

There are two ways of understanding emptiness. One is an emptiness of inexistence, seen from the metaphysical point

Two concepts of emptiness: from the point of view of being and from the point of view of function

XU:
fn..empti-
ness>

Empty and full

the later
background
to all things>

Beyond metaphysics: background as a kind of stock

from which
a brush
stroke
emerges

The emptiness prevents the fullness from becoming bogged down

of view of being or nonbeing: this is the emptiness of Buddhism (*sunya* in Sanskrit; cf. *kong* in Chinese). The other is the functional emptiness of the *Laozi* (the notion of *xu*[yy]): it operates in relation to fullness, and it is thanks to it that fullness can fulfill its full effect. The two are radically different, although some people have been tempted to confuse them, and, as a result, they have become contaminated. (It is well known that, in part at least, it was on the basis of that misunderstanding that Buddhism, which came from India, that is to say, from an Indo-European land of metaphysics, penetrated China. That is, after all, perfectly understandable, since the only way to assimilate thought from outside is by misunderstanding it.) The emptiness of the *Laozi*, which stands in opposition to fullness and functions correlatively with it, is absorbed and becomes undifferentiated; it is also out of that emptiness that fullness comes about and becomes effective. So this emptiness is not "nonbeing," but rather the latent background to all things—in the sense that one speaks of the background to a painting or a background of silence: that background constitutes a stock from which sound is produced and that makes that sound resonate, the stock from which a brush stroke emerges and thanks to which it can vibrate. (So far as I can see, only by means of such analogies is it possible to break away from our Western ontological atavism.) Continuing with the experience with a paintbrush: far from being an inane emptiness, it is more a looseness that stands in contrast to the solidity of a heavy line and in which the concrete is reduced to a minimum and becomes discreet. It makes the solidity of a painted line stand out in all its force and depth. It is an infinitely subtle emptiness and its spirit, liberated from the weight of forms and things, circulates constantly through them and animates them. If it ceased to permeate reality, the latter would be forever numb, prostrate, and fixed. Without this influx of emptiness, reality would be utterly reified.

The *Laozi* suggests a number of images to convey this (section 11). All the spokes of a wheel converge at the hub, and it is "there, where there is nothing," in the empty part (at the center, where the axle slips in) that "the cart functions" (enabling the wheel to turn and the cart to advance).

Similarly, one molds clay to fashion a vase, but it is "there, where there is nothing," that "the function of the vase comes into play." Thanks to that inner emptiness, the vase can be a container, an object with a use. Likewise, it is thanks to the door and windows pierced through the walls that light enters a room and one can live in it. It is where the fullness is hollowed out and thanks to what has been taken away in the wood, the ground, or the wall that fullness can fulfill a function and acquire the capacity to produce an effect. The *Laozi* sums all this up in a formula that can be rendered as follows: that which can be called "profit" at the stage of the actualization of things operates as a "functioning" at the level of their undifferentiated basic stock (section 11). Through the actualization of that which is full, the indefinite functioning of emptiness can emerge from its indeterminacy and manifests itself as a particular kind of profit. But it is also thanks to the undifferentiation of the emptiness that serves as the latent stock of things that each particular actualization is no longer trapped in its particularity but can communicate at the deepest level with other things and, in relation to them, can discover its own virtuality. For when an effect is realized, it is always specific; but it is what renders it indeterminate, namely, "emptiness," that constitutes the generic and generating condition that makes it possible for it to exist.

In order to assess the possibility of efficacy, we thus need to fathom the capacity that it derives from emptiness both to communicate and to deploy itself. Those two functions come together in what one might call a negative fashion: without the undifferentiation of emptiness as a common basis (the notion of *wu*[z]), one individuation would not be able to encounter others, interact with them (thanks to this "betweenness" that is operative), and produce its effect. Furthermore, were it not for the emptiness of that which is empty, which provides a circumambient milieu, an effect could not spread and propagate itself. One notion in particular conveys this efficacy of emptiness. It is expressed by the commentator on the *Laozi* (*tong*[aaa] in Wang Bi; cf. sections 14, 40, 44). Emptiness is quite simply that which allows an effect *to pass*. "Where there is nothing that is actualized, there is nowhere [one] cannot pass, [nowhere]

A nonontological logic, to which we need to accustom ourselves (for otherwise these observations will seem mere abstractions)

Empty-full, function-profit

no longer trapped in — its particularity

wu: betweenness that is operative, a circum-

Emptiness allows an effect to pass through it

ambient milieu

blockages:
Saturated:
no room
—when
in —
to operate

one cannot go." Conversely, an effect is prevented from happening when fullness is no longer penetrated by emptiness and, having become opaque, constitutes an obstacle: forming a screen, it makes reality congeal, and one remains stuck in it. With efficacy unable to circulate, one gets bogged down. This return to emptiness is stripped of all mysticism (given that nothing metaphysical is at stake). The *Laozi* recommends it in order to dissolve the blockages that threaten all reality as soon as no gaps remain in it and it becomes saturated. For if everything is filled, there is no room in which to operate. If emptiness is eliminated, the interplay that made it possible for the effect to be freely exercised is destroyed. Once reality becomes opaque and rigid, with no room for emptiness, it finds itself inhibited. This warning is relevant also (indeed, primarily) at the political level. The excessive fullness that burdens it is, as we have seen, that of regulations and prohibitions that, as they multiply, end up weighing society down so that it is impossible for it to evolve as it should. An emptiness needs to be created, those regulations must be *evacuated,* to allow reality the space in which take off. For as soon as nothing is codified any more (codification being nothing but a reification of fullness), because nothing any longer bars the way to initiative, this can deploy itself *sponte sua*. In the emptiness created by the removal of prohibitions and regulations, all that is necessary is to allow things to happen, to allow them to pass through, so that action now occurs without activity.

This emptiness is not spiritual, nor is it material. It no more refers to the physicality of bodies than to the metaphysics of the soul; its logic is functional. It is what makes it possible for fullness to remain fluid and to breathe (by remaining aerated). It is what keeps reality going, keeps it animated (and this shift is crucial: the point of view here is not that of the *soul* as an entity, but that of *animation*, as a process). Chinese painting provides a telling example of how emptiness interacts with fullness—this interaction is precisely what is conveyed by such paintings. The blank spaces of the drawing on the scroll allow the full, thick lines to communicate with one another. The spaces constitute an area left vacant in which relations can be woven.

At the same time, the blank space allows those relations to deploy their effect, opening up what is drawn there to infinity. One only has to erase a little of what has been drawn, making it elusive, to find that the fathomless fund of reality surfaces. Through the slightest gap the farthest horizon can be glimpsed. In this way that horizon becomes disseminated right through the scroll. The whole drawing is penetrated by the beyond; the sky is no longer confined to a particular place but is everywhere (or rather, it is not, but it *operates* everywhere). Inhabited by emptiness, the drawing becomes the momentary imprint of an absence. Instead of displaying its subject fully, it captures an invisible flow— the flow of the invisible (*shen* [bbb]). The lines traced by the drawing become a trace. That is the source of the ceaseless effect of emptiness. Whereas that which is full is always limited, for one can see where it ends, emptiness is inexhaustible, a bottomless source. The *Laozi* spells this out (section 4): "The *dao* is empty, but when you use it, you can never exhaust it" (a better reading than "you never have to refill it"; section 35). Furthermore, "when you use it, you do not have to strive" (section 6). Since emptiness is not confrontational, never opposes anything, it can never provoke any resistance, and so it can never be exhausted. That is borne out by the *Laozi*'s images that represent emptiness, images that express the possibility of things *passing through*. Here are some examples. A *valley*: we know already that an invisible efficiency constantly passes through it and, on that account, it "never dies" (section 6); a *door*, including that of a Mother, through which beings are engendered (sections 1, 6); and *bellows*, which are empty but never collapse, and "when you move them, you always get more to emerge from them" (more effect) (section 5). So the question that the *Laozi* asks is the following: "This between heaven and earth," all this emptiness in which life comes to be, is it not itself "like a great bellows"?

(handwritten margin note) The sky operates continuum

What is traced in the drawing becomes a trace

Conclusion (to which, however, we shall return): emptiness is an inexhaustible fund of effectiveness :

(handwritten margin note) the possibility of things passing through

3

This interaction between emptiness and fullness, which lies at the heart of any effect, is exemplary. It reveals the interdependence of the opposed aspects of reality thanks to

reality

How can the logic of a nonexclusion of contraries engender thought on efficacy?

ceases to operate

It is on the basis of interdependence and reversibility that strategic thinking operates

instead of wearing himself out in efforts of his own

which reality never ceases to operate and, through doing so, endlessly comes about. Just like emptiness and fullness, all contraries "engender each other," the *Laozi* tells us (section 2): you can see one aspect fully but, unseen, the other is also at work. "Everyone knows beauty as beauty, yet already it is ugliness"; "everyone knows good as good, yet already it is not-good." Instead of excluding each other, contraries mutually condition each other, and this constitutes the logic from which a sage derives his strategy. For, instead of seeing no farther than the opposed aspects of things, as common sense pictures them, and keeping them isolated, the sage is able to discern their interdependence and to profit from it. This is what he exploits instead of wearing himself out in efforts of his own. That interdependence is quite enough to keep reality moving, so he is content to allow it to operate; he no longer needs to take action and can allow himself to be carried along. This brings us back to propensity, for in the last analysis, it is what determines things (section 51). While the "way" of the *dao* "engenders," "capacity nurtures" (through immanence), and "materiality concretizes," it falls to "propensity" to "make things come about." It is propensity that, as things develop, orientates the course that reality takes. It is therefore in terms of propensity that the commentator on the *Laozi* (Wang Bi, section 9) understands that whatever is too full must spill over and a point that is too sharp must snap. One expression that he uses deserves our particular attention, for it encapsulates the nature of strategy in the neatest fashion: the particular skill of a strategist lies in "spotting a propensity" in such a way that "he has no need to strive"[ccc] (and so is "without merit"; section 64). Able, as he is, to see at the earliest stage how interdependence is working, he relies on a tendency that emanates from this and has no more need to "strive."

Seize on the immanence that will produce a tendency

how to operate. how to let things operate

to avoid taking action to succeed

Let us now see, concretely, how to operate, or rather how to let things operate to avoid having to take action in order to succeed. The *Laozi* (section 7) declares that if you decide to push yourself forward in order to be successful, this will be both exhausting and risky. You will inevitably arouse rivalry and will have to confront rivals and struggle against them. Whereas, if you stay modestly in the background, it may well happen (of its own accord) that you will be pushed to the fore. The withdrawn position in which you choose to place yourself leads to a reversal: so, rather than push yourself forward, you should *act in such a way* that others do the pushing for you. If others push you forward, they will not later challenge your advancement. Because it will correspond to what the situation calls for, it will become naturally integrated with that situation. Your reticence will, in advance, have disarmed mistrust and hostility, so others will feel no jealousy toward you but will be attracted by your withdrawal and will come, of their own accord, to seek you out. Instead of seeking to impose yourself fully by trying (by dint of action) to saturate the situation, you benefit from an effect of hollowness that makes the tension converge and that may result in a promotion (*er*,[ddd] "the result is that"; it is, once again, the "empty" word that conveys the invisible unfolding of the situation through which you achieve your end). "The last shall be first," as we also say in the West, but in this case it is not a matter of a reward (at the Last Judgment and brought about by transcendence). Instead, it happens in the immediate present, purely through immanence (which stems from the situation). Furthermore, this choice of withdrawal does not express any self-denial. If one prefers to remain in the background, the *Laozi* tells us, it is in order to "bring about one's own personal interests" (and, similarly, if one treats the "self" as something "external," it is the better to make it exist). It is purely a matter of efficacy.

We still need to understand more precisely how this self-abasement (which is supposed to lead to one's promotion by others) fits into the general logic according to which contraries elicit each other, since one aspect conditions the other. We are told (section 67) that "not daring to put oneself forward" so as, later on, to be all the better placed "to direct others" is like being economical in order to be liberal (or being compassionate in order to be brave enough to attack). If one aspect can be converted into its reverse in this way, that is because basically it simply turns around on itself, thereby constituting a reserve for its contrary, from which the latter derives its possibility. One aspect

Example: instead of pushing forward, allow yourself to be pushed

The withdrawn position in which you choose to place yourself leads to a reversal

it simply turns around on itself, thereby constituting a reserve for its contrary

exhausted — it has nothing to draw upon

One aspect serves as a fund from which the contrary can result

(liberal from the start is dead)

prepares for the other, stores up within itself something that can subsequently emerge fully. One is only able to attack resolutely if, conversely, one has been capable of pity; one can only possess the resources to be liberal if, conversely, one has been sparing. In contrast, the *Laozi* tells us, if one tries to be liberal right from the start or forward right from the start, "one is dead." For that kind of liberality, or resolution, or forwardness is immediately exhausted; it has nothing to draw upon, no *fund* from which it can result.

One should not seek an effect but should simply welcome it

(we should not seek the effect ourselves, but place)

So we should not count on "calling forth" an effect but should simply allow it to come about. We should not seek the effect ourselves but should place ourselves in the right position to welcome it. An effect is something that one harvests. So the most promising position to be in is a lowly one, where our abilities are not solicited and so can remain "constant" and "not abandon us" (section 28). An image of this ability to allow effects to converge upon us is provided by the sea receiving water from the rivers (sections 32, 66). "The way that large rivers and the sea can reign over all other water courses is through their ability to position themselves below them": the sea allows rivers to flow toward it, following their downward course, and dominates from below. In the same way, a sage dominates the ordinary people by placing himself "below them, through his words" (even the emperor might refer to himself as "I, the humble one," or "the lonely one"; cf. section 39). Then, when he discovers himself to be above the people, the latter do not find him "heavy" to carry and are "happy to push him forward"—in fact, they never tire of doing so (section 66). Conversely, a sage can effortlessly use the energy of others (section 68). This humility (literally, the choice to put oneself below) is neither moral nor psychological; it is purely strategic (section 61). The *Laozi* then proceeds to develop this theme at the level of diplomacy: instead of imposing its hegemony, which would inevitably be challenged, a great country, by its own choice, places itself "downstream" so as to allow smaller countries to "flow" toward it: in this way it gains its "ascendency."

The sea: it is by being lower that one can dominate

(ourselves in the right position to welcome it)

(start below, to become full)

Put the other way around, this idea finds expression in formulae that the *Laozi* particularly favors; "Whoever

draws attention to himself is not well regarded" (or "whoever approves of himself is not recognized"; "whoever is
boastful is without merit"; "whoever glorifies himself will
not last"; section 24). In other words, whoever attempts
to obtain what he wants directly blocks the possibility of
achieving this. This is not because he is impatient (seeking
to achieve his determined goal too quickly), but because he
is fundamentally mistaken about the way in which reality is
realized. For something to be realized in an effective fashion, it must come about as an effect. It is always through a
process (which transforms the situation), not through a goal
that leads (directly) to action, that one achieves an effect, a
result. So one is mistaken if one thinks it possible to obtain
it by force, by grabbing it instead of following the way, the
dao, which allows an effect, which is progressively implied
by a situation, to come about of its own accord. That is how
it is that "by not drawing attention to oneself, one can be
well regarded" ("by not approving of oneself, one can gain
recognition," and so on; section 22). All this is borne out
by moral experience: whoever lays claim to greatness possesses only a false greatness; his greatness is pretentious
and will irremediably remain petty. In contrast, because,
"to the very end, he never seeks to be great," "the sage is
in a position to have his greatness come about" (section 63)
and is truly great.

Any strategy thus seems, in the end, to come down to
simply knowing how to *implicate* an effect, knowing how
to tackle a situation upstream in such a way that the effect
flows "naturally" from it. By pushing this logic as far as it
will go, we arrive at the following conclusion: a fine strategist is a person who knows how to cope with a lack at the
center of a situation (a condition that is lacking) in such a
way that a compensatory effect, operating in his favor, then
must inevitably result. The *Laozi* delights in expressing
ideas such as the following: "Being pliable [or partial]
results in one becoming whole," "being bent results in one
becoming straight," or "being empty results in one becoming full" (section 22). By placing yourself in an extreme
position, you produce and maximize the propensity that
will carry you to the opposite extreme. Thus, if you choose
to place yourself at the negative extreme, thanks to the

Margin notes:

An effect cannot be achieved directly

What is needed is a process

tension that regulates reality, as if despite yourself, you are swept along to a converse plenitude. According to the *Laozi*, an understanding of this is "a subtle intelligence" that one can also use the other way around, against one's opponents. "If you want something to be folded up, you must first unfold it" (this refers to an initial situation whose effect must be enabled to stem from it in an "intrinsic" fashion; cf. the meaning of *gu* ᵉᵉᵉ). Similarly, if you want something to be weakened, you must first strengthen it; if you want it to be eliminated, you must first promote it; if you want it to be withdrawn, you must first grant it" (section 36). The commentator (Wang Bi) does not hesitate to extract the consequences on the political level: if you want to get rid of a despot, let him follow his own inclinations and sink into the extremes of tyranny, for then he will provoke his own downfall all by himself and far better than if you set out to punish him. The lesson to be learned is the following: China should expect its liberation to stem from the self-regulation of reality rather than from revolution.... Revolution constitutes a paroxysm of action that, like any action, focuses on its goal, trusting to a particular model and adopting an epic mode.*

If one did not know better, one could suppose the following lines from the *Laozi* to come from the New Testament: "Given that it is for others, one has more oneself" or "Because you give to others, you yourself have more" (section 81). However, the commentator leaves us in no doubt about the matter: if you derive an advantage that is because "others respect you"; if you have more, that is because "others come naturally to you." Such an attitude

Marginal notes:

गु
(intrinsic
destiny)

Regulation (through propensity) versus revolution (through action)

Generosity and humility bring their own reward (because they imply a necessary compensation)

---

*At the beginning of the twentieth century, China did borrow the notion of a revolution, breaking with its traditional idea of a "mandate" that is "cut off" *(ge-ming),* and thus, by dint of a readjustment, found itself able to adopt the term "revolution." At any rate, it did borrow a model and, more important, the very idea of a model. The idea was that, on the basis of a revolutionary theory (Marxism-Leninism, copied from the country judged to be the closest to China both socially and politically, whose revolution was believed to be successful: namely, the Russian revolution of 1917), it is possible to change reality through praxis. I wonder if China still believes that today.

certainly expects no retribution from another world. Its gain is immediate and temporal. At the same time, though, that attitude is real, not false. It is no good pretending, as a Machiavellian prince might do: the world cannot be split into appearance and truth (in order to get away with cruel behavior or to dupe others with a deceptive external appearance). It is by reacting to effectiveness that such an attitude wins over others; effectiveness can win over the whole world. Nevertheless, this kind of "generosity" or "humility" does remain suspect from a moral point of view. Even in China itself, Confucian scholars were horrified that, under the cloak of wisdom, the *Laozi* revealed the most devious of strategies to serve self-interested ends (cf. Lin Yin, twelfth century, *Jingxiu xiansheng wenji*, "Tui-zhaiji"). Starting from the principle of the interdependence of contraries, which establishes every aspect of reality in a polar relationship, and counting on the fact that the propensities that stem from this "seek each other out" and are mutually attractive (for each must convert into the other or else become exhausted), it is possible to use reality's logic of compensation deliberately in order to make a situation react as one wishes it to. To this end, all one needs to do is "set out walking against the current" of the result that one hopes to arrive at (for example, as we have seen, one withdraws, backing away, in order to be swept forward; one takes up a lower position in order to rise; and so on). Thus, "before one even enters," one has "an eye on the exit,"[fff] and, without anyone else "noticing a thing," one garners all the profit for oneself.... Basically, for our most selfish ends to result as effects, we need no longer bring our will to bear on things by exerting pressure. All we need do is implant those ends in the trajectory of things. In this way, left to its immanence, the desired effect is realized.

There is no transcendent retribution

No pretence

A back-to-front strategy of the most twisted kind

8

From Efficacy to Efficiency

1

The beginning of a
split between effect
and effectiveness

It was thus apparently unnecessary to elaborate a psychology of will. In fact, that notion never even arose in China. All that was needed was a phenomenology of effects, or rather of "effectivity"—as in affectivity—that is to say, effectiveness. For an effect is at once too simply causal and too purely explanatory, too much a product and too final to account for the effectiveness that is at work. The very concept of an effect is at once too clumsy and too narrow. An effect is too separate from the overall procedure that produces it, too much simply a flat result; and as such it is too noticeable and demonstrative (to the point of possibly seeming artificial, as when it is a matter of seeking to create effects in music or poetry, for instance, or when one speaks of "a fine effect." Such an effect is both too theatrical and too technical). In contrast, and if one remains closer to the root of the word *"efficere"* (to make happen), effectiveness is the operative dimension to an effect. It is what leads to an effect and makes it effective. It is an effect in the making, an effect in pregnancy that stems from an ongoing process that has started (and never ceases to stem from it), so it belongs to a logic not so much of production but of coming about. An effect is thus the full, saturated aspect of effectiveness, and, as such, it is too complete. Effectiveness, in contrast, is an effect that is still empty and so is inclined to deploy itself. It is an effect in opera-

An effect is deliberately aimed for; effectiveness stems from a process

tion, in motion, and on that account is never completely manifest, as if lacking something yet inexhaustible.

Chinese thought never ceased to endeavor to plumb this capacity for effectiveness. It was not concerned to set being in opposition to appearance or to becoming. It did not wonder where reality came from (or why: which is why it developed no myths). Rather, the question that it asked was *how* reality comes about, how it "works" (the notion of *yong*[ggg]) and makes itself "viable" (by being regulated: the *dao*). For, constantly subject to its own affects (*gan*[hhh]) as it is, reality never ceases to become effective: although it never ceases to deploy itself, and precisely because it is coherent and regulated, reality never stops coming about and can never be exhausted.

We need to forge the notion of what might be called "a thought of processivity" (if we are prepared to force the vocabulary at our disposal somewhat, as indeed we must if that is the only way to open up to that which is different). All reality is a process, so, at the level of things coming about, only that which is the object of a process— that is to say, only that to which a process leads—becomes real. Unlike an effect (at which one aims through action involving a "means-leading-to-an-end"), effectiveness is not something that one "seeks," steering toward it directly and deliberately. It needs to stem "naturally" from a process that is unfolding. So strategy is always a matter of knowing how to impinge upon the process upstream, in such a way that an effect will then tend to "come" of its own accord. Because this efficacy is by nature a consequence and so, to be realized, implies passing through a process that is its very precondition, it achieves the envisaged goal only in an indirect fashion. It resembles a fruit that, changing imperceptibly, eventually ripens; it is not a heroic gesture designed to seize something by force. For, as Mencius too tells us (II, A, 2), one cannot hope to take reality "by assault" or "by surprise." One must always allow it to unfold (for that unfolding is the precondition for its deployment). As we all know, it is impossible to pull "directly" on a plant to make it grow (MZ, ibid.); one must allow it to grow by itself.

One might, however, imagine there to be a paradox

Margin notes:

yong : works
Effect/affect

dao : viable

The central notion of processivity

stem naturally

impinge

Effectiveness is not sought as a goal but results as a consequence

up stream

unfolding is precondition for its deployment

here: "Superior virtue [or a superior capacity] is not virtuous; that is how it is that it incorporates virtue [or capac-
ity]; inferior virtue [or capacity] does not lose virtue, and
that is how it is that it is without virtue" (LZ, section 38).
The truth underlying this contradiction is clear: it is only
if one does not explicitly see it as such (I want to be virtuous) and it flows out *sponte sua*—flows directly from
source, so to speak—that virtue (or capacity) is super-
abundant and inexhaustible, always there to be used. In
contrast, if one constantly wishes to attain to virtue, fixing it as the goal to which one is "attached," and strives,
whatever the circumstances, to be virtuous, always acting
deliberately "to that end"—never losing sight of virtue,
never swerving from the aim of achieving it—then one will
never find oneself sufficiently rich in virtue or capacity.
What makes this proposition, in its succinct form, a paradox is the fact that—the better to imply it—it only hints at
the process that, upstream, constitutes the sole condition
that can lead to the full effect (through effectiveness).
Whoever attempts to do without that process and insists
on aiming directly for an effect will always fall short of
effectiveness. For that "aiming" undermines the effect,
paralyzes it. If "there is [something] in view of which one
takes action" and that action is deliberate, it is necessarily
"partial" (Wang Bi), for from the start it has had to priv-
ilege whatever is *the aim* of the action. If its effect is
brought about deliberately, it is bound to be slight. That is
because it has been diminished in advance by the motiva-
tions behind it and cannot rise above one's momentary
assessment of the situation. In contrast, when carried
along by that situation as it evolves, an effect can unceas-
ingly renew itself.

All this is borne out by the subtle distinction that has
been drawn, in this connection, between the virtues of
"humanity" and "equity" (LZ, section 38 and later). To
the extent that they both "take action," both are inferior
virtues, but one of them is nevertheless superior to the
other. Humanity is superior to equity, since, when one acts
out of humanity, one "acts" but without "aiming to act"
and even without foreseeing one's action, moved suddenly
as one is by compassion. In fact, we *react* rather than act,

Margin notes:

A contradiction serves
to illustrate the case

Intending an effect
kills it, dries it up,
exhausts it

Two degrees of action:
action without a spe-
cific aim is generous,
abundant; concerted
action is limited

and the feeling that arises in us, unforeseen and unbidden, incorporates a global principle (we feel pity for all human beings, simply because they are human beings). This virtue of humanity thus "embraces" the whole of humanity generously, "covering" it all. In contrast, when this love directed toward others does not extend so widely, one acts through "equity," simply to be just, so this action is actually adjusted, adapted, and measured out case by case, so that its virtue withers through its very specificity. All it can achieve is the formalism of a rite, and this ranks lower than the virtue of humanity. So it could be said that, while equity, which proceeds step by step (or blow by blow), can achieve no more than an effect, the virtue of humanity, for its part, is capable of effectiveness (which is itself rooted in its affective capacity). For in the case of humanity there turns out to be a *fund* of effects that, although it is usually latent, allows an effect, when produced, not to exhaust itself but, on the contrary, to exercise its effectiveness to the full (cf. *Zhouyi,* "Xici," A, 5).[iii] The intentionality of an effect, on the contrary, confines that effect to a superficial level. Once produced and proclaimed, it is striking because it is forced (cf. the meaning of *yi,*[iii] which conveys intentionality; also LZ, section 20, and MZ, VII, B, 33). This reflects on the respective phenomenology of humanity and equity. Because it does not aim for an effect, the superior capacity of humanity passes unnoticed (which explains how it can be said, as above, that "the superior virtue is not virtuous"). Because it is indistinguishable from effectiveness, that superior virtue cannot be named (as something "on its own") or recognized (Wang Bi; cf. the great general whom no one thinks to praise). Meanwhile, because it aims ostensibly for effect and reaches higher and higher to achieve it, it is the inferior capacity of equity that is generally called "effective." Its effects are so spectacularly clear that they might be taken for the true capacity. They might be, except that, of course, as soon as this equity draws attention to itself, it lays itself open to refutation and provokes resistance (which makes it noticeable). It is proclaimed but also challenged.

What needs to be developed is the phenomenology not of the visible effect, but of that which happens upstream

The former is generous because it proceeds from a fund of effects

What moral experience can reveal about reality (by moving from a metaphysical to a processive view of reality)

In consequence, because it does not aim for effects, the superior capacity of humanity passes unnoticed

Toward a phenomenology of effectiveness

and out of sight; for it is not by placing oneself at the same level as the effect itself that one can obtain its full force. One cannot claim great "depth" or "consistency" for the virtue of humanity that lies within us if one deploys it directly (Wang Bi, section 38). Similarly, one cannot achieve the continuous uprightness of equitable behavior simply by applying oneself to the virtue of equity any more than one can achieve the purity of respect for the rites simply by meticulously performing all of them (nor can one get rectitude to reign by introducing rules, for rules immediately encourage deviation; cf. section 57; likewise, what is pure does not lead to purity, nor does what is full lead to plenitude; section 39). For if one only barely manages to produce an effect and has to use every possible means to do so, one lacks what it takes truly to fulfill that effect (Wang Bi, section 4). If I limit myself to "the capacity of a home," I cannot "make my home complete"; and if, at a higher level, I limit myself to "the kingdom's capacity," I cannot "make that kingdom achieve its full potential." The level one believes to be sufficient is never high enough. Effectiveness is quite different from a full or saturated effect (for, as we have seen, an effect that is full is quite the opposite of a full effect). For an effect to have full play, a reserve fund of efficacy must always be available. Or, to put that another way, what allows an effect to work *effectively* is precisely that hidden "fund" of effectiveness—the polar opposite of a showy effect—that will never be exhausted however much it is used.

The effectiveness of an effect is always drawn from a prior wellspring and contains the overflow of an earlier effect from which it derives its resources. Therefore, the process that leads to it must begin upstream, at the source; if not, the effect is soon exhausted. "Going back to" the process' point of departure is a movement of return that is characteristic of the way, the *dao* (section 40), and the whole of the *Laozi* is bound up with this logic of regression (cf. the theme of "the untutored person" or "the newborn infant"; section 28). Such regression is not set in opposition to progression. On the contrary, it safeguards the possibility of progress farther downstream. This resource (in the sense that a person may be said to possess a deep

[margin note:] The effect that is full, in opposition to a full effect (containing emptiness and stemming from a fund of effectiveness)

[handwritten margin note:] going back to the process' point of departure

fund of resources or *effectiveness*) is constituted by the effect's fund of immanence. In traditional Chinese images, this fund of immanence is portrayed as the root or trunk of the tree from which branches grow naturally like so many separate effects (cf. Wang Bi, section 57); or it is described as "the mother of effects" and effects are its "children" (section 52; cf. Wang Bi, sections 32, 38).[kkk] If one places oneself at the level of the "mother of effects," one no longer needs to push at an effect in order to make it come about, for the capacity "appears" without one needing to "draw attention" to it; it manifests itself "without competition." If, on the contrary, ignoring the fund of immanence from which an effect will spontaneously flow (as *effectiveness*), one remains fixed at the stage where the effect comes about (Wang Bi, section 39), however much one forces it, that effect is bound to be dissipated. The difference between those two stages is one not of essence, as in Western metaphysics, but of actualization. And it is by going back to the stage of preactualization that one can always make the realization of an effect complete. For, by tracking back upstream to well above the point where the effect begins to become concrete by differentiating itself (cf. the *Laozi*'s idea of the original *one*), one not only can open up the possibility of the effect having maximum impact but, above all, can hold it back from definitively coming about and keep it surging onward in its infinite capacity for effectiveness. Thanks to this fund of potentiality, one can keep it going, keep it actual.

> Get back to the effect's fund of immanence

> Beyond metaphysics (cf. processive logic): through its potential dimension an effect remains actual

Thanks to this fund of potentiality

2

In the last analysis, this is how we should understand the "nonaction" of the sage or, to be more precise, the fact that he can "act without taking action." What might have seemed a paradox now dissolves: the sage "acts," we are told, but does so "before reality is yet actualized"[lll] (section 64). Action certainly does take place but *upstream;* and it happens so far upstream that it is not noticed. For instead of trying to manage reality by grappling with it head-on and hoping to succeed by dint of great exploits, a sage knows (and he who knows is a sage) that it is always

> Nonaction is action upstream

necessary to pass through a process in order to reach an effect. He knows (to quote the adages that the *Laozi* delights in repeating) that the tree "whose trunk one's arms encircle" "was born from the tiniest slip"; and that to build a tower, one must begin by "heaping up the earth at ground level"; and that every long voyage begins "under our feet.". . . Whatever one seeks to undertake (be it a tower or a journey), one always comes back to the notion of a process (the tree grows). So however tenuous and modest the beginning, that beginning is the *start* (to the process that it sets off); and the sooner you act in the

Upstream, reality does not resist

course of things, the less you need to act *upon* it. By the stage of the actualization of things, actuality has become both rigid and exclusive: it now resists whatever one undertakes with regard to it. So one is led to force one's "action" upon it, to focus wholly upon it, and this draws attention to it as action. At the stage of actualization, action encounters resistance on the part of reality, and this hampers the action. The action becomes exhausting, and the effect that it produces is minimal. Upstream from actualization, however, reality is still flexible and fluid; one does not have to confront it head-on, since whatever one might need to pressurize has not yet come about (cannot come about until the stage of concretization). At this early stage (the stage of *pu*,^{mmm} cf. sections 28, 32), reality is still largely at one's disposition, its functions not yet channeled. So one can steer it gently, and the slightest inflection will be decisive, since the progressivity of things inclines it to deploy itself.

pu: the early stage.

Strategic consequences

the slightest inflection will be decisive.

The *Laozi* points out the consequences for human behavior. At this upstream stage, it is easy to work out a strategy with regard to "that which has not yet revealed any symptom" (section 64; see also 73). Of course this is particularly relevant to military affairs. The Chinese arts of warfare emphasize the fact that one can vanquish the enemy far more easily if one does so at the stage when an antagonistic situation has not yet developed. The graded set of possibilities listed by the *Sunzi* has been mentioned above; it should now be read in descending order to show how effectiveness becomes degraded. The best strategy is to attack the enemy when he has barely begun to work out his own strategy; the next best is to attack him in his "alliances" (or "when armies are joining together"); the next best is to attack him "in his troops"; the last option is to attack him in his "places" or positions (SZ, chap. 3, "Mou gong"). Efficacy diminishes as the course of things becomes more definite: the more reality is determined concretely, the more cumbersome it is to manage. The more the conflict takes shape and the farther the process advances, the more our behavior is hampered—the more "action" and increasing effort are required. At the level of the above mentioned "places," in siege warfare, when the antagonistic situation is already fully deployed (to the point of become immobilized), our initiative becomes bogged down; our need for material means is greater, and consequently we suffer heavier losses; success takes longer to achieve and requires more effort.

The earlier one intervenes, upstream, the less one needs to act

efficacy diminishes as the course of things becomes more

"Winning a hundred victories in a hundred battles" is really no more than "a mediocre result," however grandiose it seems. In truth, the acme of the military art is to get the enemy to "give in" in advance and to do so discreetly, by intervening upstream before the conflict unfolds and thus without having to join serious battle subsequently (SZ, chap. 3, "Mou gong"). Intervening upstream makes it possible to obtain an effect *from a distance*. Instead of waiting for an effect from a confrontation, it is better to get at the enemy indirectly, from as far away as possible: "If one knows how to discover the intentions of the enemy," one can kill the leader "from thousands of *li* away" (SZ, chap. 11, "Jiu di"). For, as we have seen, victory can be determined long before it is confirmed by any event. Again, it is "mediocre" to see victory only when it happens and when everyone else can see it too. A real strategist possesses the skill to perceive the "seed" even before it has grown (SZ, chap. 4, "Xing"; cf. Cao Cao). By detecting the conditions for various possibilities in advance, such a strategist can mastermind the evolution of a situation from a distance, steering it in the desired direction.

The art is to win before having to fight

definite

There is thus a subtle distinction to be drawn between two ways of envisaging success: on the one hand, as "a configuration in which I triumph" and "everyone knows it"; on the other, as a configuration in which I "determine" or "control" this triumph "with nobody noticing" (SZ, chap. 6, "Xu shi"). The arrangement that is efficacious is, of course, the configuration that antecedes the situation in which one's triumph is actualized and becomes clear for all to see. (In truth, it is far more than an "arrangement," since it makes use of all the phases in the process through which I get my enemy to pass in order, progressively, to paralyze him.) A second, complementary, distinction allows us to pinpoint the imperceptible nature of this predetermination (cf. the commentary of Mei Yaochen): people notice the tangible marks or "traces" that indicate success but not the "implicit configurations"[nnn] the lineaments of which have conditioned the earlier evolution and through which I eventually achieve success. In other words, people see an effect (once it has come about and takes on a particular and limited aspect in the guise of a result), but they do not see the source of the effect, to which its "traces" point: they do not perceive the whole past of its *effectiveness*.

Another way of representing these two stages is to use the opposition between *round* and *square*, as the ancient treatise on diplomacy does. So long as nothing has taken on a visible form, particularly on the side of one's enemy or interlocutor, one directs the course of negotiations within a "roundness"; later, when signs appear, one needs to manage the situation in a "square" fashion (GGZ, chap. 2, "Fan ying"). In other words, one should be "round" before the situation actualizes itself and "square" once it has become actualized. "Round" means that one remains mobile, open to different possibilities, without stiffening into any definitive position and without any sharp points or angles; "square" means that, once one has fixed on a rule (or direction) for oneself, one manifests determination and, sticking fast to one's position, one refuses to budge. At first (upstream), one "tries to adapt to" the circumstances; then, as the situation takes shape, one manages it by taking certain "measures." At first, one "evolves" diplomatically; then a decision that is taken "halts" that evolution (as a stone that is square comes to a halt; GGZ, chap. "Ben jing"). At the initial stage, when nothing is yet determined, one gets to "know," through roundness, thanks to its perfect adjustment to anything that may get started. Later, once the process has begun, one proceeds in a square way, maintaining stability. Similarly, heaven, which imitates the course of things, is "round," while the earth, which materializes them, is "square." (At a technical level and in the context of divination, the roundness refers to the stalks of milfoil, which slip through the fingers and make it possible to apprehend an invisible (unforeseeable) evolution. The squareness is that of the figure of a hexagram, the fixed framework of which makes it possible to identify the type of the case in question, in all its constancy (cf. *Zhouyi,* "Xici," A, 11). Of the two stages, it is of course the first that is strategically determinative, so that is the one on which the treatise on diplomacy concentrates. At that stage one is constantly ready to turn in any direction and is sensitive to the least eventuality. Always keeping abreast of the beginnings of things, one can from the start make the most of the slightest possibility.

3

This initial action takes place upstream, at the stage when everything is still flexible and offers no resistance. It responds to the slightest opportunity that arises and conforms to every modification as it takes hold, so it never allows itself to reify or codify anything. It consequently encounters "no ruts," as the *Laozi* puts it (section 27). A rut constitutes the imprint of something that has exerted pressure, indicating the repeated passage of heavy loads. In contrast, true efficacy never ceases to improvise, becomes stuck in no ruts, does not need to exert pressure. Were that not so, the following aphorisms taken from the *Laozi* (ibid.) might be regarded as a vestige of magical thought: "he who excels at going leaves no trace of the wheel"; "he who excels at closing never uses a bolt or a lock yet defeats all attempts to open"; "he who excels at attaching resorts neither to ropes nor to bonds, and yet it is not possible to undo." However, there is no supernatural power at work here. Rather, as the commentator Wang Bi stresses, it is, on the contrary, because one simply sticks to whatever "happens of its own accord" that "without insisting" or "exerting pressure" of any kind, one easily

*Action upstream
"encounters no ruts"*

arrives at a result. That perfect ease stems from immanence, with which the action has merged.

This efficacy that is not magical is not technical either (although we tend to regard technology as an alternative to magic: efficacy that is not technical often finds itself summarily relegated to the domain of irrationality and magic). If we intervene at the earliest point, at the stage when nothing is as yet rigid or complicated, we have no need to descend into the particularity of things (cf. section 47) nor to struggle with their instrumentality (no need to *man*euver [or handle things, *"main"* being French for hand; Trans.]). At this stage, there is no such thing as "things"—neither individual things nor individual causes nor, in fact, anything that creates confusion. A rut that is left by a wheel and a recourse to tools both, as it were, constitute deficiences in comparison to pure processivity; all such traces are stains (cf. the series of formulae, "He who excels in speaking leaves no stain"; the commentator tells us that this is because he does without "analyses" and "distinctions," for these only become operational at the level of reality that has become differentiated by becoming actualized). Traces, stains, and tools are appurtenances of a reality that has already completely come about and become concrete and so can only be worked upon by dint of action and force. In contrast, the commentator concludes, if you operate at the stage before actualization, you do not need to determine the course of what is to come by means of things that are "already actualized."ᵒᵒᵒ

On the one hand, there is a stage before actualization; on the other hand, is a stage when individuation has already taken place. So we need to switch to a different metaphysics, or rather to renounce metaphysics altogether (the kind of metaphysics in which eternal being is opposed to becoming or absolute being is opposed to appearance). We need to accept a different primary distinction, one that, however, rejects any separation (for, on the contrary, it emphasizes the constant *transition* of reality). By so doing, we shall be able to enter into this logic of processivity. (Even the Aristotelian distinction between potentiality and actuality does not fit here; in fact, it is completely beside the point, since, on the Chinese side, it is clearly not a mat-

Traces, stains, and tools: these are only needed downstream, where one must strive in the face of the concrete

Not two levels, but two stages in a process

ter of "form" that, "when in actuality" will guide the development to its proper end.) This logic of processivity produces a concept of efficacy that we may find easier to seize upon by considering its opposite. The mistake that we make when we aim directly for an effect is that we are led to take individual measures in order to achieve that effect. We do not realize that everything that is individualized necessarily presents a particular individual aspect that immediately reveals a reverse aspect and opens up a path leading in the opposite direction. Thus, once something is particularized or characterized as being "good," the possibility of "evil" looms up; everything that is recognized to be "upright" implies that other things may be "crooked." And those notions of "evil" or "crooked" will then make headway. In similar fashion, whoever adopts particular measures in order to achieve a particular effect (directly) reveals the implied existence of opposed possibilities and thereby generates a *countereffect*.

Act before the stage of concrete individuation, because all individuation summons up its opposite (and so, at this stage, every effect, its countereffect)

It is in order to elude this trap of individuation that the efficacy recommended by the *Laozi* refuses to be characterized by visible measures intended to act directly upon the situation (downstream). Instead, it elects to remain in a state of "indistinction" (sections 20, 58), upstream in the unfolding process, before dichotomies become explicit. It is because the plenitude of the way has been lost that we resort to speaking of "humanity" and "equity." Only since the country sank into disorder has there been talk of "loyal and devoted" ministers (section 18). The commentator (Wang Bi) points out that if the country remained in order of its own accord, "nobody would have the slightest idea where these loyal and devoted ministers were to be found." The capacity of a process only coagulates, so to speak, or becomes ostentatious where there is some deficiency. Otherwise it remains fluid, diffuse, present everywhere in equal measure—and is consequently imperceptible. And, just as all virtues draw attention to any absence of virtue, every effect that is well adjusted draws attention to all that remains ill adjusted (cf. Wang Bi, who, at section 35, puts that the other way around: "as soon as it seems as if nothing is deliberately aimed for [like a target], the possible use is endless"). One then becomes

it elects to remain in a state of

Virtues are only differentiated (downstream) because the plenitude of capacity (upstream) has been lost

indistinction in the plenitude of the way

imperceptible! fluid, diffuse, present everywhere

caught up in a frenzied race to make all those other adjustments that each new adjustment reveals to be a crying necessity. . . . As can be imagined, this is theoretically bound to turn into an endless race in which one scours the whole world in search of an efficacy that, in order to achieve its goal as quickly as possible (always seeking the most direct means, what the *Laozi* calls "false shortcuts"; section 53), in fact leads farther and farther away from its goal.

In order to break away from this negative concept of efficacy, it is necessary to call into question the elements on which its very principle rests: not only the means-ends relationship, which is at once instrumental and selective (and resorts to individual measures), but likewise its chancy nature (will one succeed or not?: a crucial and tragic moment of uncertainty) and all the effort that this implies (in the performance of all the tasks that we set ourselves as means to success). However much we try to resolve the notion, that kind of efficacy always remains too dependent on action. Just as we needed to work back from a patent effect to *effectiveness,* we ought to be able to unearth from beneath efficacy a notion that is not so burdened with the weight of tangibility. Right from the start Chinese thought has shown us how to look at things from the point of view of transformation so as eventually to lead us to the idea of indirect efficacy (an efficacy that can only be indirect, which suggests a paradox within the notion itself). But in the last analysis, what Chinese thought has been purveying is not, strictly speaking, the idea of efficacy but—more radically—that of *efficiency.* Now we are at least in a better position to set out what this concept of "efficiency" amounts to. The qualities peculiar to efficiency stem from the fluidity and continuity of a process: efficiency opens up efficacy to an aptitude that has no need of the concrete in order to operate. Proceeding, as it does, from a comprehensive system, it requires neither a goal nor effort. And given that, instead of being willed, it stems from the conditions implied in a situation, it never suddenly proves inadequate or misdirected. It belongs not so much to the domain of action (and events) as to that of happening-and-accomplishment. Whereas efficacy can be localized

more radically :

The end of the discrepancy: not efficacy but efficiency

fluidity

Now let us forge the concept of efficiency

Continuity

and its results are therefore directly perceptible, efficiency rightly passes unperceived, since particular effects relate to it only indirectly, and do not affect it. In short, there seems to be the same difference between efficacy and efficiency as there is between a remedy and the sun (we call the sun an "efficient" cause, whereas we say that a remedy is effective). In Chinese thought, efficiency, unconnected to the notion of a cause, seems to be an efficacy that is no longer linked to any particular occasion and therefore seems to dissolve into the basis of things. It moreover itself becomes the source or fund from which everything that comes about constantly stems. In this respect it merges with immanence. And it is this basis (fund) of efficiency (immanence) that a Chinese sage hopes to find beneath all the superficial clutter of things (and the chain of causes). A military strategist likewise seeks to tap it in order to succeed.

a remedy and the sun

Efficiency is identified with immanence

If, by opening efficacy up to something beyond itself, one then discovers it to be everywhere, deep within everything, and accordingly sets it up as an absolute principle, one instantly finds oneself faced with the following alternative: either it becomes *efficacy,* which, as a property of transcendence, eludes the will of human beings; or it becomes *efficiency,* the processivity of which stems from a fund of immanence. At a theological level, it was easy to bring dualism into play and develop the European notion of God's efficacy as opposed to human effort. But why not think the reverse and turn that hypothesis upside down? Instead of setting two levels in opposition, bring them together (not for the purpose of worship, but simply to "proceed"). Root your action in the processivity of things (to the point where that action becomes altogether unnecessary). In other words, plug efficacy into efficiency (or, to use the metaphor of the tree stump and branches that is archetypal in China), graft efficacy onto efficiency. It is clear that two separate lines of thought have resulted from that alternative. As we know, the first, by introducing the hypothesis of two separate levels, established European theology. Meanwhile, on the Chinese side, the other line of thought has served as a basis for human strategy.

Efficacy/efficiency (God or processivity)

In China, the development of the latter line of thought

At the origin of the notion of efficiency in China

led to the religious notion of the Invisible (first and foremost the spirits of the dead, *shen*[PPP]), referring to the efficiency stemming from the fund of immanence. The *Laozi* itself illuminates this with a string of negative propositions (section 60: of course, I am interpreting these formulae not from a strictly historicoreligious point of view, but with regard to what they can tell us about changes and with a view to revealing what is at stake here): "When you approach the human world by following the way, the spirits of the dead no longer manifest any efficiency." Here, the efficiency of the invisible *(shen)* is still close to a religious efficacy. However, the author immediately goes on as follows: "Or rather, it is not that they no longer manifest any efficiency, but rather that their efficiency cannot harm men, but neither does the sage harm men." The commentator (Wang Bi) adds that the point is that the efficiency (of the invisible) does not harm that which is "natural," "and when the myriad things preserve that which is natural, invisible efficiency has nothing to add; and when nothing is added by invisible efficiency, then one no longer notices that the efficiency is efficiency." This efficiency that one no longer notices (and that therefore stands in opposition to the Western notion of the miraculous) and

From a religious background to the concept of a fund of immanence

more effic.

less visible

that "has nothing to add" to what is natural (and so is not *super*natural) *becomes* the fund of immanence. The spirit "of the valley," which—as we know—"never dies," provides an image for this (section 6): it is the "fathomless female" through whose "door" existence endlessly pours forth, we are told, "as if that door really existed." We have already seen how it is that, by operating continually upstream, efficiency remains undetectable; and now, we are also told, "One can use it without ever exhausting it." In other words, this is a bottomless fund of efficiency from which effects never cease to flow.

A return to experience: efficacy is all the greater when (in the form of efficiency) it cannot be seen

Ancient religious thought thus underwent a series of mutations that led to a concept of efficiency that brings us back once again to what Chinese thought is constantly trying to elucidate from human experience: the more efficacious behavior is, the less it is visible (for the more it merges with processivity). This means that efficiency and visibility stand in opposition but without the invisibility of the efficiency being absolutely of a different order from the visible. (It does not take on a separate metaphysical status such as that of the "intelligible" or the Invisible that is accessible to the "soul.") Rather, the invisibility of efficiency is that of something visible that is not burdened by the stiffness and weight that are indissociable from the concretization of things (things such as "ruts" or "traces"). It has been purified of all opacity (cf. "emptiness") to such an extent that it exists only as movement and flow. It has become so infinitesimal and "subtle"[qqq] that one can no longer see it. It *becomes* invisible, because the reality within it is no longer reified and because, being ready as it is to respond to the slightest stimulus, it is constantly reactive. At this stage, reality loses all inertia; it becomes completely alert. In consequence it is never still enough to be discernible. The invisibility of efficiency is of the same order as imperceptibility, and the reason efficiency is invisible is that, unlike efficacy, it never allows itself to coagulate. That is why the ancient treatise on strategy, too, invokes it without hesitation. However, it does so without ascribing any religious connotation to it and simply in order to evoke the flexibility by dint of which a military strategist gets the better of the enemy. Both in attack and in defense, he takes care never to become bogged down in maneuvers or even to let the enemy glimpse the slightest fixity in the disposition of his troops. He too leaves no "traces" and constantly changes the pattern in which he disposes his troops. "Subtle, subtle, subtle! To the point of never allowing a sound to be heard!" (SZ, chap. 6, "Xu shi"). When military strategy achieves this degree of perfection, efficiency is transported to the level of human behavior but still retains the full measure of efficacy with which ancient belief credited it. "In this, the military strategist can be the one who directs [decides] the enemy's destiny." Because his strategic plan is always flexible and shifting" and he "is constantly changing and adapting to the enemy," it is fair to say that he is fully "efficient."

We can at last see how thought such as Daoism, which is not only not metaphysical but moreover is *nonmetaphysical,* can be productive, even if it is not foundational (i.e., if it rejects the notion of foundations of the kind that

But this invisibility is of the order of that which is not yet perceptible (upstream)

Invisibility in military strategy

**The end of the
digression**

we in the West associate with ontology). It reveals the conditions of possibility of human efficiency, illuminating the kind of coherence that it possesses and how military strategy depends upon it. Now we need to take a closer look at these strategic procedures and to compare them to our Western ones. The first thing to do is to understand how it is that controlling a situation from upstream, before its actualization, constitutes the Chinese art of manipulation.

9

The Logic of Manipulation

1

In the West, "manipulation" is only rigorous in the true sense in laboratory work, in the scientific and technological domain, where it is a matter of manipulating substances or products. In recent years, however, people have also been speaking of manipulating human beings. However, when expressed figuratively, the idea lacks consistency. It remains strongly pejorative, and we hesitate to press the analogy too far. Chinese thought, in contrast, had no qualms about conceiving of manipulation upstream, in an ongoing process. That is because, from its own strategic point of view, it never drew a distinction between the world and consciousness (or nature and the internal life of a human being, physical laws and moral laws, and so on). So it never subsequently had to bring the two orders together to repair the gap by offering analogies. For Chinese thought, everything constituted a process— everything, including human behavior. Manipulation could thus be imperceptible. At the stage when everything is still smooth and malleable, people so easily allow themselves to be controlled that one encounters no resistance (and one is not bothered by one's conscience).

> How can the "manipulation" of human beings be rigorous?

How far can the concept of manipulation be developed —and at what cost? First, let us recapitulate. As we have seen at every turn, the whole of Chinese strategy consists in getting a seemingly antagonistic relationship to evolve

the enemy being drawn to
him . at the
him there

from the outset in such a way that eventually the conflict is already resolved before it even begins. Everything hangs on that *already*, which would seem to indicate an initial move but is really a result. To the other side, it seems like a factor given from the start (at the moment when the clash began), but in reality it is the consequence of a process to which they have already been subjected without their noticing (the success of which then stems from itself, without it occurring to anyone to praise the qualities of courage or wisdom of the person who thereby manages "easily" to win the day). This discreet art of transformation, operating as a necessary condition, is the art of manip-

Manipulation upstream   ulation. There are two complementary aspects to it: one must progressively ensure that one holds the initiative, at the heart of the situation, in such a way as to make it lead to the creation of the desired conditions; and in order for this to happen one must reduce the opponent to passivity by very gradually stripping him of his ability to react. In this way one can eventually win without striking a single blow, since, by the time the fight at last begins, the enemy is *already* undone.

In the operational field, this initiative results first in the enemy being drawn to the place where one wants him, at the time when one wants him there. For instance, one waits for him calmly, and he, arriving later and in a hurry, feels "harassed" (SZ, beginning of chap. 6, "Xu shi"). The

Seduce
and
lure
him

ancient treatise makes no bones about how to achieve this: one simply has to "seduce" and "lure" him. To make sure that the enemy "comes of his own accord" to the spot where one wants him to be, one must "hold out an incentive"; and similarly, to prevent him from coming where one does not want him to be, one must "hold out a danger." Of course, one lays out this incentive or this danger as one would a trap. For that is the very principle of manipulation and is also what makes it so fascinating. To manipulate your enemy is to get him, "of his own accord,"

Get the adversary to   eagerly to want to do exactly what you, foreseeing that it
want what you have   will do him harm, want him to do (while he believes it will
already decided will be   be to his advantage). He thinks he is acting of his own free
harmful to him   will, but it is really you who are indirectly leading him on. Because he himself wants to act in this way and is already

inclined to do so, you do not need to force the situation or to expend any effort. At the same time, when he wants something that he believes to be in his interest, whereas it on the contrary plays into your hands, it is not the case that whatever you are holding out as an incentive is not profitable momentarily (for example, you may let him capture a position that he really does want). However, the profit that you offer him—and that he indeed snatches—engages him in a process that eventually turns out to serve you, not him (for example, the position offered to him has the effect of distancing him). As the treatise earlier puts it (SZ, chap. 5, "Shi"): the ability to "coax the enemy into movement," in order to manipulate him, consists in conferring upon the situation a "configuration" that will cause him to feel obliged to "pursue" it.′″ For him to "pursue" it, he must of course see profit for himself in it, and that is what you hold out to him, seemingly to your own disadvantage. But what really counts is that he should set out in pursuit of what he thinks he wants and thereby become dependent.

In the end, if you wish to join battle, however well holed-up the enemy may be "behind high walls and deep ditches," he will "be unable not to" come out and fight; or if, on the contrary, it is you who do not wish to engage in battle, all you need do to become unattackable is to "draw a simple line on the ground." For in the first case, you attack what he finds himself "obliged to come and save" and so is drawn out from his defensive position; and, in the second case, coming out to attack you would mean abandoning the path that you have made him take and to which he has become attached (SZ, chap. 6, "Xu shi"). In both cases, however uneven the material means (such as high walls and deep trenches) of the two camps may be, they carry no weight in comparison to the determining factor constituted by the orientation in which you have been able to guide the enemy's mind. For once the right conditions are set in place, the enemy will "be unable not to" behave as you wish him to, and there will be no unforeseen hitches in the unfolding of the situation. Considered literally, the observation, as formulated in the ancient treatise, appears very flat and obvious: "When on the attack, in order to be totally confident of carrying all before you, you must be attacking something that the enemy is not defending, and when on the defense, to be totally confident of preserving what you are defending, you must be defending something that the enemy is not attacking (SZ, chap. 6, "Xu shi"). However, the implicit reasoning behind that apparent truism belies its simplicity: you must first make certain, through the way in which you inflect the situation, that the enemy is no longer in a fit state either to defend or to attack; only then do you yourself venture to do either.

But what reception should you offer "numerous" enemies "in good order" who are about to arrive? The answer is as follows: "Begin by taking whatever they hold to be most important," and then "they will listen to you"; that is to say, they will begin to be reduced to passivity. So instead of engaging directly in battle, which would be risky, you must, as we have seen, begin by undermining the enemy. And to achieve that, you must disconcert, destabilize, and divert him. (This *disarticulation* is itself a systematic concept that the treatise describes in detail: act in such a way "that there is no communication between the front and the rear of the enemy's forces," that no compensation can be made between positions where there are many soldiers and positions where there are few, that those who are extremely brave are unable to come to the aid of those who are not, that no "solidarity" can be maintained between the base and the summit, and so on; see SZ, chap. 11, "Jiu di," and also Sun Bin, chap. "Shan"). As we have seen over and over again, it is a matter of starting a process the foreseen result of which will come about of its own accord, indirectly but ineluctably, thanks to the situation that develops. Infinitely preferable to the flamboyant heroics of action is the discreet work of transformation, which little by little erodes the enemy's ability to resist. Chinese efficacy does not consist in acting for or against, by launching attacks or opposing them, but simply, within the terms of a process, in *starting things* or *breaking them off* (starting that which, as it develops, will of its own accord tend in the desired direction; and breaking off whatever, however minute but already present in the situation, could prompt it to evolve in a negative fashion). All one has to do is to engage a process or disengage it, and reality will then bear its own fruits. The ancient literature thus returns repeatedly (SZ, chaps. 1, 6, 11, and Sun Bin, chap. "Shan") to the pressure to be brought to bear on the enemy right at the start, because from this victory will stem of its own accord: if the enemy is "full of ardor," you must begin by unsettling him and draining his energy; if he is "prudent" and watchful, you must start by getting him to "lose control" and act thoughtlessly (in the case of a general, you must unsettle his mind; cf. chap. 7); if the enemy forces are united, you must begin by dividing them; if they are "in good form," you must exhaust them; if they are well fed, you must starve them; if they are "calm," you must upset them. . . .

2

If you upset the enemy, you lead him not only to lose his confidence, but also to emerge from his reserve, abandoning the impassiveness behind which he remained concealed. He now reveals his own particular character and can be recognized. In this respect the strategy to adopt is twofold. On the one hand, you should lead your enemy to "adopt a definite position" so that you can establish a hold over him and work out how and where to attack him; but at the same time, you must take care not to give the enemy any hint of your own position, so as to be able to continue to elude him[sss] (SZ, chap. 6, "Xu shi"). You force him to actualize the positioning of his own forces, displaying it openly in what is always a somewhat rigid fashion, meanwhile keeping your own arrangements fluid so as to be able to adapt to anything. Whereas the enemy has "taken shape," which means that he is definitely in one place and not in another so you can easily keep an eye on him, you yourself remain inscrutable—by refusing to adopt a definite position—and continue to be ready to react to anything. For disposing your forces in a definite pattern bogs you down (you lose dynamism); it is too reifying (fewer possibilities are open to you), and it limits you to the exclusivity of all that is concrete. Your opponent is numbed, because he has been led into disposing his forces in a

The strategic ploy: get your opponent to adopt a position without adopting one yourself

The absence of a definite position makes for adaptability

definite way; but you, for your part, remain alert. The difference in the respective potentials of the two sides does not depend primarily on which has more troops, on material factors, or on the respective means that they possess. It results from the one allowing itself to be stuck downstream in the process of reality, with its degree of effectiveness lowered and trapped at the level of concrete things, where, like things themselves, it can be seized upon. Meanwhile the other, by remaining upstream, can inflect and direct everything, ever elusive and unfathomable.

We must make no mistake about the principle that is the very basis of the whole military art, rather than wrongly supposing this to be simply an extracunning ploy and failing to appreciate its overall importance. Warfare, we are told, in no uncertain terms, rests on the art of "deception" (SZ, chap. 1, "Ji"; chap. 7, "Jun zheng"). There can be no doubt that manipulation is a matter of dissembling and secrecy: "When you are in a position to do something," persuade the other that "you are not"; "when you are busy doing something," persuade the other that "you are doing nothing"; "when you are close," seem to be "distant"; when you are "distant," "seem to be close"; and so on. The first benefit, of course, is the effect of surprise that, together with the mobility that is facilitated by the absence of any definite disposition of your forces, makes it possible "to attack the enemy where he is not prepared for it" and "to spearhead an attack when he is not expecting it (SZ, chap. 1, "Ji"). Indeed the reciprocity between these contraries is such that the art of attack can be reduced to "the enemy not knowing what to defend," while the art of defense can be reduced to him "not knowing what to attack" (SZ, chap. 6, "Xu shi").

The advantage in getting the enemy to dispose his troops in a definitive order while not doing so yourself, or at least not being seen to do so, is not only that you can disconcert him by taking him by surprise. If he does not know where you may attack him, the enemy is careful to defend many positions and, by doing so, becomes numerically weak at all of them. Numerical weakness, from which defeat ensues, is thus not a given factor from the start but results from manipulation. Whereas the side that

Manipulation— dissimulation

has been led to dispose its forces in a definite formation must "divide itself up" in order to defend all approaches, the side that has not adopted any visible formation is, for its part, able "to concentrate itself." So numerical inferiority simply results from having to defend oneself against others, while, conversely, numerical superiority results from "acting in such a way that it is the others who have to defend themselves against you." In other words, the more you have to take defensive precautions, the more exposed you are. "Numbers," like "courage," as we have noted above, are not a matter of the initial conditions, but result from effects. Even if the enemy starts off with numerical superiority, he can still be defeated if the greater part of his troops, all dispersed to different points, remain unused.

Numbers, in combat, result from effects

The power attributed to manipulation is so decisive that this treatise on warfare thinks better of one of its earlier declarations. Initially (SZ, beginning of chap. 4, "Xing"), it claimed that victory could be "known" but not necessarily "obtained," and that was a claim that seemed to make good sense. For if the first thing to do in warfare is to make yourself invincible, and this is something that depends on yourself alone, it is, after all, a principle that is equally valid for your enemy and may, in consequence, be turned against you. Even if, having first made yourself invincible, you have prepared yourself to "wait" (indefinitely) for the enemy to be defeated, you yourself have no way of preventing that enemy from acting in exactly the same way, with the result that he too can remain invulnerable and never present you with an opportunity to defeat him. That being so, the conclusion that has to be accepted is that "one cannot act in such a way as to make it possible for the enemy to be defeated." Now, however, the treatise affirms precisely the contrary: victory is always "obtainable" (chap. 6, "Xu shi"). This is the strongest of claims and one that is almost scandalously defiant. The only explanation for such a switch must be that, as the writing of this treatise progressed, the very idea of an opportunity (offered by one's opponent) dissolved and was overtaken by the notion of manipulation (conducted by oneself). Between the first claim and the second, a new concept has

l ɔ f l e c t

been introduced: that of a process through which you can progressively inflect the situation in such a way that, even if your opponent makes no mistakes and refrains from taking any precautionary defensive measures, nevertheless, if he so much as *disposes his troops in a definite formation,* then you, who do not do so, can prove your superiority over him. You do not need him to reveal any flaws, for if you can but get him to draw up his troops in some sort of formation, you establish a hold over him and can transform him (for instance, you can force him to take precautionary measures and thereby to weaken himself and eventually to give way). The strict reversibility of the respective positions of your opponent and yourself (with both of you depending solely on yourselves and therefore both equally secure in your invincibility) is no longer operative, since your positions do not relate to the same levels—or

One can always defeat the enemy if one starts manipulating before he does

rather they do (the level of operations), but they differ in their degree of actualization. In this respect, the possibility of a difference between the two sides is always open (as is the bottomless fund of immanence), and the one can always prevail over the other. It is up to whoever is more skillful at intervening at an earlier point in the predetermination of conditions and, rendering himself ever more elusive in the same manner as invisible Efficiency, guiding the unfolding of the process from a greater distance.

3

When the ancient Chinese military treatise concludes with such assurance that victory is "always obtainable," it is bound to elicit a reaction, since, for once, the thesis is strikingly uncompromising—not weakened by the usual contextual accommodations and the interplay of different interpretations (although even here the philological tradition no doubt did its best to introduce qualifications). The thesis is at once too uncompromising and too crucial in its scope not to prompt us to ask to what extent this concept of strategic manipulation, which is claimed to lead ineluctably to success, has been developed on our side (the European side)—or to what extent it has been misunderstood or rejected or concealed. (And if we have not developed it so far as the Chinese, what has deterred us from doing so and why?)

It cannot be denied that, on the European side, we have always emphasized the part played by the hazards of warfare, the gods, chance, or pure genius. It is true that we too stress the effects of surprise, praise cunning, and advocate secrecy. But in comparison to the Chinese elaboration of such notions, it seems on the European side more a matter of making concessions to experience or introducing parenthetical asides into the main thesis. The various elements involved are never linked together sufficiently closely to produce an overall concept or theory. The difference between Europe and China is not so much that the one ignores what the other recognizes (or vice-versa), but rather that the respective rhetorical tools used in China and Europe to develop their respective theses seem to have been suited to exploiting more or less widely differing sources of intelligibility. As a result, what remains underdeveloped in the one context is more developed in the other. The purpose of our foray into China is not to imagine—let alone fabricate—other "mentalities" (although that is often one of the rather confused pleasures of exoticism). It is simply to make use of other possible sources of intelligibility (which are, in themselves, more global and radical than all the particular inventions of philosophy, which, for its part, does no more than simply describe those). Really, it is a matter of convenience: if it turns out that the idea of strategic manipulation fits in better with the notional framework of Chinese thought and that the Chinese perspective illuminates it, then making a detour through China in order to develop the idea further will certainly have been worthwhile.

To test this out, let us return to the Greeks. Their military treatises, faithful to the ancient tradition of *mètis*, frequently suggest traps (false fortifications, false ambushes, false information, and so on). Nor do they fail to advocate pretense and duplicity (making troops seem more numerous than they really are, appearing to be absent when one is present, and so forth; cf. the Trojan horse). Stratagems clearly do relate to strategy, even if Clausewitz, later on, was to mistrust that affinity. However, even when a treatise

> Why is strategic manipulation not organized into a theory on the European side?

foray

detour

On the Greek side, a stratagem remains an expedient

such as the *Hipparchus* sets out to show how to stand up to a numerically superior force, one does not find it explaining how to *transform* the situation in order to render the enemy numerically inferior (chap. 8). Furthermore, more generally, even when it lists many means of confounding the enemy, the treatise does not focus on them so as to make them the major factor in the thesis: however cunning they may be, they do not carve out any new line for exploring reality; they are not expected to serve as the major axis of support for a theory. When one reads the ancient Greek treatises on warfare (for example, those by Xenophon), one realizes that fundamentally their purpose is twofold. They are either technical (tactics, siegecraft, and so on) or else organizational and political (concerned with maintaining order, "keeping subordinates happy," or even "being eloquent": leading an army is like "running a household" or "organizing a chorus," we are told in the *Memorabilia*, III, 1). In whichever direction Xenophon points, it is always toward a *form* of order, but the real object of strategy seems to fall somewhere in between.

Basically, the same goes for Machiavelli, whose *Art of Warfare* is certainly the least Machiavellian of all his works. Yet sporadically one does come across points of correspondence with Chinese thought: not only the need to pretend, to surprise, and to conceal the disposition of one's troops, but also—as has been noted—the importance of not holding the enemy at bay with his back to the wall (it is better to put one's own troops in that position); also the importance of being wary of lures, "hooks hidden beneath the bait" by means of which the enemy can lead you wherever he will; and "above all" the need to try to divide the enemy forces: "Many generals have deliberately allowed the enemy to invade their country and capture a few strongholds so that, because he is then obliged to station garrisons in those towns and thereby weaken his forces, they can more easily attack and conquer him" (VI). Even the idea of the potential of a situation makes a fleeting appearance: "In war, courage is better than numerous troops, but advantageous positions are better still" (VII). Nevertheless, these are just remarks, based on experience; they are not brought together to form a consistent thesis.

Although Machiavelli draws up lists of traps and stratagems (in fact, precisely *because* they are just lists), these seem
no more than warnings in response to certain (deplorable)
current practices; they do not constitute Machiavelli's primary interest. He is above all interested in the military institution and how it is structured (how militia are selected,
the primordial role of discipline, and so on). For him,
basically, it is always a matter of describing *forms* (the
forms of battles, of marches, of camps, and above all of
recruitment): problems to do with order or with models
(the model of order is provided by the Romans). According
to Machiavelli, established order is the sole source of
strength. These are all notions that inevitably return us to
the Greeks.

Machiavelli himself is more interested in the forms of order than in strategy

As for Clausewitz, it is no doubt he who best illuminates the reticences of Western thought where strategic
manipulation is concerned. All the same, he certainly does
develop the idea of "wearing down" the enemy gradually,
over a period of time, exhausting his forces and his determination (cf. the example of Frederick the Great in the
Seven Years War), although he applies it only to defense
and resistance. Likewise, his concept of warfare is certainly
that of an armed engagement, to which he systematically
ascribes three possible objectives, namely, the destruction
of the enemy forces, the conquest of a place, or the conquest of some object. And it does occur to him to add a
"fourth category of engagement," although this too is limited, to offensive action: this, he says, is based on deception
and exercises of "reconnaissance designed to render the
enemy vulnerable" (and on "alerts aimed at exhausting the
troops" or "operations designed to prevent him from leaving a position or from securing a new one"). The earlier
types of engagement simply serve as the means of success in
this fourth category. However, Clausewitz remains attached
to his idea of destructive engagements, whether these actually take place or are simply a possible option, so he can
proceed no further. Since, for him, an engagement is conceived as action and is defined by its goal, the logic behind
it is bound to be that of direct efficacy; any preliminary
maneuver could well serve "as a guide to the efficacious
principle" but could not in any circumstances be regarded

Attached to the notion of an engage-ment, Clausewitz can conceive of no true efficacy unless it be through direct confrontation as that principle. To put that another way, Clausewitz never develops any idea of the indirect determination of an effect through a progressive and discreet conditioning of the situation and via transformation.

This is made particularly clear by the way that he envisages the effect of surprise, conceiving it, in accordance with a common logic, to be the fruit of secrecy and swiftness. Initially he places surprise "at the basis of all military enterprises" and presents it as the key to success, but subsequently he repeatedly downplays its importance on the grounds that perfect success for surprise interventions is "exceptional" on account of the friction that exists within the military machine. Besides, as soon as one takes a close look at it, one also discovers how much depends on chance. His attitude to cunning undergoes a similar reversal, despite the ancient Greeks' claim that every situation calls for "a cunning ploy." After recalling the traditionally close connection between cunning and strategy, Clausewitz seems to revise his opinion and, on the contrary, shows how ineffective it has been throughout History: "But however much we are inclined to delight in the sight of war leaders surpassing themselves in cunning ploys, cleverness, and deception, we are bound to recognize that those qualities... are seldom evident in the great mass of events and circumstances." In the last analysis, cunning ploys are nothing but a game, similar to "wordplay" in the domain of discourse, and, as such, they fail in the face of the "serious" nature of warfare, in which "bitter necessity" makes "direct action so urgent." Clausewitz concludes that we must perforce recognize that in warfare the pieces on the checkerboard "lack the agility that is the very element of cunning and cleverness."

In contrast, strategic manipulation as seen from the Chinese position is far more than mere "cunning" and "cleverness." In fact, fundamentally, it is something altogether different, even though those qualities may constitute indications of it and may lead to its detection. We in Europe have often tended to psychologize the familiar figures of "cunning" and "cleverness," and subsequently to moralize about them or even demonize them and therefore dismiss them as anecdotal. But on the Chinese side they are, on the contrary, considered to conceal an art that consists in "conducting" reality so gradually that one never has to clash head-on with it at all. Or rather it is the art of, so to speak, "inducing" reality, for "conducting" is somewhat too interventionist and showy, since its aspect of an accompaniment ("con" or *cum*: with) is suggestive of externality to the situation and so also of too much interventionist activity and effort on the "subject's" part. We can thus distinguish two types of mastery, which stand in contrast (possibly to the point of excluding one another). In one type (as in Clausewitz' theory), the exercise of force takes the form of a clash that is produced by a maximal concentration of action being focused on the one point and the one moment that are judged to be crucial and that now coincide to produce an event (the "principal battle"; cf. Clausewitz' study of the enemy's centers of gravity, the purpose of which is to reduce them to one single center on which the entire impact of the military clash can be concentrated).* In the other type, the process is predetermined by its evolution being inflected so gradually that the process consists solely of successive moments, not one of which is distinguishable, and the very *possibility of an event is dissolved*. In the course of such manipulation, efficacy is indirect and discreet, but in an engagement it is direct and manifest.†

Inducing while manipulating

Moments/event

---

*"It is not only rash generals who have sought to complete their work by venturing to fight a decisive battle, but great and successful ones have also done so.... Therefore a deliberately planned great battle is always to be regarded as the central point of the whole system. The more imbued a general is with the true spirit of war, with the feeling and idea that he must and will conquer, the more will he strive to throw every weight into the scales in the first battle and do everything in his power to win it." *On Warfare*, IV, 11, English translation T. D. Pilcher (London: Cassell and Co., 1918), pp. 223, 224.

†The difference between these two kinds of strategy is not purely theoretical, as I think became evident in the war in Vietnam. On the American side, the strategy was always to seek a pitched battle involving a maximum use of material power and a clash of maximum impact. On the Vietnamese side, that strategy was foiled by a process of continuous manipulation—to the point of achieving victory by bringing about a collapse and without the major event ever taking place.

4

But who, precisely, is to be manipulated? The enemy, of course, but also, as must be recognized, one's own troops, so that it is these who find themselves at bay, with their backs to the wall and forced to fight. It is not only the enemy who must be kept in ignorance of the maneuvers that you are undertaking; secrecy is also essential vis-à-vis your own men and in your own camp. The very logic of manipulation makes this essential. To the embarrassment of today's commentators, who consider this principle immoral, the ancient Chinese treatise declares that a good general must be "able to block the eyes and ears of his soldiers and officers so that nobody realizes [what he is doing]" (SZ, chap. 11, "Jui di"). In order to exploit the potential of the situation most profitably, he "pushes his troops forward like a flock of sheep, urging them now in one direction, now in the other, without any of them knowing where they are going." Exactly the same happens at the political level, in China, and again the strategy is openly acknowledged: an "enlightened" sovereign, alone with his secret, treats all his subordinates as pure automatons, not as people, as we would say, but as objects. Not only are the domain of warfare and that of internal power interconnected, but they are analogous, with a common logic and similar "arts" (far more so in China than in Machiavelli). Already in Antiquity, within the framework of thought on despotism, inappropriately known as "legalist," which we have considered above (chaps. 2 and 6), the Chinese produced a fully developed theory of political manipulation.

The manipulation of power

In this context, the idea is closely related to our own etymology: manipulation refers explicitly to what is "taken in hand." What an "enlightened prince" "takes in hand" are rewards and punishments, which he draws on as if "from two sleeves" or in "two handfuls"""" (HFZ, chap. 7, "Er bing"), thereby eliciting from his subjects the opposed, but equally distinctive, reactions of fear and self-interest— reactions from which submission flows *sponte sua*.

The above notions of strategic manipulation can thus be recapitulated to construct a notion of political manipulation that covers and interrelates every aspect of despotism: (1) as we have just noted, the secrecy that the prince shares with nobody, not even his family or his intimate associates (HFZ, chap. 48, "Ba jing," I); (2) the complete assymetry of roles and the antagonism that sets his position apart from every other: to preserve the full potential of the situation constituted by his position as sovereign, the ruler must regard all the other individuals in his kingdom as so many opponents who must be forced to submit to his authority; (3) his control over others, which enables him to dominate them: just as a general can force the enemy to knuckle under, thanks to the latter's disposition of his troops, the ruler maintains a hold over all his subjects by rendering them transparent through the discipline and control that he imposes upon them (while he himself is careful never to reveal any internal disposition of his own— toward joy or anger, for instance—so that nobody gains any hold over him); (4) the reduction of all others to passivity: since he alone is always in command (of all rewards and punishments), the ruler concentrates all authority in the throne, and no one can resist him; (5) and finally, the illusion that his people foster as to their own interests: in their desire for rewards and their fear of punishment, every one of his subjects believes he is promoting his own personal interests, without realizing that in truth he is simply bolstering the power of his oppressor.*

And what about Mao?

We can now see how the two principal characteristics of Chinese efficacy come to operate within the political domain. In the first place, this efficacy is indirect and stems from a process of conditioning. The pitiless rigor of the "law" produces absolute power purely as a consequence, without the ruler needing to take any action or even issue any commands: there is no need for him to "seek" authority, as this stems ineluctably from the regime that has been established. Second, true efficacy dispenses with the need to exert oneself. The theorists of despotism explain that, whereas a moral man constantly puts himself out in order to influence others, a true tyrant can direct everything

A perfect despot does not need to seek authority

---

*It seems hardly necessary to note the degree to which Maoism was faithful to this tradition. It is not hard to see why the Gang of Four itself regarded the "legalists" as progressive.

Nor does he need to exert himself

without having to make the slightest effort or even involve himself personally: the mechanism of power operates in such a way that others are obliged to put their services at his disposal (ibid., II). Just as the general did, the ruler proceeds by invisibly predetermining the situation, without the knowledge of his subjects, like a "ghost" (ibid., I), that is to say, he intercedes at the root of their desires and aversions, while he himself remains ever unfathomable. His influence, like that of nature, is so assimilated, so constant and general, and so inexhaustibly replenished that it passes unnoticed.

Nothing eludes this logic. Right from the start it is extreme; and its radical nature is instructive. It is amazing to see this ready-made "canon" of all totalitarianisms emerge as if, on this point, thought never even had to feel its way: its rigor is unfailing; its power is unwavering; every slightest tremor of humanity is eliminated. Nobody receives any recognition, any gratitude; the very idea of rights is engulfed by the omnipotence of the "law"; there

Leviathan

is no room here for values of any kind. While everything converges upon the ruler and propels him forward, he, for his part, effaces himself, renouncing all desire for glory, even shedding his own individuality. As a perfect manipulator, he is dissolved within his manipulation. As a result of treating others as automatons, he too becomes one.

10

Manipulation versus Persuasion

1

Now let us consider a treatise written for the use of diplomats and chief ministers. It is called after its presumed author, the Master of the Valley of Ghosts, *Guiguzi*. No doubt the Valley of Ghosts was the name of the place to which this master retired at the end of his life, but by setting its seal upon this work, the title cloaks it in secrecy and surrounds it by mystery and suspicion. The manipulative powers that man deploys in this work make him seem very close to the ghosts and spirits. He haunts rather than acts, seemingly unaffected by the uncertainties and rigidities of ordinary modes of behavior, impervious to any tangible influences and meeting with no resistance. Yet there is nothing diaphanous or supernatural about the world in which he evolves. On the contrary, it is a most realistic and opaque world, concerned with conflicts of interest, the conquest of power, and politics.

Manipulation and danger

This is a strange book. Like the other works that we have considered, it certainly dates from late Antiquity (the fourth century B.C.), but it was later attributed to a variety of authors and always remained somewhat clandestine, disdained if not despised by the literary tradition. It is one of those books that were read in private, for one's own purposes—even by emperors—but that it was better not to mention and that was certainly too dangerous to cite. For thousands of years people pretended to be unaware

extreme
book:
solely.
relations
of
force

of it (and the sinological tradition paid it no attention). It is one of those rare books that suddenly reveal a rent in the ideological covering of reality and proceed to set things out baldly, as they are. It seems solely and undisguisedly bent on efficacy, without the slightest pretention to moral sentiment. It is an extreme book, possibly unique in its rigorous determination to consider human relations solely as relations of force. I, at any rate, know of no European equivalent. In it, the language is terser and dryer than elsewhere, making sudden aggressive lurches that are somewhat at odds with the harmony that, in China, is usually expected in a sentence; and the style, steering clear of all inflation and even all subjective coloring, is so spare that it sometimes reads more like a code than a written language. Or perhaps, in truth, the meaning becomes so dangerous, because of all that the words lay bare, that it instinctively becomes cryptic. For this book's subject, which is clearly of burning importance in China but is generally considered too dangerous to put into words, is this: how to be successful in one's dealings with the ruler so as to win his approval yet be in a position to dominate him.

Indeed, this Master of the Valley of Ghosts is said to have produced in his school the most prestigious of all the ministers of this period of late Antiquity (Su Qin and Zhang Yi), ministers whose renown rested on both the authority that they acquired in their ruler's court and the skill with which they set up alliances abroad. For the China of late Antiquity was the China of the "warring states," in which, as the earlier sovereign power collapsed, all progressively affirmed their own independence, only to find

A struggle to the death for dominance

themselves locked in endless rivalry. By forming clever but constantly changing confederations, each of them strove to restore a hegemony with itself as leader. Betrayals, plots, and revolts became commonplace, and every word pronounced was immediately suspect. Nobody was fooled by professions of morality, for sure. There was no belief in any form of transcendence that brought retribution or punishment, no illusion as to the existence of a beyond. Ambition was one's guide, and strength was the measure of all things.

In the course of the present work, we have already come across this treatise. It teaches the reader to consider relations with others, in particular the ruler, in terms of the potential of the situation (see above, chap. 2). It dissolves the notion of an offered opportunity into that of exploitation of the slightest "cracks" detectable in one's opponent's position (cracks that tend to grow, chap. 5). It recommends intervention upstream, at the stage when everything is still "round" and can easily be managed (chap. 8). But its interest does not lie solely in what it thus teaches us about human manipulation within a framework that is not strictly either strategic or political. It also lies in its implicit revelation of a contrast with the European tradition, a contrast that concerns the status of speech. For here, although it certainly is a matter of speech between two people, the adviser addressing his prince, rhetoric does not come into it. Or rather, this is a treatise on antirhetoric. Instead of learning how to persuade the other person by making him see the justice, or at least the advantage, of your advice, it teaches you how to establish total influence over him before offering him any advice that he will be inclined, of his own accord, to heed. The emphasis here is thus not on how to organize your speech as discourse, but rather on the conditions to be created, upstream, between the other person and yourself—conditions such that the least suggestion that you voice will be so welcome to the other person that he will immediately agree with it. Straightaway he will place his trust in it, without ever thinking to question it—let alone disagree with it. As we know, persuasion always involves an effort—the effort of rhetoric—and it is, moreover, never foolproof. Persuading someone else is always a battle. Whereas if the other person has no mistrust (has been led not to distrust you), you need make no effort at all and immediately get your way.

Antirhetoric

Rather than persuade the other person, simply condition him, in advance, to agreeing

The fact that speech is involved here thus in no way affects the two earlier points: the importance both of transformation undertaken in advance and of indirect efficacy achieved through conditioning. We are all aware of the importance that the Greek world attached to the prestige peculiar to discourse and how seriously the Greeks studied the best way to use that discourse. In ancient China, in contrast, little interest was shown in the procedures of argumentation, the different parts of discourse, and the figures of rhetoric. In Greece, eloquence and the prestige for which it aims seem linked with action and the spectacular. Without doubt, oratory is a type of action, and an orator performs in public. By increasing the vehemence of his speech, using all the means provided by rhetoric, and setting out his arguments "before the very eyes" of his audience, as is recommended, he aims for an ever more direct effect. In this Chinese treatise, in contrast, whoever "speaks" does so as little as possible, or rather *is not seen to speak.* Instead, we see how, very discreetly, upstream and by gradually inflecting the situation one way or another, just as a general does, such a person prepares for a situation in which he will be heeded. For him, the business of speaking and advising will happen a long way downstream, just as the battle will for the general.

To be sure, it is sometimes said that rhetoric is also a means of manipulation. For it does not simply instruct whoever it addresses but should also, as we know, seek to please and touch the listener. In fact, it often aims to get him to react unconsciously, at the level of his "passions" rather then his reason (for "reason" and "passion" constitute one of the old European oppositions that rhetoric played a part in establishing). Nevertheless, the fact remains that arguments clash with one another, and a choice between them is possible: the interlocutor reaches a conviction. A logic is spelled out based if not on truth, then on likelihood; and because the listener is always more or less in control of how he will receive it, he may well reject it. On the Chinese side, meanwhile, everything depends on how the listener has been predisposed before you begin to give him any advice. Here too, the battle, the battle of speech, must be won before any engagement takes place, that is to say, before one even opens one's mouth to speak. The assumption is that the process of securing the goodwill of the listener does not take place during one's speech, as it does in the case of eloquence, but is completed beforehand; not in broad daylight, however, but by night; not all

Eloquence, action, spectacle

Everything is prepared upstream from speech itself

Speech, like a battle, lies in the distance, downstream

at once (during the event of the speech), but gradually yet without pause. Thanks to the relationship of trust into which the other person has been lured and the power that you therefore hold over him, a "propensity" gradually develops—a propensity that inclines him to listen to your advice.

Foreseeably then, a relationship involving speech is conceived on the basis of the very chain of ideas upon which military strategy is based. The important thing is to "lead" the other person and not "be led" by him;[uuu] you must hold "power" over him and not allow him to decide his own destiny (GGZ, chap. 10, "Mou"; cf. SZ, chap. 6, "Xu shi"). For, as this treatise sees it, the interests of the two interlocutors are bound to clash, with each clinging to his position, so your listener must always be considered as an enemy. You must therefore do all you can to win the other's trust, and that trust must always constitute a trap. The preliminary stage always consists in "seducing," "attracting," and "luring" the enemy, as in military strategy, in order to gain influence over him (GGZ, chap. 2, "Fan ying"; chap. 8, "Mo"). The comparison usually drawn is that of bait and a fishing net. You must offer the other person what he thinks is in his interest in order to get him to be "receptive" (GGZ, chap. 11, "Jue"), meanwhile progressively ensuring that all the initiative remains with you. Then, even if the other person is the prince, he will allow himself to be sent in one direction or another, "to the east or the west, the north or the south." He becomes your plaything (GGZ, chap. 3, "Nei qian"; chap. 5, "Fei qian"). Then you yourself go forward with such ease that not the slightest "gap" remains between the two of you, and nobody else detects any sign of that dependence.

> A relationship involving speech is governed by strategic manipulation

In itself, what this treatise proposes is not astonishing, for one can see the logic of it clearly. Rather, what is astonishing is its absolute tone. Such behavior is not treated as manipulation using a series of more or less shameful expedients, but as the normal—even the ideal—course to follow. Let every other possibility be excluded and let the other person (but is it really still a matter of an "other") be reduced to complete passivity. Even our own Machiavelli never envisaged such a state of affairs.

Opening and closing: to sound him [handwritten annotation]

2

The treatise makes it quite clear that its sole objective is manipulation through speech. It does so by its choice of the two terms that, from the outset, serve to define the use of speech and dominate the entire treatise. The terms are "opening" and "closing"ᵛᵛᵛ (GGZ, chap. 1, "Bai he").

Two operations: "opening" and "closing" — These constitute two deliberate operations—two actions really. We are told that "to open" is to incite the other person to reveal freely what he thinks so that you can make out whether his sentiments chime with yours. "To close" is to move in the opposite direction in order to force your listener to react and thereby to check whether he is speaking the truth. These two operations should be practiced alternately, because they complement each other: either, by indicating your agreement, you lead the other on to "open himself up" and, abandoning his reserve, to lay his own feelings completely bare or, on the contrary, you deliberately block his way forward so that, faced with this "barrage," he suddenly reveals his true feelings, whereupon you can draw your own conclusions as to the veracity of what he has said.

The first maneuver is exploratory; the purpose of the second is verification. The first, by encouraging the "other" to be expansive, reveals what he wants; the second, which elicits a reaction from him, reveals whatever he was trying to conceal. Combined together, these maneuvers serve to "test out" and assess the other: either you go along with him so that he himself lets himself go; or else you move in the opposite direction so that, in reaction, he enables you to measure the strength of his resistance. Even his reticence and silence are revealing. In either case, whether he "opens" or "closes" his mouth, whether he speaks freely or is reticent, the other is revealed, or rather, he is manip-ulated, used purely as a tool. We are told that he can be manipulated in exactly the same way as the two opposed and complementary factors *yin* and *yang* (which consti-

The "other" is a tool to be manipulated — tute the whole of reality). That polarity can be exploited equally successfully where speech is involved: on the one hand, there are positive themes *(yang)* that can be used to "open"; on the other, negative ones *(yin),* that can be used to "close." You resort to the former in order to encourage the other in whatever he has undertaken and to the latter in order to force him to give up his plans. In this way, "opening" and "closing" is all that is necessary for "there to be nothing that does not emerge" (from deep within the other—his hidden feelings, for instance) and vice-versa, and, in consequence, "there is nothing that cannot enter" (such as advice that you wish him to follow). In short, "there is no longer anything that is not possible," whatever the scale of your operations and whether you are dealing with an individual, a family, a country, or the "whole world."

This omnipotence attributed to speech chimes with all that is said by the Greeks and the Latins, except that the means employed are fundamentally different. Speech here is not used for speaking but for getting the other to speak. It aims not to express your feelings, but to get the other to reveal his: in this way, you can adapt to him and, in consequence, be well received by him and, again in consequence, be believed by him. Once the other has rendered himself transparent, he no longer offers any resistance, as our theorist of despotism also shows. According to the terms used in this treatise, the prime objective of "opening" and "closing" is to subject the other to an examination that will reveal "what there is in him" and "what there is not in him." On the basis of what is thus shown to be "full" or "empty," true or false, you will then be in a position to "embrace his desire" and thereby to discover his deepest secrets. (As in military strategy, these constitute the other's true "disposition," and here "disposition" means internal dispositions: his intentions and feelings.)

> You speak not to tell the other something, but to get him to speak

Dispositions and manipulation, nets and secrets: in this arid human desert, all subjectivity is excluded, or rather it is negative (since it allows one person to establish a hold over another). It is true that you establish an intimacy with the other, but the sole purpose of this is to flush him out. The writer never imagines, for example, that intimacy will reveal itself of its own accord, in a burst of sincerity. Nor does he even expect the other quite simply to say what he thinks. That is why speech is conceived primarily as a trap in which to capture the speech of the

How do you force the other to reveal himself?

other, which you then proceed now to "open," now to "close," in order to force him to reveal himself without pretense. Two methods may be adopted to this end (GGZ, chap. 2, "Fan ying"). The first method is to keep quiet while the other speaks, and, as soon as something seems out of place in what he says, you "go back over it" to discover the truth. For given that speech is used to "represent" reality and that facts "are linked together," when you compare them all, speech is revealing and makes it possible to see "what lies behind it." It is thus possible for you (through silence), without offering any hint of your own position, to catch the other in a "net." However little he says, and even if it is to speak of matters other than whatever concerns you, you can always discern hints and deduce the rest by making comparisons. Here is the second method. Suppose the other does not speak at all and so reveals absolutely nothing: then you need to change your tactics and suggest certain views of the situation that take him aback and force him to react. The information that you supply to him amounts to "almost nothing," but he will nevertheless soon reveal himself. To achieve this, all you need to do is play on the polarity between the other and yourself: you go one way, thereby forcing him to come toward you; or else you fabricate a lack that prompts him to compensate for it. If you wish him to speak, you retreat into silence; if you want him to take action, you pull back, and so on. If you yourself deliberately move in the opposite direction to that in which you wish him to go, you will make him react and will lure him to where you want him. You lead him into playing the role that will fall to him given the situation now developing. It is enough for you to stimulate this effect, covertly, in order for it to be produced, positively, through immanence. The other will now *respond*—not simply by communicating with you but acting fully in accordance with the developing situation—and will produce all that you want from him.

Yet another tactic to fathom the feelings of others and force them to hide nothing is to push them into an extreme emotional state (chap. 7, "Chuai"): either you choose a moment when the other is full of contentment and you go along with him in the direction in which his ideas are leading him so that, at the height of gratification, he allows his most intimate feelings to surface; or else you choose quite the opposite moment and proceed in the same way. When his fear reaches the highest pitch, he will likewise deliver himself utterly into your hands. When he is pushed to the limit, whatever his feelings may be, they will make him lose control of himself or at least, thanks to the modifications in his position that they will bring in their train, will reveal a number of symptoms. For, in principle, everything that alters "within" becomes detectable "without." "On the basis of what you see," you become aware of "what you cannot see" (chap. 7). Then, once you have fathomed the feelings of the other in this way, you can be sure that he will be true to himself in his behavior (chap. 8). If, despite all this emotional provocation, he manages to elude you, you should "dump him" and no longer speak to him. Instead, reengage in your detection work from another angle and even more indirectly, this time by making inquiries among his entourage and seeking a better understanding of the "basis" of his personality. For as a result of your "rubbing up against him" and polishing him as you would a piece of jade (the meaning of *mo,*ᵂᵂᵂ cf. chap. 8, "Mo"), the other will end up by revealing all his dispositions in a transparent fashion. From this you must conclude that there is no pure appearance in which he can any longer take refuge.

> **Lead the other to lose control**

> **Everything in the other becomes symptomatic**

In parallel, just as in military strategy, you must never reveal the slightest hint of your own disposition. As the treatise says, never allow your "door" to be seen, and always remain a kind of ghost or spirit to your interlocutor (chap. 2, "Fan ying"). Even if your speech is one day "displayed openly" *(yang),* it will have come to maturity in the dark *(yin).* Whether you are engaged in "opening" or in "closing" in your dealings with the other, you should do so as discreetly as possible (chap. 1, "Bai he"); and if you are rubbing up against him so as to be able to see right through him, you must, of course, make sure that he does not notice, both by "plugging all holes" and by "concealing all loose ends" (chap. 8, "Mo"). The fruit of speech is definitely to encourage that contrast: while the other renders himself transparent, you render yourself opaque. Speech is

Back-to-front speech: making the other transparent and yourself opaque

certainly efficacious, as rhetoric declares, but it works back to front. Not in the simple and naive way that would be implied by a refusal to communicate and a straightforward decision to lie, for it turns out that the symptomatic nature of speech renders that impossible; but through a far more twisted subversion that alters the functions of speech. You speak not to tell the other something, but to get him to tell you something; and you listen to him not to follow his advice, but to gain a hold over him.

3

Conform with the other in order to dominate him

This point is as crucial in a relationship based on speech as it is in military strategy. You conform with the other but purely in order to dominate him. To make the point more clearly, one might even say that it is by adapting to his disposition and so, in a way, initially submitting to his views that you can be certain eventually to gain the upper hand over him, and you can be certain not only of your power to do that, but also of the way that you must proceed to that end. Or, to make this point even more incisively and to push the paradox as far as it will go: you follow him *in order to lead him* (that is to say in order to have the power to do so). Is that a paradox, or is it glaringly obvious? By stretching the formula used to express the idea and forcing it to be totally explicit, we may think we are playing the paradox game and pushing discourse to its limit, but really what we arrive at is obvious, so obvious that at first we do not notice it and can only begin to see it when we have turned it into a paradox. Chinese thought, for its part, is content to glide constantly over this fact, never bothering to investigate it but always treating it as an underlying assumption. It never wastes time in setting it up as a principle. This being so and given that it is so implicit in the entire treatise, but always deeply so rather than in an eye-catching way, the danger is that we may overlook it or fail to appreciate its importance.... But let us return to the theme of manipulation: "As you drive the other to react, by means of the views of the situation that you express, you can go along with what he has in mind and his inner dispositions become manifest to you. So by following [his inner dispositions], you are in a position to guide him" (GGZ, beginning of chap. 2, "Fan ying": "guide him" in the fullest sense of the expression, *mu,* as a shepherd guides his flock of sheep).

This is certainly a far cry from the demiurgic, and therefore heroic, European myth of the pure power of initiating things. To be the first to undertake things, to become engaged in them: this always involves solitude and personal investment, risk and effort—no doubt along with jubilation and fascination with the unknown. But in acting in that way we lose sight of efficacy and swing over into a different logic: the logic of desire and audacious effort. For if we are bent on efficacy, it turns out to be far more productive to "go along with" reality, as Chinese wisdom and military strategy never cease to tell us, and to behave "in consequence" of that reality. *In consequence* means "by following" what is given so as to profit from it by *con*forming with it.

The risk and effort involved in initiating

It is time to dispel an ambiguity that might otherwise make this concept unintelligible: wanting progressively to monopolize the initiative to your own advantage, both in warfare and in relationships based on speech, does not mean that you have to initiate situations. On the contrary, in fact, since whoever initiates something is always more or less bound to take a risk and, because he does so, then exhausts himself in seeking a way forward. In contrast, whoever follows benefits from knowing all the necessary landmarks and does not have to venture into unknown territory. His progress is much easier, since he knows what points of reference to make for. He has a *hold* on the situation, while the one who initiates it does not. The behavior of whoever follows along thus acquires a rigor and a sense of direction and from this stems an authoritative force. All this affects the original relationship in a covert fashion to the point where, even when he ceases to make an outward show of adapting to the other, he progressively acquires the ability to control the latter's inner impulses. In other words, even as he continues to follow and allows himself to be carried forward, he accedes to a position that affords him, with his unassuming ways, the possibility of far greater efficacy than the one who, with all his wearing

Initiative does not mean initiating

The capacity for initiative is acquired as the situation unfolds

responsibilities, has led the way. A capacity for initiative is revealed not at the beginning but rather at the end, for it too stems from an ongoing development, is acquired little by little, and is manifested in the form of a result. Somewhere along the line, the initiative slips from one to the other, and the power that they hold is reversed. This is not a dialectical reversal such as that between Master and Slave, although in a sense it is an extension of that, since it proceeds from a continuous transformation that, unlike an event, leaves no datable mark on History. Nobody else is aware of it, not even the one to whom it happens and who, thanks to your having conformed to his behavior and espoused his feelings, you can now discreetly push forward in whatever direction you choose.

This treatise presents the relationship as one between a prince and his subject (chap. 3, "Nei qian"). As we have seen, it is essential to detect the inner dispositions of the prince. That is so as to enable you, the subject, to espouse his logic and win his good opinion (by whatever means available: "morality" or a "partisan" alliance, or through his desire for "wealth," or through "sex," and so on). By always supporting whatever he desires, you manage to "enter into intimacy with him" in the same way, as the saying goes, as a key in a lock, and it then becomes possible to set about "implementing" your own ambitions. For,

Use the intentions of the other to determine the measures that he takes

we are told, knowing how to "make use of his intentions," you can guide him as you wish, without him offering the least resistance: "if you wish him to seek you out, he will seek you out"; "if you wish him to think of you, he will think of you"; and so on. You, the subject, align yourself so closely with the desires of the prince that the prince becomes inseparable from you. Not only has the relationship of dependence been reversed, but it is now all the stronger because it is purely internal and allows "no sign of it to appear." Once again, the resulting efficacy is all the greater because its mode of determination is as of a consequence; it does not operate directly, imposing force, but simply *results*. Here, it results from what would appear to be the very contrary of a recourse to force: it is the fruit of trust.

Similarly, as is suggested by the title of another chapter (chap. 5, "Fei qian"), you make your partner "take to flight" in response to the praises that you heap upon him, and then you seize him "with pincers." The commentator's gloss runs as follows: to acquire a "hold" over the other, you should "start by praising him to the skies so that he takes to flight. All of a sudden he will reveal his feelings totally, leaving nothing concealed, and then, knowing what it is that he wants so desperately, you can draw him along in pursuit of it and attach him to it so securely that he can no longer turn or move." Your words make the other "fly off" so that you can then grab him, both in order to "harmonize" your relationship with him and, in accordance with your own intentions, to "direct" him toward your own goal. This maneuver is what our treatise describes as "setting off empty and returning full." Making him take to flight simply by means of a few words is "setting off empty"; and once the other has poured out his heart and revealed his feelings in such a way as to pass entirely under your influence and become wholly dependent on you, you "return full."

Even the manner in which you "praise" and then "nab" the other depends on him. The fact is that there are many ways of "rubbing up against" the other in order to polish him and be able to detect his inclinations, and in each case the manner chosen must be appropriate. One way is to be "pacific," another to observe "strict" principles, another to follow whatever gives the other "pleasure," or whatever makes him "angry," another to rely on his desire for "glory," and so on (chap. 8, "Mo"; cf. chap. 10, "Mou"). Even if what the sage (here, the strategist of speech) sets up is something that "all men are equally capable of doing," only he knows how to adapt the stratagem completely to the other person involved. It is from this knowledge that the entire success of this use of words stems—success in this instance consisting in "gaining his ear totally" (chap. 8, "Mo"). This treatise even makes a closer analysis of the reason why such adaptation is so beneficial. If adaptation is such an efficacious ploy, it is by virtue of the very principle that the present work has been invoking right from the start, namely, *the creation of propensity.* Here, the propensity in question is that of like to

> Make him "take to flight" in order to "nab" him

> A return to the logic of propensity: here, getting him to listen to you

seek like through *affinity* (just as, we are told, dry wood, when tossed on a fire, is the first to catch or damp earth absorbs water thrown on it more quickly than dry earth does). Like attracts like, *sponte sua*. If you adapt yourself to the other, you make yourself like him, and, for this reason alone, he is attracted to you.

4

Echoing this treatise on diplomacy, the theorist of authoritarianism, the so-called legalist, declares that the whole "difficulty of speech" lies in "knowing the mind of the person we are addressing so as to make our words equate to his thoughts" (HFZ, chap. 12, "Shui nan"). The point, then, is not to persuade the other by dint of reasoning but to fit in with the situation. If the man you address is besotted with glory and you speak to him of material advantages, "he will look at you with scorn and eject you as a vile individual." If, on the contrary, he is thinking of material advantages and you speak to him of glory, he will consider what you say to be "of no interest" to him, because it is "too far removed from reality" and "he will not be receptive to it." But the matter is even more complicated. It may be that deep down inside he is thinking only of his own interests but wishes to appear to desire glory. If you speak to him of glory he will pretend to listen but in fact will distance himself from you; and if you speak to him of self-interest, he will secretly follow your advice but, so as not to lose face, will feel obliged to dismiss you....

It is not hard to see how it is that, unlike in Greece, rhetoric never developed in China. On the Greek side, that is to say in a Greek city, an orator usually addressed a group of men who were deliberating on the issue that was at stake, men who would constitute a court, a council, or even an assembly. He had to bear in mind the likely state of mind of his public, but he could certainly not enter into the personal logic of each of his listeners. Furthermore, his speech was generally set within the framework of a pro-and-con debate, one *logos* against another. His *logos* would either refute the other or be refuted by it. His best course was therefore to support his discourse with the reasoning

Why did rhetoric not develop in China?

One logos
a l.
another

that he judged to be the most objective, even if it was based only on probability, and to appeal to the rigor of the argumentation as a common denominator of thought. But in China, as in any monarchical regime (and China has never conceived of any other kind, not even today: hence the Party), speech, because it is addressed to the prince, never completely sheds its private character. Inclined as it is to set the highest value on the perspective of its addressee, it seeks not so much to prove as to insinuate itself. It seldom leads into head-on contradictory debates but instead, like military strategy, operates in an oblique manner. The reasoning itself, legitimately enough, adopts a devious line in response to a captious situation. As the theorist of despotism explains, if there is something that the prince is anxious, through personal interest, to do, you must "urge him to do it," making it appear to be "a public duty." If he is inclined to some base action and cannot hold back from it, you should "maximize the more advantageous aspects of it" and "minimize its reprehensible side," and so on. In these circumstances, winning the benevolence of the prince is simply a preamble. "If you get the prince to like you, your enlightened views will be welcomed and, furthermore, you will enjoy his favor; but if you are disliked, your enlightened views will not be welcome, you will be rejected as a criminal, and you will be dismissed." The center of gravity moves from the "mouth" (of the divine Peitho, the fetish organ of Greek rhetoric) to the ear: to win the ear of the prince is to guarantee success.

Public speech/private speech: argumentation or insinuation, a head-on or an oblique procedure?

captious situation

However, since the objective of the theorist of authoritarianism is to render the prince's authority absolute, he consequently adopts the point of view of the despot and not that of his subjects. Indeed, his perspective is quite the opposite to theirs, since the subjects are regarded as the prince's antagonists. It is to be expected that this question of winning the ruler's benevolence is here mostly seen from the opposite angle. Everything that was advocated by the theorist of diplomacy is converted into a warning (HFZ, chap. 14, "Jian jie shi chen"). The principal task that falls to the prince, if he is to protect his authority, will be to be wary of all those who try to use winning words in order to insinuate themselves into his intimacy. All

Antithesis

their attempts at insinuation need to be unmasked by the prince and recognized to be insidious. His response to any secret plot to acquire his trust will be an all-embracing distrust. Actually, his wariness is directed not so much toward others as toward himself in his dealings with them, for he knows that, "because of the agreement that existed between an interlocutor and himself in the past," he will be inclined "to trust what that interlocutor says today," and he also knows that by expressing agreement with him today, his interlocutor is seeking to win his favor in order, rather, to abuse it and seize his power. The prince responds to compliancy with suspicion—in order to preserve the full potential of his position.

An example from outside (from China) thus confirms the link between rhetoric and democracy. But the two procedures—persuasion and manipulation—that are here set in opposition overspill the respective historical frameworks that favored their development. The Greek framework was public, the Chinese private; and the former promoted confrontational discourse, whereas the latter favored an oblique relationship. Once disentangled from their contexts, they stand as alternative models of behavior. One alternative is to exert direct pressure on one's listener, through speech, showing him why and why not and setting out the whole matter before his very eyes. One uses all the oratorical vehemence at one's command but at the same time sticks fast to the logic required by reason, for in Greece eloquence was certainly a matter of theatricality as well as logic. The other alternative is to manipuate the situation so as to influence one's adversary indirectly, progressively getting him to move in a particular direction so that, without ever showing one's hand, and purely as a result of what is involved in it, the situation itself enfolds the other and disarms him.

Long ago Duke Wu of Zheng wished to attack Hu. So—the theorist of despotism tells us (HFZ, chap. 12)—he began by marrying his daughter to the prince of Hu "to turn his mind toward pleasures." Then he said to his ministers, "I wish to use my troops. Who can I attack?" His chief officer, Guan Qisi, replied, "Hu can be attacked." Duke Wu was angry and had him put to death, saying, "Hu

Persuasion by means of argument: an expenditure of energy

Alternatively, disarm resistance by manipulating the situation

is a brother country: how can you think of advising me to attack it?" "Hearing of this, the prince of Hu thought that Zheng was well intentioned toward him. So he took no precautions. The men of Zheng suddenly attacked and took the principality."

11

Water Images

1

One particular image runs through the thought of ancient China, both irrigating it and linking it together: the image of water. The *Laozi* (section 8) tells us that water is what is closest to the way, the *dao*. Of course water itself is not the way, since it constitutes a particular and therefore exclusive reality, whereas the way embraces the whole of reality in its entire plenitude, and in it all incompatabilities are absorbed and vanish: water is one of the realities already "actualized," whereas the way takes us back to the deep, undifferentiated fund of things. Nevertheless, because it is infinitely flexible, *fluid*, with no form or sharp edges, and it never ceases, inexhaustibly, to flow, water guides us toward the Way; it takes us back toward that which is undifferentiated, that which we cannot see (in isolation) or name (separately), from which everything ceaselessly proceeds, and to which everything ceaselessly returns. Of all the realities that are actualized, water thus seems to be the one that is least so: it is not fixed in any definite aspect, never immobilized in any particular place. It is the least thinglike of all things—the most alive, the most alert.

Water has so often been celebrated for its purity; elsewhere, in the aridity of the desert, it has served to staunch thirst, even the thirst of the soul, and so has seemed a source of life. Heraclitus' "everything flows" (or "you can

Water is "the closest
thing to the way"

never enter the same river twice," fr. 134 [91]) expressed
a poignant sense of the ephemeral and the ceaseless shifting of things, the fleetingness and insubstantiality of existence, the fact that "we are and we are not" (fr. 133 [49a]).
Confucius, standing on a riverbank one day, produced an
equally laconic exclamation: "To pass by like this, with
no let-up, day and night!" (*Analects*, IX, 19). But in the
Chinese tradition this is said to express admiration for the
continuous flow that so resembles the great process of the
world, the source of which is inexhaustible (cf. MZ, IV,
B, 18). On the Greek side the seemingly commonplace
image points toward nonbeing; on the Chinese side it
points to the inexhaustible fund of immanence. Because it
constantly renews itself and, flowing from some invisible
point upstream, its course never stops proceeding, water
represents efficacy. Or rather—and the image of *flowing*
helps us to seize upon the difference—it suggests what the
nature of efficiency might be.

Two aspects of the same image: Heraclitus and Confucius

In fact, it even illuminates a number of aspects of efficiency, reflecting all that has been said above about it. The
Laozi even declares that discourse about water seems to
be back to front and to indicate—yet again—a paradox:
"In the whole world there is nothing more flexible or
weaker than water, but to attack that which is hard and
strong, nothing can surpass it"—or "replace" it either (LZ,
section 78). Similarly, "that which is most flexible bestrides
that which is most hard" (LZ, section 43). Because it has
no rigidity, there is nothing into which "water cannot insinuate itself"—but water itself can never be "broken" (cf.
Wang Bi). Meanwhile, whoever seeks to "keep strength
within himself is not strong"; "it is by keeping flexibility
within oneself that one is strong" (LZ, section 52). Likewise, by offering no resistance, a person or thing is more
resistant. In this respect, water is the opposite to stone.
Because stone is solid, it gets worn away and breaks, even
if it is as brilliant as jade. Through its immobility and
hardness, it embodies that which "has completed its actualization" (LZ, section 38, cf. Wang Bi's commentary),
that which has become fixed in its configuration. The flexibility of water, in contrast, calls to mind the flexibility of
the body of a newborn child (LZ, section 76): when a man

The "flexibility" and "weakness" of water make it stronger than strength

Water/stone

is born, or when plants grow, the tenderness and flexibility of his limbs and likewise the swaying grace of a sapling's branches joyfully exhale life; whereas at a man's or a tree's death, the body is invariably hard and dry. The *Laozi* goes on to observe that the same applies to military strategy: once the troops have become "hard" and "rigid," they can never triumph.

It is through "weakness," which generally prevails over strength, that the way, the *dao*, is said to proceed (LZ, section 40). For true strength is strength that is contained, implied, not that which, in order to show itself, has to stiffen and in stiffening is led to snap, or at least to become worn. In other words, true strength is not power that is displayed, but potential power. In military strategy, it is the power that lies in the potential of the situation, as is illustrated by an accumulation of water. "In combat, troops are used by the victor like accumulated water for which one opens up a breach in the precipice" (SZ, end of chap. 4, "Xing"). Because of the great distance of the drop and the narrowness of its channel, the violence of the water can even carry stones along (ibid., chap. 5, "Shi"). Despite the fact that the nature of the water is "flexible and weak," while that of stones is "hard and heavy" (Du You), the water triumphs over the weight of the stones purely thanks to how it is disposed.

True strength is definitely characterized by the fact that it is not forced. Chinese thought never tires of this theme: it is in the nature of water to flow downward; and the reason why it can even carry stones along with it is that it is content to follow the slope offered to it. Water is the very image of that which never ceases to seek for a way out in order to flow onward but does so without doing violence to its natural inclination, simply going along with its propensity: "The conformation of troops must resemble water. Just as it is in the conformation of water to avoid what is high and incline toward that which is low, similarly, the conformation of troops must be to avoid the points at which the enemy is strong and attack it where it is weak" (SZ, chap. 6, "Xu shi"). The strong points are where the enemy is "full" and may act as a barrage; the weak points are those where the enemy is "empty"—deficient or

Margin notes:

display
stiffens
snaps
wears
out

true

An accumulation of water constitutes an image of potential

strength
is
potential
power
held
back

water
can
slope
potent

Strength—propensity: to advance, water follows its inclination unprepared. The general, like water, steers clear of obstacles and insinuates himself wherever the way before him is free; like water, he always sticks closely to the line of least resistance and at every moment seeks out where it is easiest to proceed.

2

That low level to which water never ceases to flow, as it follows the downward incline, is what will eventually allow it to dominate. As we have seen (LZ, section 66, and chap. 7, above), the reason why large rivers and the sea are able to "reign over the hundred tributaries" is that they have the advantage of being situated at a lower level. That gives them the ability to reign supreme. The obvious message here is one with which we are already familiar. An effect is obtained at the bottom of the slope, downstream, and the sea is filled by all the world's waterways without having to seek them out. The waters tend and converge toward it simply because that is where they incline: all the sea has to do is receive them. But just below that surface meaning lies another, one that is more adroitly strategic even though it appears to run contrary to military strategy or even to wipe out the very possibility of it. Water, with its tendency to flow downward, manages to avoid any head-on "confrontation" (LZ, section 8). Having reached the lowest level, there is no need to fight. The best strategy is to begin by disengaging every adverse strategy by removing all competition, and the effect of this is devious. For whoever avoids all confrontation can never be confronted (LZ, section 22). Not only would no one ever dream of it, but it would be impossible to achieve—because there is nothing on which to establish a hold. By deliberately placing yourself below, where the other would hate to find himself, you deprive him of the possibility of a confrontation and rivalry, and by doing so you undermine his resistance. By defusing antagonism, you disarm the enemy in advance.

Once again, everything depends on the condition to which you have reduced your enemy simply by the position that you adopted. By deliberately placing yourself in

Water flows to a lower level: rivalry is suppressed

a position withdrawn from everyone else, you deflect their desire to challenge you and paralyze their aggression. "He who possesses within himself a full capacity is like a newborn child": impossible to attack (LZ, section 55). In contrast, anyone who uses his strength and intelligence vis-à-vis others prompts them to do likewise vis-à-vis him and himself thereby provides them with arms and delivers himself up to their blows (cf. Wang Bi, section 49). Hence the following principle, which is established in the most general terms: the "way of Heaven," which is the most natural way, is to "manage to win without confrontation" (LZ, section 73). The *Laozi* then applies this principle to military strategy. A good leader in war is not "bellicose," that is—as the commentator Wang Bi understands it—he does not try to take the initiative and be aggressive. In other words, "he who is capable of defeating the enemy does not engage in battle with him," and it is purely through this "ability to avoid confrontation" that one becomes able to "use the strength of others."

But how can we conceive of such a relationship with the enemy in which we can defeat him without ever clashing with him? The *Laozi* explains the situation using a set of paradoxical expressions in which the complementary object of the verb is in each case withdrawn (as in "acting-without-action"): "marching on an expedition without there being any expedition" or "rolling up one's sleeves without there being any arms there" or "pressing forward to battle without there being any enemy" or "holding absent weapons firmly in hand" (section 69). The meaning of all this, the commentator laconically tells us, is "that there is no resistance due to any engagement." Let us unpack those expressions: pressure is certainly exerted upon the enemy—for pressure, tension, and threat are certainly in the air—but it does not find expression in offensive action (in fact, one is perfectly ready to retreat). It does not manifest itself at all in a localized fashion: one does not need to come face-to-face with the enemy in a particular place, at a particular time, in the course of a particular expedition, taking up arms on a particular day and proceeding to attack. There is certainly some kind of "expedition" afoot but no specifically identifiable one;

Winning without confrontation

How to paralyze resistance by presenting nothing tangible to oppose

there is certainly an attitude of "rolling up one's sleeves," but it does not find expression in any man-to-man confrontation. In other words, a gesture is certainly made but without any (particular, limited, individual) object in mind. In short, nothing is *tangible,* so there is nothing to provide the enemy with the chance and support of an opportunity that would at last allow him to find his feet and make a stand. He will be defeated without ever having joined battle—and without ever encountering his opponent. Pressure is exerted upon him but without ever taking a completely concrete form (so without being reified and thereby limited). That pressure has never been allowed to focus on any particular point or goal so has never made it possible for resistance to crystallize. In this constantly flowing and elusive process, which runs as smoothly as a current of water, the enemy has never been able to lay his hand on any hard edge to which he could cling.

In contrast to the event constituted by a battle, which gives rise to resistance, there is a continuously unfolding process in which the strength of the antagonist is progressively dissolved: not so much worn away—for that would involve an expenditure of effort—but frustrated, paralyzed, rendered vain and pointless. The treatise on diplomacy (GGZ, chap. 8, "Mo") echoes these ideas: it is a matter of "winning day by day," "by dint of combat that is constant [but] avoids confrontation." This kind of combat, though constant, is diffuse, all-pervading. One takes care not to be seen taking part in it. It "costs" the country "nothing"; the others do not even notice "how they were overcome." The chapter devoted to military strategy even advises against confrontation in its chapter devoted to "attack"! (SZ, chap. 3, "Mou gong"): "To win a hundred victories in a hundred battles is good but belongs to the order of that which is not good. The height of excellence is to manage to overcome the enemy without having to fight." Thus, "those who are expert in the art of warfare defeat the enemy army without engaging in battle, take towns without attacking them, and overthrow a hostile country without protracted operations." In the long run, such a progressive unfolding of the situation proves decisive in less time than a series of battles that are spectacular and dazzling but give rise to a whole sequence of ripostes, the outcome of which, right to the last moment, risks reversing the victory.

3

This military treatise uses an image that illustrates even more precisely the source of a possibility of success: "Water determines its course by the lie of the land; and victory is determined by the nature of the enemy"(SZ, chap. 6, "Xu shi"). This image is worth studying closely. For it is not introduced to illustrate any earlier principle, nor is it further explained later on. The strict parallel encompasses and accommodates the theory as a whole. Or rather, the idea has been implicit everywhere but is here made explicit. By itself, water has no form of its own: it constantly conforms and adapts; in fact, it is because it always adapts that it always tends to progress. Similarly, as we have seen, it is only by adapting to the enemy that one can triumph over him. The situation of your opponent plays the same role for you as the lie of the land does for water: you mold yourself upon it, go along with it rather than opposing it. In short, you do not stiffen into any form of your own; instead you *con*form. Victory is then as irresistible and irreversible as the flow of water is. Carried along, as it is, inclining ever lower, it never goes astray, never hesitates.

The form of water "is not in the water itself" but is produced by the lie of the land. Similarly, "the potential is not in me" (Du Mu) but is produced by my opponent. Or rather, it is not in me (it would exhaust me), nor is it exactly in him, but *I draw it from him*. In other words, potential is not a matter of strength, my own potential clashing with that of my opponent. The potential lies *in the situation* and through it, as the situation unfolds, one can continually and effortlessly strengthen oneself. It lies in the possibilities that the situation opens up, just as the lie of the land allows the water to pass; and one exploits the situation just as the water does, knowing how to flow through it. Thus "potential is constituted by adapting to one's opponent" [xxx] (Mei Yaochen), and it can be deployed

The course of water is determined by the lie of the land; victory is determined by the enemy

Conform, as water does

Potential comes from conforming

because it lends itself to manipulation; if the enemy troops are "carried away," you insult them, and if they are "full of go," you relax them; if the general is "full of pride," it is advantageous to "humiliate him"; if he is "covetous," you "capture his interest"; and so on (Li Quan). Because it is not disposed in any particular way, water can make the most of the slightest crevice to advance. And similarly, the more I make myself constantly adaptable (not only do I never adopt a form of my own, but I never get fixed in any of the positions with which I conform), the better I can profit from the slightest breach offered by the situation and so continue to progress. Generally speaking, I always determine my own strategy *in relation to* the enemy: if I am "ten against one," I must "surround him"; "five against one," "attack him"; "two against one," "fight him"; "equal in strength," "divide him"; "weaker in numbers," "flee from him and avoid him" (SZ, chap. 3, "Mou gong"). For just as water moves around the obstacles that stand in its path, there is never anything to be gained from resisting. "If the party in the inferior position determines to resist, he becomes the prey of the more powerful party." In this logic of a potential that stems solely from the situation, there is no room to accommodate the—gratuitous—surplus constituted by human effort. Sacrifice is useless—let alone dangerous—heroism.

Just as water moves around obstacles, never resist

Nor is there a place for a plan drawn up in advance; and every general is declared to have the right to disobey the orders he has received the moment they become unsuitable. Nothing is essential except the demands of the situation: the situation is the only thing that counts; it is what makes it possible to decide "what should be done" and "what should not be done" (SZ, chap. 3, "Mou gong," cf. Jia Lin), and it is also the source of all dynamism. As is well known, nothing could be worse than wanting to repeat what has previously led to success, for since the situation is new, so is its potential, so any precedent is out of date. If, on the contrary, you determine your victory "by adapting to the enemy's configuration," the potential is "inexhaustible" (SZ, chap. 6, "Xu shi"): the strategy that you adopt will constantly take the enemy by surprise and will throw him off course. Its whole "mainspring" "is to be

the situation is the only thing that counts

found in this constant *con*formation," which is a "motivating" force (Mei Yaochen, cf. the meaning of *ji*[yyy]). Any disposition that is isolated and depends principally on itself remains relatively inert; its function is scanty, and there is no tension. In contrast, if it is adapted to the adversary, it possesses a mobilizing force and becomes reactive; its coherence is concentrated, and it holds itself alert and ready for anything.

4

The comparison continues. Just as water "has no constant form," "likewise, troops have no constant potential" (SZ, chap. 6, "Xu shi"). Not only does water symbolize a potential through its ability to adapt; it also illustrates it through its variability. It is not hard to see that, since the enemy's configuration always tends to become slightly modified, if I continue to conform to it, I shall ceaselessly be *transforming* myself. It is important to distinguish between the two notions, for although they are linked (*bian hua*[zzz]), they correspond to two different degrees of involvement. When the *modification* undergone by your opponent begins, it is always in response to particular circumstances, but you, for your part, must mobilize yourself completely each time such a modification occurs in order to react and adapt to it. By *transforming* yourself totally in response to that modification, you renew yourself entirely from within and thus remain dynamic—to such a degree, in fact, that this effect, which is constantly manifested through the unfolding of the situation, should strictly speaking no longer be called "efficacy," for once again that notion turns out to be too narrow. Rather, it is deployed as "efficiency." "To be capable of transforming yourself in response to the modifications to your adversary, in such a way as to obtain victory, is what is called [divine] efficiency" (ibid.). This is an infinitely "subtle" efficiency and so is unfathomable. It merges with the efficiency of the fund of immanence, whence the great renewal of the world—that of its "days" and "seasons"—ceaselessly proceeds. Because it never fails, this is the most "divine" kind of efficiency and, at the same time, the most natural.

Water, an image of strategic variability

It is therefore necessary to distinguish between what is "constant" and what is "changing." In warfare, the "logic" is constant but the "potential" is not,[aaaa] in the same way as the "nature" of water is constant but its "form" is not (Wang Xi). For, although the constant nature of water is to tend downward, it has no constant form, since that is determined by the terrain. Similarly, although the constant logic, in warfare, is to attack the enemy's weak points, the potential is constantly changing, since it depends on the enemy to whom you are responding and because those weak points never cease to vary depending on the situation. That is why it is impossible to *construct a model* for warfare, that is to say, a form (*eidos* in Greek) that will remain valid even though every case is different: "Attack and defense are infinitely subtle; one cannot give them a form by making a statement about them" (Li Quan). For by seeking to slot the form into a statement and set it up as a paradigm, one would lose all the potential of the situation.

With no constant form, it is impossible to construct a model

In default of being able to construct a model of conflict, given that any conflict is constantly changing, the only possible "statement" about it must be *variable*. Rather than construct a theory of forms, Chinese thought sets up a system of differences. Instead of seeking to pick out common features that are more or less fixed, more or less stable, it sets out to explore the limits of the possibilities of change. In Chinese thought, it is a matter not of *identifying*, in a quest for essences, as we do in the wake of our Western metaphysics, but rather of making an *inventory* (of resources). So, after expounding the single "logic" inherent in warfare, all that remains for this military treatise to do is to draw up a table of differences. Not differences at the level of any application of its logic, as if, from being abstract, it could now take on form; for that is only suitable with a model (cf. all the differences and frictions in practice). No, these are differences that arise from the diversity of possible situations, all of which are permeated, through and through, by the same single logic, which makes it possible to draw up a table of differences and compare them. The concluding chapters of this treatise carry titles such as "The Nine Variables" or "The Nine Terrains" (where "nine" does not have a limiting sense but

The only system possible is one of variability

In Chinese thought, unity does not stem from the abstraction of essences, but rather from "communication" between differences and from "threading" all the different cases together

represents an extreme number that "can encompass all the extremes of change"). They list a wide range of different possibilities. The terrain may be "sloping," "convenient for establishing communications," "cut off from everything," "enclosed," "lethal," and so on. Or else the term "terrain" may be given the wider sense of a place for an antagonistic configuration. This may be of "a dispersed nature," "light," "confrontational," "heavy," "difficult," and so on. All these differences are listed so that each may be exploited in the appropriate way and also—indeed, above all—to show how a general can move from one to another: "If the general does not understand the advantage of the nine variables" *(tong)* [bbbb] and see the possible communications between them, however well he understands the configuration of the terrain, "he will not be able to exploit it" (SZ, chap. 8, "Jiu bian").

These lists of differences do not really constitute a veritable typology. Their purpose is not to identify each case separately (as is proved by the fact that the labels attached to them overlap from one list to another), but rather to draw attention to the possible variations. For, as is recognized in warfare, nothing is more dangerous than immobilizing yourself within one particular case; and nothing is worse than setting up rules and imperatives for yourself, for these make your conduct inflexible and prevent you from the variation from which all potential stems (and the same applies to morality). The treatise insists that there is nothing to which you should "cling at all costs" (the meaning of *bi;* [cccc] SZ, chap. 8, "Jiu bian"): not "risking your life," nor "saving your life," nor "being ready to rush in," nor the wish to remain "pure" in your honor, nor even "loving your people" (your soldiers). Not that any one of those particular attitudes is to be condemned in itself. It is simply that to cling to any one of them is blameworthy, for then you would be led by it no longer to go along with the situation as it changes. Eventually, depending on the circumstances, it would lead you to be "killed," "taken prisoner," "hoodwinked," "insulted," or "embarrassed." Like the sage (cf. Confucius, *Analects,* IV, 10), a general "does not dig his heels in"; all his skill lies in varying from one extreme to another—as widely as reality does.

In military strategy, the essential is to know how to slip from one case into another

5

The overlap between warfare and diplomacy is illuminating. In warfare, the alternative is to attack or to defend; at court it is to "associate yourself" or "separate yourself," to set up alliances or to break them (GGZ, chap. 6, "Wu he"). But in every field that is affected by polarities, just as nature is, the logic is the same: "In general, whether it is a matter of *inclining toward* or *going against,* the best strategy is to adapt: transformations follow one upon another without interruption every time there is a particular configuration with a particular potential. You determine whether to go one way or another, depending on the situation." A diplomat, like a general, not only adapts to the situation but also embraces its variations. "Embraces" here means depending on the "circumstances," noting "what they add up to momentarily," and also depending on what is "increasing" and what is "diminishing" in those circumstances so that he can "anticipate" the situation in advance and "change his behavior to fit in with it." Since nothing is stable, particularly not "that which one honors," there is nothing to which the "sage" (here, the diplomat) will link himself to forever or from which he will distance himself "definitively." Since "to associate himself" with one party is to "dissociate himself" from another, he goes from one side to the other, to sound out where his own interest lies and so as to be able, later, when no longer in doubt, to rally to whichever offers him the most profit (which is exactly what important ministers must have done whenever there was a change of dynasty). And when one is close to the prince, it is also by "varying" that one tries to worm one's way into his intimacy (GGZ, chap. 3, "Nei qian"). Hence all the varying cases that this treatise, too, lists, setting them out systematically as points of reference by which to plot one's conduct. The author addresses the powers of one's partner (chap. 10, "Mou"), the ways of associating with him (chap. 8, "Mo"), and the different modalities of speech that suit different types of situation (speech that is "flattering," "compliant," "resolute," "intimate," "serene"; chap. 9, "Quan"). Whereas in Greece rhetoric set up lists of rhetorical figures, as *forms* peculiar

Diplomacy, too, is an art of variation

A system of variation replaces all models

Discourse itself is conceived in relation not to forms of speech, but to different situations

to discourse, this Chinese treatise conceives of the diversity of speech purely in relation to lists of different circumstances and opportunities.

There is one notion that confirms the importance of the situation (*quan,*[dddd] cf. GGZ, chap. 9). Literally it relates to scales and the operation of weighing, but it also serves to illuminate both power, in particular political power (*quan-li* [eeee]) and also what we understand by circumstances or expedients (*quanbian, quanmou* [ffff]): all that which, through its variability and in contrast to the fixity of rules (*jing* [gggg]), makes it possible for the situation to remain unblocked and to continue to evolve in conformity with the logic of the process that has already begun. Now, the fact that those two meanings meet in the same word and are both conceived on the basis of the flexibility of weighing scales suggests that the only way to determine reality, in the last analysis at least, is by the extent to which the situation tips to one side or the other. "Circumstances" means *the way in which* reality never ceases to change in order to continue to deploy itself (the notion of *biangtong* [hhhh]); and the weight of power simply results from such a tipping from one side to the other. In our interpretation of reality, we in the West grant to circumstances no more than the status of an accessory, relegating them, in the final analysis, to morphology and limiting them to surrounding *(circum)* the hegemonic perspective of the case under consideration (and its essential relation to its object). In contrast, in China, this uninterrupted flow of variance, so well illustrated by the course of flowing water, is regarded as constituting the *very course* of reality. In the twentieth century, admittedly, China has added a new meaning to the notion in order to convey the new idea of "rights" that it discovered in the West (cf. *renquan:* [iiii] human right[s]—literally "human power"). However, it is easy to see how this added meaning, which seems to be justified by the fact that "rights" too should take into account the difference between one case and another, remains stuck with the same notion or even seems to contradict it (as can still be seen today in Chinese political life). For, whereas power stems from the situation, rights transcend it. At the level of values, they imply an absolute recognition of the individual, at the

[margin notes:]

Sit-cation:
guan

Balance, power, and circumstances all have the same meaning in Chinese

We should rethink what we mean by "circumstances"

The course of water or of reality has no fixed form

China thinks in terms of power, not rights

level of behavior, an absolute recognition of the autonomy of the subject.

The Greeks too were conscious of variability—in fact, as they saw it, it could elude all formalization, and in that case it could not be controlled. Aristotle recognizes that in navigation, with which he associates military strategy, there is no possibility of a general knowlege that encompasses all particular cases. The winds that plow across the waters are too diverse to codify. According to her mythical ancestry, Tuche, chance, was the daughter of Ocean and Tethys, and the sister of Metis. But this particular water motif was developed very little in the literature and thought of ancient China. The navigator carried this way and that by the waves and striving to find a way out, a *poros,* praying to the gods and studying the currents with all his cunning, is unknown in Chinese imagery. When disappointed at seeing his way so little followed, Confucius one day spoke of "taking to a raft designed for the deep waters and setting out to sea" (*Analects,* V, 6); but when a disciple took him at his word, he soon admonished the latter, saying that he was only joking. . . . In China, there really was no elsewhere to which to sail. In Greece, in contrast, the sea is everywhere, infiltrating the land on every side and breaking into it; its ever heaving "back" is a place where adventures are always possible not only for a sailor but likewise for a military strategist or a philosopher. Odysseus, seeking Return, yet drifting toward the unknown, was already if not the first philosopher, then the father of philosophy.

In China, the sea borders the earth at the lowest point of a downward slope. It does not encourage one to set out across it; it is neither threatening, nor does it lure one on to confront its dangers. It does not encourage thought to become *deterritorialized.* Immanence is not presented by it as a "level," with the sea "cutting through chaos" (Deleuze). Rather, it appears as a great fund (of the processivity of things). So there is no reason for the general to risk setting out to cross it. Nor is the sage in any doubt on that score.

In Greece, infinite variability could elude the system

The Greek image of water as a sea on which one adventures is unfamiliar to the Chinese

Odysseus, the father of philosophy

A level or a fund of immanence

12

In Praise of Facility

the hardest thing of all
to express: water, a dragon
(ceaselessly realized in an unremarkable ¹ and   unnoticed fashion

The course of water,
the body of a dragon

what
is dynamic
ic ?

presents
any fixed
tangible
shape

The image of what constantly flows past our feet—water forever closely embracing every hollow in the terrain, conforming to its shape so as to move onward—is totally unexceptional, yet its repercussions at a theoretical level are endless. And the more unexceptional the image, the more endless its implications are. Chinese thought has always drawn inspiration from this image to find words for the hardest thing of all to express: the evident "facility" of that which is ceaselessly realized in an unremarkable and unnoticed fashion. As if to interpret the message more clearly, Chinese thought projected this onto the sky, giving it the emblematic form of the body of a dragon, whose shape is almost impossible to make out, so quickly does it change, coiling and uncoiling as the clouds dictate.

A covert comparison is implied here. Water has no consistency of its own, or rather it does have a consistency but this is constantly remolded and transformed, which is how it is that it is never worn out or decomposed and water never loses it. In similar fashion, if the dragon is the most magical of beings, to which only a sage or an emperor bears comparison, that is because it so closely follows the course of the world that its dynamism is continuously renewed. Neither water nor the dragon presents any definite, fixed, tangible shape, which is why they are always so dynamic. To put that another way, Chinese thought,

always so anxious to capture the capacity invested in natural processes, is wary of anything that seems to stand on
its own and is visible. It does not declare there to be no
subject or ignore it, let alone suggest that a subject should
deny its own existence or condemn itself (for its aim is certainly to succeed). It is simply that the subject always
remains smooth, fluid, and discreet.

It is a well-known fact—and one that becomes even
more obvious when seen from China—that European
thought can be interpreted as a history of the progressive
buildup—to its modern extreme—of the autoconsistency
of the subject. Or rather, although a great deal has been
said on the subject of knowledge, that fact is perhaps less
fully realized where action is concerned. Let us return to
our earlier analysis. From Aristotle onward and in the
wake of the categories elaborated by epic and the theater,
we note the introduction, for ethical purposes, of the various elements of a theoretical framework for what was to
become the subject in action, elements that included both
points of reference and criteria. The full range of a subject's autonomy was determined by the faculties of "wishing," "deliberating," "choosing," and, most important, the
distinction between what is done "willingly" and what is
done against one's will. However, we can now see that
these are distinctions that were never spelled out in China.
In Europe, the next historical period that reinforced the
autonomy of the subject was the Renaissance, when, particularly in Machiavelli's works, the autonomy of the subject received a considerable boost. Machiavelli no longer
believed that the ideal for action was to be discovered by
contemplation of the order of things, for—as he saw it—
there was no order of things. Instead, a Machavellian subject was bent on making his mark on the world by imposing his own order. In the face of the caprices of fortune,
Machiavellian *virtù* was an ability to confront a situation,
however risky, and impose upon it a form that suited his
own plans. Finally, with Clausewitz, when post-Kantism
moved beyond morality, that affirmation of a subject confronting a situation boiled down to willpower. "Resistance,"
according to Clausewitz, is the product of two combined
factors: the extent of one's means (material forces) and

The autoconsistency
of the subject, in
Europe

That autoconsistency
culminates in
willpower

"strength of will." When one overcomes an opponent, one "stamps him out." In fact, in the last resort, a general can count only on his will to enable him to get out of the indecision into which he is plunged by the chancy nature of a situation (which is why, Clausewitz says, one needs more will at the level of strategy than at the level of tactics). Only through willpower can he subdue the doubts that are bound to arise on account of the slowness and difficulty of "execution" and do away with all "friction."

Amazing willpower.... European thought converged from all sides to set it up as an ability to confront the world and as the source of the subject's power to affirm himself and fulfill himself. It is even through our will that we most resemble God, thanks to the infinity that it reveals within us (Descartes). In short, man's use of will is his way of being God. And then, just as European thought killed God, it also killed the will. (Its death is clear in Freud but came about in Nietzsche or, even earlier, in Schopenhauer, in whose work will is at once affirmed and denied.) Yet it still could not do without it. Chinese thought, in contrast, never explored or expounded on the will, any more than it sought to postulate God. That can be seen as clearly from Chinese ethics as from Chinese military strategy. For Chinese thought, the opposition is between what one "does" and what one "can" do rather than between what one can do and what one wants to do (cf. MZ, I, A, 7). It is all a matter of force, even within oneself (cf. the common notion of *li* [iiii]). Chinese thought no more expounded on will than it conceived of rights or liberty. In other words, it never tried to think through human personality by isolating and abstracting it from a situation in order to set it up as a subject (of action). Instead of ultimately exalting human willpower, the ideal that Chinese thought advocates is to slip into the world so discreetly that one no longer seems to make any intervention (nonaction) and to melt into its processivity in order to succeed.

"He knows himself but does not show himself," says the man of the "way," or *dao*, in the *Laozi* (section 72). He "loves himself" (*ai:* [kkkk] that is to say, he is concerned for his person) but "does not value himself." Chinese thought thus refuses to set a high value on the subject just

In China, will is never explored or explained

as on its ascetic opposite (which is paired with it, the "hateful self"). As often happens in Chinese thought, the essential point is conveyed through a nuance. It is also said of the man of the "way" that he "illuminates" but does not "dazzle" (section 58). He tends to soften his light and "harmonize" it with his surroundings, because he knows that only he who does not draw attention to himself can avoid confrontations (cf. Wang Bi). Better still, he knows that shows of virtue or capacity are designed to make up for some lack, a deficiency that cries out to be compensated by merit and prowess, taking the form of excessive effort producing excessive effect (cf. sections 17, 18). He knows that any quality that is made to stand out as an individual characteristic can be no more than a flash in the pan, which, as such, is never completely adapted (for if it were, it would merge with the course of the world and become invisible). Besides, such a quality, which draws attention to the subject, blocks regular processes, which alone can ensure the unimpeded regime of efficacy (or rather, efficiency; cf. section 19). Manifestations of virtue or ability are excessive impulses, spurts, or eruptions, which seem the more sensational the less they are integrated with reality. That is why a sage/general is a man without qualities. If you operate in timely fashion, before the antagonistic configuration has taken shape, as strategy— as we have seen—constantly recommends, then you can prevail without anyone noticing, and the enemy knuckles under with no need for bloodshed (SZ, chap. 5, "Xing"). That, at least, is the "way" (although, of course, carnage is not unknown in China . . .). But what really concerns Chinese thought and what it sets out to explain is precisely the nonbattle, the nonconfrontation, the nonevent, that is to say, in short, the ordinary. For the ideal (the ideal of processivity) lies in what is ordinary (cf. in particular ZY, section 11). In ideal circumstances, there is nothing left to praise or even to see, no trace of an exploit, and "it" has all happened without being noticed ("it," which eludes specification and so remains undifferentiated). "Sagacity," at its peak, no longer needs to "dazzle" (Mei Yaochen), and "merit" is so great that it no longer needs to "be deployed."

A show of virtue betrays a deficiency

Ideally the effect goes unnoticed

2

The history of philosophy is constituted by the series of old cleavages through which philosophy took shape but in which, today, it can no longer quite recognize itself—cleavages that have neither been resolved nor absorbed, whether they were conceived from the point of view of "knowledge" (for example, matter and spirit) or of action (liberty as opposed to necessity). But now another cleavage is detectable, one that repeats the earlier cleavages but at the same time shifts them: namely, a split between subject and situation. This both overlaps and upsets the earlier cleavages (for despite the many efforts made in China in the past, it turns out to be as impossible as ever to present Chinese thought in terms of either materialism or idealism; nor can it be classified as determinism, since it never encountered the notion of liberty). The alternative that we now see surfacing seems to concern whatever it is that is postulated at the point where reality begins. Instead of setting God up as both an archetype and a magnified subject, the Chinese explain reality by the tension that is manifest in the slightest of situations, a tension out of which it then evolves. "A *yin*–a *yang* (now *yin*, now *yang*) is what is called the way, the *dao*" (*Zhouyi*, "Xici," A, 5). The *dao* or way, which is the ultimate term in Chinese thought, itself consists simply in the uninterrupted interplay of these factors—*yin* and *yang*, or whatever other names they may go by—for the polarity of the situation rests in them.

Inevitably, this prompts us to rethink exactly what it is that constitutes a "situation." For it cannot be reduced to the set of circumstances *in* which a subject finds himself or herself, although that is how we, in the West, usually define it. A situation is not a frame into which the subject's action inserts itself or the ambience in which he or she exercises his or her capacities. It cannot be limited to something that incorporates the subject and sets off his or her qualities. It is neither a screen (onto which his or her faculties can be projected), nor is it a setting. As we have seen, if you are cowardly or courageous in battle, it is not because you possess this or that quality. Rather, it is because the situation causes you to react in that manner. "The cow-

It is the polarity of the situation that determines everything

ardice [of one individual] stems from the courage [of another]" (or the weakness of the one stems from the strength of the other) (SZ, chap. 5, "Shi"). In warfare, the polarity of the situation stems from the antagonism between the forces involved (which is why Chinese thought, which conceived of reality in terms of polarity, was predisposed to strategy). Not only is courage the result or even the product of the situation; but furthermore, as the above military example implies, it cannot be radically distinguished from the "objective" aspects of the situation, such as the relation of the forces involved and the degrees to which these, respectively, are well organized. Whoever is skilled in warfare seeks success from the potential of the situation "instead of demanding it from the men under his command." His art is "to rely on the potential," and he "chooses his men" accordingly.

> Victory is to be expected not from the fighting men, but from the situation

Furthermore, a situation can never be pinned down. It is not a place, not a site. Pulled this way and that by its polarity, its configuration is constantly changing; it is always oriented by a propensity. When one of the two corresponding factors increases, the other decreases, and the situation is regulated by that ceaseless compensation, as the one factor draws its potential from its relation to the other and is renewed by it. Whatever disappears later reappears in a different form and what may appear to be a stable situation really consists in a succession of mutations. To repeat: "A *yin*–a *yang* (now *yin*, now *yang*) is what is called the way, the *dao*." The "way," which is the fruit of those endless interactions, is what reality follows as it comes about and what a general seeking to succeed sticks closely to. It never ceases to be logical, even when seemingly traversed by "crises"; but it is always unprecedented.

> Situation—evolution by a propensity

To summarize the difference between Western and Chinese thought: one *constructs* a model that is then projected onto the situation, which implies that the situation is momentarily "frozen." The other *relies* on the situation as on a disposition that is known to be constantly evolving. It is a disposition that functions as a device—and, once again, this is a term that needs to be given a new twist. For although it is generally used in the context of military strategy, this disposition-device does not carry the same meaning as we in the West ascribe to it ("a collection of means disposed in conformity with a plan"). Rather, it means something that we now see to be back-to-front (from the Western point of view): namely, a particular configuration that can be manipulated and that *in itself* produces an effect. Chinese thought found an emblematic image for this device: a two-winged *door* (*men*^IIII). Its two facing wings, each on its hinge, represent the polarity that is inherent in every situation. Considered generally, a door is something that constantly alternates, now "opening," now "closing." More specifically, with a door one can either prevent things from entering or allow them to pass through. In short, as a device, it makes a regulated flow possible (it is what makes both the flow and its regulation possible). Through such a door, the infinite success of reality passes—an "unfathomable" success, which is constantly renewed, as the *Laozi* puts it in its opening paragraph. The door constitutes an ultimate—or rather, extreme—image, which is pushed to its limit in the interests of coherence. It suggests that nature itself may be seen as a "door," whether that of the Dark Female, through whom life ceaselessly comes (section 6) or that of Heaven, whose alternating "opening" and "closing" one must espouse, "as a woman would," in order to allow an effect to result, instead of assuming the initiative oneself, right from the start (section 10, Wang Bi).

Similarly, the preface to the treatise on diplomacy (GGZ, beginning of chap. 1, "Bai he") declares, "By considering the opening-closing of the *yin* and the *yang*, so as to name and determine the lot of all existing things," the sage/general "knows the door of life and death" and of "success and failure." Nor is this merely theoretical knowledge—since strategic success consists in "guarding" this door. If one is able both to "calculate every kind of end-beginning" and to "apprehend the internal logic of human consciousness," in other words, if one is capable of understanding the inner coherence of regulation, "one can perceive the precursory signs of change" and "control the door" of success. The door continually swings one way or the other, and it is the swing in one direction that makes it possible for it to swing in the other. It is thus by "opening" and "closing" that natural transformation proceeds, alter-

Images for this device: a door, a hinge

nating between *yin* and *yang* (cf. the renewal of day and night, and that of the seasons). And it is also through such an opening and closing that "modification" should operate in our (diplomatic) relations with others, through speech:^mmmm is not the mouth itself like a "door" (the door of consciousness), since it is an organ for both allowing things to "pass" and for "blocking" them? Another image used to convey this opening and closing device is that of the "hinge" or "pivot" on which the door is fixed but that, on that very account, allows it to move this way and that (cf. GGZ, chap. "Chi shu"). As the commentator explains, "To assume the position of the hinge is to occupy the center so as to produce an opening outward, to remain close in order to regulate from a distance." The hinge itself— like the sage—never moves. It attracts no attention, even passes unnoticed, but it is the hub that offers no friction or resistance on which all the rests pivots.

This brings us back to *mètis*. To explain why this notion of cunning intelligence, perceived at the dawn of Greek thought, was never cogently theorized, Marcel Detienne and Jean-Pierre Vernant tell us that *mètis* is characterized by the way that it "operates by continuously oscillating between two opposite poles (*Cunning Intelligence in Greek Culture and Society* [Atlantic Highlands, N.J.: Humanities Press, 1978], p. 5). The reason why *mètis* was soon banished from Greek thought and even from the Greek language is that, as we know, Greek thought eventually came to define "two mutually exclusive spheres of reality": on the one hand, "the sphere of being," "the One," the "limited," and "true and definite knowledge"; on the other, "the sphere of becoming, the multiple, the unstable and unlimited, and oblique and changeable opinion" (ibid.). This division is perhaps somewhat schematic, but it nevertheless served as a basis for Western metaphysics: the way forward for *mètis* was barred, because philosophy opted to think in terms of essences and antinomies. However, that in itself illuminates two particularly striking aspects that seem to predispose Chinese intelligence to (military) strategy: one aspect is, of course, the polarity that it perceives in all reality; the other, its keen sense of constant to-ing and fro-ing between the two poles

China may make it possible to illuminate *mètis*, which Greek thought never theorized and its awareness that the one both implies the other and turns into it (the meaning of *fanfu;*[nnnn] cf. in particular GGZ, chap. 2, "Fan ying"). That is a compensatory reversal, but, on that very account, it is ceaselessly innovatory. It may not be at all "dialectical," notwithstanding the Chinese claims sometimes made today with a view to having it recognized as philosophy. Nevertheless, in that it reveals the reactivity of the factors in play, it has certainly favored a *situational* approach—both contextual and predispositional—to what we would smugly call the "efficacy" of a subject.

If you begin by constructing a model, your only possible relation with the future takes the form of a projection (and anything that will not fit into the project has to be relegated to the domain of chance). But if your starting point is the potential of the situation, your relation to the future is one of *anticipation*. Sticking closely to the regulatory curve of its evolution and detecting in the existing situation a sign of the beginning of the change that will happen, you have, logically enough, a head start over its unfolding. So, rather than detect omens in the universe, interpret their meaning, and deploy their symbolism—in short, rather than behave hermeneutically (Western hermeneutics being linked to the origins of divination)—a Chinese general pays close attention to the least indications-premonitions of change (cf. the notions of *zhen, zhao;*[oooo] GGZ, chap. 1). This implies a fundamental difference in the status of the invisible in Greece and in China. What is invisible in a Greek model-form *(eidos)* belongs to the order of the intelligible, the "mind's eye," or theory. Meanwhile, the kind of invisible that interests the Chinese is that which is *not yet visible* in the undifferentiated basis of all, way upstream from any process. The intervening stages of "the subtle" and "the infinitesimal" (*wei*[pppp]) make the transition possible, and it is on these that the sage/general relies to orientate himself. Thus, even though he knows that there are no rules or norms to codify the future, since the flow of reality is constantly innovating, he feels no anxiety (in contrast to the latest Western mode of ideology—which is concerned with "uncertainty," "turbulence," and "chaos"...).

Projection or anticipation

A difference in the status of a sign: symbolic or premonitory

The invisible conceived as what is intelligible or as what is not yet visible

3

On the Chinese side, everything seems to lead to praise for "facility." On the European side, in contrast, the highest value is placed on difficulty, and the effects that are expected tend to be proportionate to the difficulty of the task undertaken. That is certainly so in the task of "foundation," in Machiavelli. The new prince acquires his sovereignty by dint of great effort, for "there is nothing more difficult to take in hand, more perilous to conduct or more uncertain in its success than to take the lead in the introduction of a new order of things" (*Prince,* VI [English translation, W. K. Marriot (Chicago: William Benton, 1952)]). Initially he encounters great obstacles and "dangers at every step"; but subsequently, he will preserve that sovereignty with all the greater ease. The difficulties he encounters in the world not only allow him to stamp the mark of his project upon it the more vigorously, but are also productive where he himself is concerned, since it is through those difficulties that the prince achieves greatness. He has to demonstrate outstanding abilities—abilities that he would otherwise never deploy, never even suspect that he possesses. To surmount the obstacles, he has to surpass himself: the all-pervasive theme is exaltation of the self-subject and his heroism. That same theme resurfaces in Clausewitz: "It has seldom happened in war that any great enterprise has been achieved without correspondingly great exertion, pain, and privation" (*On War,* III, 7 [English translation T. D. Pilcher (London: Cassell and Co., 1918)]). You could even set up, as a law, the proposition that efficacy is proportionate to difficulty, as can be seen from the effect of surprise in warfare: "It is clear that whatever surprise gains in facility, it loses in efficacy, and vice-versa" (ibid., III, 9).

On the one side praise of heroism and all that is difficult

On this point, the Chinese thinkers explicitly take up the opposite position. The treatise on diplomacy (GGZ, chap. 10, "Mou") declares that a clever man "manages" things and situations "with facility," whereas a man who is not clever "manages with difficulty." It is not that the sage/general despises or underestimates difficulties; on the contrary, he is most attentive to them (cf. LZ, section 63),

On the other side, praise of facility

he approaches the situation by placing himself at the

but he knows that, as the *Laozi* teaches, far from being antinomic, the easy and the difficult, just like any other pair of opposites, "make each other come about" (LZ, section 2). Far from being two irreducible or even mutually exclusive states, they are two stages that are produced by the deployment of reality. The one leads into the other—in fact the one "already" is the other. In the same fashion, the "undifferentiated fund" and "concrete actualization" "engender each other" (instead of being categorically opposed, as being and nonbeing are), and "before" and "after" follow on from each other (instead of being independent). Given that in this processive logic everything is in transition and unfolding, the best strategy is to tackle the situation at the stage when it is easy and then allow it to carry you along, through the deployment of its implied logic, to the stage of difficulty. The sage/general envisages and "plans" the difficulty "at the stage of facility," we are told, just as he "accomplishes great things at the stage when they are still infinitesimal" (LZ, section 63). Thus, "the difficult things that need to be done in the world must be undertaken at the stage of facility, just as great things in the world must be undertaken at the stage when they are still infinitesimal." For the sage expects effects to come from what is infinitesimal (cf. ZY, sections 14, 15). Instead of confronting difficulty directly, he approaches the situation by placing himself at the point of the beginning of the evolution that will carry it in the desired direction. Similarly, instead of immediately undertaking great exploits, he starts off by making a minimal intervention that passes unnoticed but that, through the conditions it generates of its own accord, makes it possible to achieve the greatest of results later on.

In short, he "does" nothing, commits himself to nothing unless the situation that he is approaching is prepared for it. The *Laozi* points out that whatever is stable and at rest "is easy to hold," and whatever is fragile "is easy to break" (LZ, section 64). This means that, to start taking things in hand, one must first attain that stability; and to think of breaking anything, one has to wait until that fragility comes about. The whole art lies in an ability to predispose (the enemy or the world: for example, predis-

Tackle the situation at the stage when it is easy, then allow it to carry you on to the stage of difficulty

the diff. or great things

The effect comes from the infinitesimal

to be done ... must be undertaken at the stage of facility

1. c

Predispose the situation to make it inclined to deploy the desired effect

infinitesimal

pose the former "to listen" or to be defeated, and so on). Thus, the sage/general is only seen to intervene when it is a matter of responding to the way that things are inclining to go, so he never "does" anything "difficult"; and given that he is content to start processes off discreetly and then leave them to develop on their own, nor does he ever do anything "great." But by those very means he is able to accomplish what, in the end, "will turn out to be great."

Win easy victories

The military art provides a good illustration: a good general "wins where/when it is easy" (SZ, chap. 4, "Xing"). For, as we have learned, "he attacks only that which can be vanquished" (Cao Cao). In the meantime, from a great distance, he arranges the conditions for success. It is by "going back" to that most "subtle" stage for determining things that he "makes victory easy to win." While there are not yet any "signs" of conflict, "he evolves in a subterranean fashion," in an underhand way, so as to attack the plans of the enemy. At this stage, "the strength brought to bear is slight," and "victory can be determined by an infinitesimal factor," "so it is fair to say that the victory is easy" (Du Mu).

Facility stems from the potential of the situation

Logically enough, this returns us to the potential of the situation—in fact, from this point on, there is no getting away from it, no chance to digress, nothing more to say, nothing to do but repeat the obvious: "If one uses men in accordance with the potential of the situation, it is easy; whereas whatever one demands of them by resorting to force is difficult" (SZ, chap. 5, "Shi," Mei Yaochen). If one can but obtain that potential, "victory comes by itself"; there is no longer any need to demand anything "special" (He Shi). However heavy the logs or boulders, thanks to the slope it is easy to move them, "whereas it is difficult to shift them by force." The same argument is equally valid for the theorists of despotism (HFZ, chap. 34): it is easy to exact obedience if one relies on the potential of one's position but difficult if one has to count on merit or goodwill.

Morality, too, makes the most of the facility of success

In this respect even the moralists cannot be faulted, since they too claim that the easiest way to attain success is the way of virtue that they recommend. In late Antiquity, the various schools were unanimous in their praise of facility. The mistake that people make is "to seek the way in the distance when it is close at hand," Mencius declares, and "to seek at the level of difficulty that which, in reality, is easy"—and that is why they are not successful (MZ, IV, A, 11). Whereas, if they start from what is most simple, which lies at the basis of the evolution of things, and then allow the effect to spread and propagate itself, they can spin the world around "on the palms of their hands" (MZ, I, A, 7). All they need to do is to conform to the order of things, which is well within their grasp. They should "treat as close to them those who are close," "treat as their elders those who are their elders." And to do so is not really to obey a set of rules; it is not even prescriptive, since, "for the whole world to be at peace," it goes without saying (i.e., one remains in a tautology). In fact, the harder the times and the more the world is prey to violence, the more sensitive people are to the slightest signs of humanity: the more ready they are to run to welcome a prince who is less cruel and, ardently accepting his authority, they will soon ensure his success (MZ, II, A, 1).*

Greece celebrated the figure of Heracles as the hero of *ponos,* the man who performed a series of dangerous and costly labors; and China seems to offer an equivalent in the shape of Yu the Great. At the time of the flood, when the waters covered the earth, which was then inhabited by many monsters, and men no longer knew where to turn, the Great Yu dug out riverbeds and, directing the water into the sea, made the world once more inhabitable for them (cf. MZ, III, B, 26). But Mencius points out, precisely, that in order to evacuate the water, Yu made it flow "where it was easy to do so," making the most of the gradient and without having to labor, and therein lies the lesson to be learned (ibid., IV, B, 26). "What I detest about people who claim

they can spin world around on the palms of their hands [handwritten marginal note]

Heracles or Yu the Great [margin note]

---

*Even more significant, the title of the classic *Book of Changes (Yijing),* which is the most fundamental book of Chinese thought, could equally well be translated as *The Book of Facility,* as "*yi*" means both "to change" and "easy." This suggests that change always comes about in reality by following the line of least resistance (as water does), where it is easiest to move forward; cf. *Figures de l'immanence* (Grasset, 1993), p. 201.

to be clever is that they are forever 'boring away' and 'forcing,' always doing violence to nature and ending up by making things worse." Even to bring the flood to an end, the Great Yu forced nothing. He took the situation into account (the lie of the land slopes down toward the sea). He relied on propensity, never needing a confrontation.

But, of course, there is a price to pay. And it is a price that, sad to say, none of the Chinese thinkers, whatever his tendencies, seems ever to have noticed. To confront the world is a way to free oneself from it. Not only does this provide the substance of heroic stories and jubilation for the subject, but, through resistance, we can make our way to liberty. After all, we should remember all that this extremely coherent Chinese concept kills. By dint of identifying with that coherence and allowing ourselves to be carried along by it, possibly or even manifestly to the point of being unable to do without it, we may well forget all that we have jettisoned along the way: under the heading of "subject," the infinite possibilities of subjectivity; passion, of course; and the pleasure derived from exerting ourselves; but above all relating to "others" who really are *others* (and who are there to be discovered, not simply "others" defined as our polar partners/adversaries). It is certainly enough to make one dream of Heracles, mounting his pyre, happy to have exerted himself for nothing. . . .

One can imagine what his retort to a Chinese general might have been: "And what if not just the greatest pleasure, but even the greatest 'profit,' as you would say, was not to win but to lose: really to lose—and to lose forever, so as to experience the weight of that 'forever,' as Sisyphus and Prometheus did (not so that that loss, thanks to the ricochets of reality, should later turn into gain)? And what if the best way to feel alive—finally beyond the world—was not efficacy but the very opposite?" In that case, this essay would have to be rewritten the other way around. It would be titled: *In Praise of Resistance*—or of the nontolerance of reality—*In Praise of Counterefficacy.*

Glossary of Chinese Expressions

a   *Xing* 形; *shi* 勢
b   *Yong li shao er de gong duo* 用力少而得功多
c   *Xiao* 校; *ji* 計
d   *Ji li yi ting, nai wei zhi shi, yi zuo qi wai* 計利以聽，乃為之
     勢，以佐其外
e   *Bing fa wu ding, wei yin shi er cheng* 兵法無定，惟因勢而成
f   *Li shi er zhi shi* 立勢而制事; *Shi zhe, li hai zhi jue* 勢者，
     利害之決
g   *Shi bu de yi* 勢不得已
h   *Bu qiu er de* 不求而得
i   *Ze* 則
j   *Bu te* 不忒
k   *Bi* 必
l   *Fan qi ben* 反其本
m   *Yong* 用 and *ti* 體
n   *Hua* 化
o   *Bu jian er zhang* 不見而章
p   *Wu wei er cheng* 無為而成
q   *Jiu er hua cheng* 久而化成
r   *Wu fang* 無方
s   *Zhu shi ri cheng er ren bu zhi* 主事日成而人不知
t   *Jie* 節

u   *Ji zhi shi* 幾之勢

v   *Ji wei zhi jue* 幾危之決

w   *Ji* 幾 and *ji* 機; *wei* 危 and *wei* 微

x   *Ji wei zhi dong zi wei zhi zhu* 幾危之動自微至著

y   *Zhi yu wei zhao, cha yu wei xing* 知于未兆，察于未形

z   *Bi xun jian er dong* 必循間而動

aa   *Tui jian* 推間

bb   *Shengren yi wu wei dai you de* 聖人以無為待有德

cc   Cf. *Bi yu shen qi bian hua* 必像審其變化

dd   *Bian hua wu qiong, ge you suo gui* 變化無窮，各有所歸

ee   *Mo hua* 默化

ff   *Wu wei er wu bu wei* 無為而無不為

gg   *Bu gan wei* 不敢為

hh   *Wei zhe bai zhi* 為者敗之

ii   *Shi-wei-zhi-ge* 施為執割

jj   *Yin* 因 — *wei* 為

kk   *Tian xia shen qi* 天下神器

ll   *Wei wu wei* 為無為

mm   *Wei er bu zheng* 為而不爭

nn   *Ziran* 自然

oo   *Xi yan zi ran* 希言自然

pp   *You de wu zhu* 有德無主

qq   *Xuan* 玄

rr   *Cheng* 誠, *ren* 仁

ss   *You* 有, *wu* 無

tt   *Gui* 歸

uu   *Shun* 順, *yin* 因

vv   *Ying* 應

ww   *Ying yu wu fang* 應于無方

xx   *Guo er bu de yi* 果而不得已

yy   *Kong* 空, *xu* 虛

zz   *Wu* 無

aaa   *Tong* 通

bbb	*Shen* 神
ccc	*Mou zhi wu gong zhi shi* 謀之無功之勢
ddd	*Er* 而
eee	*Gu* 固
fff	*Fang shi er ni qi zhong* 方始而逆其終 / *Wei ru er tu qi chu* 未入而圖其出
ggg	*Yong* 用 in relation to *ti* 體
hhh	*Gan* 感
iii	*Xian zhu ren, zang zhu yong* 顯諸仁，藏諸用
jjj	*Yi* 以 in *wu yi wei* 無以為, *you yi wei* 有以為
kkk	*Gong bu ke qu, chang chu qi mu* 功不可取，常處其母
lll	*Wei zhi yu wei you* 為之于未有
mmm	*Pu* 樸
nnn	*Xiang* 象 opposed to *ji* 跡
ooo	*Bu yi xing zhi wu* 不以形制物
ppp	*Shen* 神
qqq	*Wei* 微
rrr	*Xing zhi, di bi cong zhi* 形之，敵必從之
sss	*Xing ren er wo wu xing* 形人而我無形
ttt	*Er bing er yi* 二柄而已
uuu	*Gui zhi ren, er bu gui jian zhi yu ren* 貴制人，而不貴見制於人
vvv	*Bai he* 捭闔
www	*Mo* 摩
xxx	*Ying di wei shi* 應敵為勢
yyy	*Bu zhi gu tai, ying xing you ji* 不執故態，應形有機
zzz	*Bianhua* 變化
aaaa	*Bing you chang li er wu chang shi* 兵有常理而無常勢
bbbb	*Bu tong yu jiu bian zhi li* 不通于九變之利
cccc	*Bi* 必
dddd	*Quan* 權
eeee	*Quanli* 權力
ffff	*Quanbian* 權變, *quanmou* 權謀

gggg	Cf. Wang Bi: *Quan, fan jing er he dao* 權，反經而合道
hhhh	*Biantong* 變通
iiii	*Renquan* 人權
jjjj	*Li* 力
kkkk	*Ai* 愛
llll	*Men* 門
mmmm	*Bai he zhe, dao zhi da hua, shui zhi bian* 捭闔者，道之大化，說之變
nnnn	*Fanfu* 反復
oooo	*Zhen* 朕, *zhao* 兆
pppp	*Wei* 微

About the Author

François Jullien, philosopher and sinologist, is a professor at the University of Paris VII and director of the Institute of Contemporary Thought. Among his publications are *Figures de l'immanence* (1993), *Le détour et l'accès* (1995), and *Fonder la morale* (1996).

Production Notes for
Jullien / *A TREATISE ON EFFICACY*

Cover designed by Santos Barbasa, Jr.

Interior designed and typeset by Lucille C. Aono
in Sabon and GillSans

Printing and binding by
The Maple-Vail Book Manufacturing Group

Printed on 55# Sebago Antique, 360 ppi

transition . p 79   (opportunities)

opening and closing of 2 poles

of reality . p 73

particularity and rigidity (to be
liberated from) . p 72

orient : error posses in the
great logic of reality .
always at work beneath the
surface of things
crack / fissure, gap , crevasse
(to spot it first) (union.
separation : yin yang) , p 70

        December   26, 2008

others have simply no
way of perceiving it . p 91
design : partial and rigid
elements . p 89
constantly   cutting back on one's
    actions . p 87

December 28, 2008

at this stage, reality loses
all inertia, p. 135

(efficiency is maximum)

the constant transition of
reality. p. 130:   →

it elects to remain in
a state of indistinction
.... present everywhere

all one has to do is
engage a process or
disengage it. and reality
will bear its own fruits
p. 141

the determining factor—
constituted by the
orientation. p. 139

Chinese efficacy, simply
within the terms of a process, in starting things
or breaking them off   p 140

Opening and closing: to
   sound them   pp 158-159

the stage of docility, (difficult
   taken at)
the not intestines (great things
   taken or)   p. 194

opening, closing,   p 190 —
   by these transformation
   comes about

turn oz my will power   p 185
   the source from which
   one imposes himself

a situation is always
orientated by a propensity
p. 189

by transforming yourself
you renew yourself
entirely from within
and remain dynamic p 178

the potential lies in the
situation p 176

water and slope → potential
p 172

we need to accept a different
primary distinction (from
being /becoming): it
emphasizes the constant
transition of reality →

by so doing we
may enter into this
logic of processing

---

p.130

begining by constructing
a model. for Piaget
p.192

9 780824 828301